D1254011

Education, Refugees and Asylum Seekers

Other titles in the Education as a Humanitarian Response Series

Education and HIV/AIDS, Nalini Asha Biggs
Education and Reconciliation, Julia Paulson
Education as a Global Concern, Colin Brock

Also available from Continuum

Comparative and International Education, David Phillips and Michele Schweisfurth
Multiculturalism and Education, Richard Race

Education, Refugees and Asylum Seekers

Education as a Humanitarian Response

Lala Demirdjian

continuum

Continuum International Publishing Group

The Tower Building
11 York Road
London SE1 7NX

80 Maiden Lane
Suite 704
New York NY 10038

www.continuumbooks.com

British Library Cataloguing-in-Publication Data
A catalogue record for this book is available from the British Library.

ISBN: 978-1-4411-3627-5 (paperback)
978-1-4411-9371-1 (hardcover)

Library of Congress Cataloging-in-Publication Data
Education, refugees, and asylum seekers / edited by Lala Demirdjian.
p. cm. – (Education as a humanitarian response)
Includes bibliographical references and index.
ISBN 978-1-4411-3627-5 – ISBN 978-1-4411-9371-1 –
ISBN 978-1-4411-6345-5 – ISBN 978-1-4411-5065-3 1. Refugees–Education–Cross-cultural studies. 2. Political refugees–Education–Cross-cultural studies. 3. Humanitarian assistance–Cross-cultural studies. I. Demirdjian, Lala.

LC3715.E385 2011
371.826'914—dc22

2011002479

Typeset by Newgen Imaging Systems Pvt Ltd, Chennai, India
Printed and bound in India

This is dedicated to the memory of all the students who have lost their lives during violence and armed conflicts.

Contents

Acknowledgements

The current volume on *Education, Refugees and Asylum Seekers* would not have come to light without the dedicated work of the contributors. I am deeply appreciative of the contributors for the time and effort they put into compiling this volume. Special thanks to the series editor, Dr. Colin Brock, for his guidance and great support.

Many thanks to Harvard Graduate School of Education for granting permission to access the Monroe C. Gutman library for the purpose of this research. Last, but not least, I would like to thank my family and friends who supported me continuously throughout the course of this volume.

Series Editor's Preface

Underlying this entire series on *Education as a Humanitarian Response* is the well-known adage in education that 'if we get it right for those most in need we will likely get it right for all if we take the same approach'. That sentiment was born in relation to those with special educational needs within a full mainstream schooling system. In relation to this series it is taken further to embrace the special educational needs of those experiencing disasters and their aftermath, whether natural or man-made. Much of value to the provision of normal mainstream systems can be learned from the holistic approach that necessarily follows in response to disasters. Sadly, very little of this potential value is actually perceived, and even less is embraced. Consequently, one of the aims of the series, both in the core volume *Education as a Global Concern* and in the contributing volumes, is to bring into the mainstream the notion of education as a humanitarian response, and those seeking to serve it as teachers, other educators and politicians. The theme of this book , one of the first of the volumes in the series, is particularly apposite in that the number of countries hosting refugees, as well as the overall number of refugees, is rising across the world.

Refugees and asylum seekers are found in low-income and middle-income countries as well as in the most developed, exhibiting a very wide range of contexts, problems and responses. Such needs and responses to those needs are well documented by the Inter-Agency Network for Education in Emergencies (INEE). They should be in the forefront of radical thinking about the type of education we need to be fostering in order to be successful in the vital challenge of sustaining the human and physical environments on planet Earth.

Colin Brock,
UNESCO Chair in Education as
a Humanitarian Response, Oxford, UK.

Notes on Contributors

James Dada has received an MA in Migration, Mental Health & Social Care from the University of Kent, MEd, Advanced Diploma-Educational Studies-University of Hull-1982. He was a teacher and education administrator in Nigeria. He has taught for 35 years. Currently, James does voluntary work as a member of charity organizations for refugees and asylum seekers: trustee member of Kent Refugee Support Group, member of Kent Refugee and Asylum Network, member of the Board of Governors Temple Secondary School, Strood in Kent, now Strood Academy.

Lala Demirdjian is a researcher focusing on Palestinian refugee education in Lebanon. She has received her MSc degree in Comparative and International Education from the University of Oxford, UK. She has worked as a consultant for the United Nations Relief and Works Agency for Palestine Refugees in the Near East (UNRWA), Lebanon, the National Association for Vocational Training and Social Services (NAVTSS) and as a campaign coordinator for the Welfare Association in Lebanon. She is currently engaged in a teacher exchange program and teaches in a community school in Boston, Massachusetts.

Susan Downs-Karkos is the Director of Integration Strategies at the Spring Institute for Intercultural Learning, USA, where she leads efforts to strengthen immigrant integration policy and practices across Colorado and nationally. Prior to this, she served as a senior program officer at The Colorado Trust, where she led the design and management of the Supporting Immigrant and Refugee Families Initiative, a $10 million investment in immigrant integration in Colorado. She is also the former national board co-chair of Grantmakers Concerned with Immigrants and Refugees, a network of US foundations working to address the challenges facing newcomers and their host communities.

Candice Lee has received her MSc and DPhil in Comparative and International Education from the University of Oxford, UK, and her BA in English Literature and Political Science from the University of California, Berkeley, USA. She has been involved in a variety of professional activities related to arts education, advocacy and research, with a particular interest in targeting marginalized immigrant and refugee communities. She is currently working for a gallery in London, UK, where she curates and oversees the management of the company's art academy, while continuing to write for various trade magazines and journals as an art correspondent.

Megan McCorriston has published on refugee issues in education with a focus on social justice and education inclusion. Her research and publications are primarily on English experience; however, she has also worked extensively in international refugee education. She was a researcher for the British Refugee Council's Inclusive Secondary Schools Project and held a UNESCO Chair research fellowship at Oxford University, UK. She received an MSc and DPhil in inclusive education policies for refugees and asylum seekers from Oxford University in 2006. She currently works in her native Hawaii as the Executive Director of an education non-profit serving native Hawaiian students in public charter schools.

Su-Ann Oh is a sociologist specializing in education and is currently a Research Fellow at the Institute of Southeast Asian Studies, Singapore. She is a graduate of the London School of Economics, UK, and completed an EdD at the University of Oxford. She has been working on research on the education of refugees along the Thai-Burmese border since 2005. Her research to date has examined the educational experience of Burmese and Palestinian refugees and the needs of marginalized students in England and Singapore. Su-Ann is also a co-founder of Room to Grow Foundation, a charity based on the Thai–Burmese border, which provides basic necessities to migrant and refugee children living in camps and in migrant areas (www.roomtogrowfoundation.org).

Janet Shriberg is an Assistant Professor in the International Disaster Psychology Program at the University of Denver, USA. She has extensive experience working in contexts affected by armed conflict and other disasters worldwide, focusing on the important roles that teachers can play in supporting post-conflict reconstruction efforts and child protection. She serves internationally as a technical consultant to the INEE and is a lead researcher on several projects in Colorado related to the education and health of newly arrived immigrants and refugee families. She holds a doctorate in international educational development from Columbia University.

Stacey Weisberg has worked as the Director of Mental Health & Community Services for Jewish Family Service of Colorado (JFS), USA, since 1995. She received her Masters in Counseling Psychology from Temple University, USA. She is a certified marriage and family therapist trained Philadelphia Child Guidance Clinic. Prior to her work at JFS, Stacey spent four years at Johns Hopkins Hospital providing mental health services to children and families. She developed the KidSuccess Program providing school-based mental health and consultation to public and private schools. She was one of the developers of the International KidSuccess program for international students and their families. She co-developed the Refugee Mental Health Program for refugees who have experienced trauma.

Introduction: Education, Refugees and Asylum Seekers – A Global Overview

Lala Demirdjian

Chapter Outline

The word *asylum* (*asylia*, in Greek) was first used in ancient Greece and later in the Roman Empire. In Greece, the temples, altars, sacred groves and statues of the gods generally possessed the privileges of protecting slaves, debtors and criminals who fled to them for refuge. The laws, however, do not appear to have recognized the right of all such sacred places to afford the protection which was claimed, but to have confined it to a certain number of temples or altars which were considered in a more especial manner to have the 'asylia'. In ancient Greece the term *asylia* was also applied to the security from plunder and piracy (asylia on land and sea), which one state sometimes granted to another, or even to single individuals (Rigsby, 1996).

In today's world, the use of the term *asylum seeker* has changed as a consequence of many wars and, later, agreements by international organizations.

The main international agency coordinating refugee and asylum seeker protection is the Office of the United Nations High Commissioner for Refugees (UNHCR). UNHCR (2010) defines 'asylum seekers' as 'individuals who have sought international protection and whose claims for refugee status have not yet been determined' (p. 23). Unfortunately, under the present conditions, the number of asylum seekers and refugees is increasing in most countries experiencing conflict or post-conflict situations. The majority of refugees who leave their country seek asylum in countries neighboring their country of origin. The 'durable solutions' to refugee populations, as defined by UNHCR and governments, are voluntary repatriation to the country of origin, local integration into the country of asylum and resettlement to a third country (UNHCR, 2003). The term *refugee* is sometimes applied to people who may have fit the definition, if the 1951 Convention was applied retroactively. After the Edict of Fontainebleau in 1685 outlawed Protestantism in France, hundreds of thousands of Huguenots fled to England, the Netherlands, Switzerland, South Africa, Germany and Prussia. Repeated waves of pogroms swept Eastern Europe, propelling mass Jewish emigration (more than two million Russian Jews emigrated in the period 1881–1920). The Balkan Wars of 1912–13 caused 800,000 people to leave their homes. Various groups of people were officially designated refugees beginning in World War I.

The first international coordination on refugee affairs was by the League of Nations' High Commission for Refugees (Zurcher, 2003). The Commission, led by Fridtjof Nansen, was set up in 1921 to assist the approximately 1.5 million persons who fled the Russian Revolution of 1917 and the subsequent civil war (1917–21); most of them were aristocrats fleeing the Communist government (Hassell, 1991). In 1923, the mandate of the Commission was expanded to include the more than one million Armenians who left Turkish Asia Minor in 1915 and 1923 due to the Armenian Genocide. Over the next several years, the mandate was expanded to include Assyrians and Turkish refugees. In all cases, a refugee was defined as a person in a group for which the League of Nations had approved a mandate (The Nobel Foundation).

As a result of the convention concerning the exchange of Greek and Turkish populations (Treaty of Lausanne, 13 January 1923), a mutual exchange of peoples took place. Even though the exact figures differ, it is generally thought to be around 1.5 million (Clark, 2006). The US Congress passed the Emergency Quota Act in 1921, followed by the Immigration Act of 1924. The

Immigration Act of 1924 was aimed at further restricting the southern and eastern Europeans from entering the United States. Restrictions on entering the United States also existed for Asian immigrants, specifically the Japanese. The Immigration Act of 1924 aimed to preserve American homogeneity which, at that time, was more important than establishing good ties with foreign countries (US Department of State, undated).

In 1930, the Nansen International Office for Refugees was established as a successor agency to the Commission. Its most notable achievement was the Nansen passport – a passport for refugees – for which it was awarded the 1938 Nobel Peace Prize. The Nansen Office was plagued by inadequate funding, rising numbers of refugees and the refusal by League members to let the Office assist their own citizens. Regardless, it managed to assist over one million refugees and convince 14 nations to sign the Refugee Convention of 1933 (a weak human rights instrument (Nansen International Office for Refugees).

The rise of Nazism led to such a severe increase in refugees from Germany that, in 1933, the League created a High Commission for Refugees Coming from Germany. Article 1 of the 4 July 1936 agreement signed under League auspices defined a refugee coming from Germany as 'any person who was settled in that country, who does not possess any nationality other than German nationality, and in respect of whom it is established that in law or in fact he or she does not enjoy the protection of the Government of the Reich' (League of Nations, 1936, p. 1). The mandate of this High Commission was subsequently expanded to include persons from Austria and Sudetenland. Around 150,000 Czechs were displaced after 1 October 1938, when the German army entered the border regions of Czechoslovakia that were surrendered in accordance with the Munich Agreement (Horakova, 2003).

On 31 December 1938, both the Nansen Office and High Commission were dissolved and replaced by the Office of the High Commissioner for Refugees under the Protection of the League. This coincided with the flight of several hundred thousand Spanish Republicans to France after their loss to the Nationalists in 1939 in the Spanish Civil War (Nansen International Office for Refugees).

The conflict and political instability during World War II led to massive amounts of forced migration, mainly due to evacuation and expulsion. By the end of World War II, Europe had more than 40 million refugees. In 1943, the Allies created the United Nations Relief and Rehabilitation Administration (UNRRA) to provide aid to areas liberated from the Axis powers, including parts of Europe and China. This included returning over seven million refugees, then commonly referred to as displaced persons or DPs, to their country of origin and setting up displaced persons' camps for one million refugees who refused to be repatriated (*Time*, 1979).

Between the end of World War II and the erection of the Berlin Wall in 1961, more than 563,700 refugees from East Germany traveled to West Germany for asylum from the Soviet occupation (Bocker et al., 1998).

During the same period, millions of former Russian citizens were forcefully repatriated into the USSR (Elliott, 1973). On 11 February 1945, at the conclusion of the Yalta Conference, the United States and United Kingdom signed a repatriation agreement with the USSR (Hornberger, 1995). The interpretation of this agreement resulted in the forcible repatriation of all Soviets regardless of their wishes. When the war ended in May 1945, British and US civilian authorities ordered their military forces in Europe to deport to the Soviet Union millions of former residents of the USSR, including numerous persons who had left Russia and established different citizenship many years before. The forced repatriation operations took place from 1945 to 1947 (Tolstoy, 1988).

At the end of the World War II, there were more than five million displaced persons from the Soviet Union in Western Europe (Marek, 2005). About three million had been forced labourers in Germany and occupied territories. Of the 5.7 million Soviet prisoners of war captured by the Germans, 3.5 million died while in German captivity. The survivors, on their return to the USSR, were treated as traitors. Over 1.5 million surviving Red Army soldiers imprisoned by the Germans were sent to the Gulag (North, 2006).

The UNRRA was shut down in 1947, at which time the newly instituted International Refugee Organization (IRO) took over. The IRO was a temporary organization of the United Nations (UN), founded in 1945 with a mandate to largely finish the UNRRA's work of repatriating or resettling European refugees. The IRO was dissolved in 1952 after resettling about one million refugees. The definition of a refugee at this time was an individual with either a Nansen passport or a 'Certificate of Eligibility' issued by the IRO.[1]

The UNHCR, headquartered in Geneva, was established on 14 December 1950 to protect and support refugees or assist in their return or resettlement at the request of a government or the UN. As governments were recovering from the calamities of World War II, they wanted to ensure there was a stable organization protecting those who had become refugees and asylum seekers as a consequence of the war. Refugees worldwide, with the exception of Palestinian refugees living in host countries, are under the UNHCR mandate.[2] Palestinian refugees are most often described as 'protracted refugees', a term UNHCR applies to refugees in a situation 'in which 25,000 or more refugees of the same nationality have been in exile for five years or longer in any given asylum country' (UNHCR, 2010, p. 6).

Even though UNHCR's mandate was initially established for only three years (and constantly being renewed at the end of each third year), the UN General Assembly abolished the requirement to renew the mandage in December 2003, because of the continuously increasing numbers of refugees and asylum seekers worldwide (UNHCR, 2009). UNHCR provides protection and assistance not only to refugees but also to other categories of displaced or needy people. These include asylum seekers, refugees who have returned home but still need help in rebuilding their lives, local civilian communities directly affected by the movements of refugees, stateless people and internally displaced people (IDPs). IDPs are 'people or groups of individuals who have been forced to leave their homes or places of habitual residence, in particular as a result of, or in order to avoid the effects of armed conflict, situations of generalized violence, violations of human rights, or natural- or human-made disasters, and who have not crossed an international border' (UNHCR 2010, p. 23).

UNHCR followed the IRO as the main UN agency concerned with the issue of refugees. The UNHCR was established by the UN General Assembly in 1950 on the basis of Article 22 of the UN Charter, in order to provide 'international protection' as well as to seek 'permanent solutions for the problems of refugees', especially after the World War II (Goodwin-Gill, 2007, p. 21).

The 1951 Convention Relating to the Status of Refugees is the key legal document in defining who is a refugee, the rights of refugees and the legal obligations of states towards them. (UNHCR, 2010).

The practical determination of whether a person is a refugee or not is most often left to certain government agencies within the host country. This can lead to a situation where the country will neither recognize the refugee status of the asylum seekers nor see them as legitimate migrants, treating them instead as illegal aliens. Governments or non-governmental organizations (NGOs), such as the International Committee of the Red Cross, build makeshift camps to receive refugees. Refugees in these camps receive emergency food and medical aid until it is safe to return to their homes or until other people outside the camps retrieve them. In some cases, often after several years, other countries decide it will never be safe to return these people to their native country, and the refugees are resettled in 'third countries', away from the border they crossed. Resettlement is seen as a tool for protecting those refugees who either cannot or are unwilling to return to their country of origin due to the risk of persecution or the lack of fundamental human rights in their countries (UNHCR, 2009). However, more often than not, refugees are not resettled. In the meantime, they are at risk for disease, child soldiering, terrorist recruitment, and physical and sexual violence.

Today's refugees and asylum seekers

According to the 2009 report of the UNHCR, 43.3 million people were forcibly displaced worldwide at the end of 2009. This is the highest number reached since the mid 1990s. Out of this number, 15.2 million were refugees, 10.4 falling under the UNHCR mandate and 4.8 million Palestinian refugees falling under the UNRWA mandate. The figure above also includes 983,000 asylum seekers and 27.1 million IDPs (UNHCR, 2010). By the end of 2009, 6.6 million stateless persons were identified in 60 countries, though UNHCR estimates this number may be as high as 12 million. Moreover, 5.5 million refugees were identified as protracted refugees.

The number of refugees was greatly composed of Afghan (2.9 million) and Iraqi (1.8million) refugees who fall under UNHCR's mandate. Afghan refugees were located in 71 asylum countries, whereas Iraqis found refuge mainly in neighbouring countries. Pakistan hosted the highest number of refugees (1.7 million, mostly from Afghanistan), followed by the Islamic Republic of Iran hosting 1.1 million refugees (mostly Afghan) and the Syrian Arab Republic hosting 1.05 million Iraqi refugees (based on government estimates).

Precarious political situations in many countries, humanitarian crises and natural disasters have uprooted millions of men, women and children. Since 2004, the number of refugees returning home is decreasing year after year, while the number of resettled refugees is rising. Developing countries hosted 80 per cent of the global refugee population. The regions of the Middle East and North Africa hosted 19 per cent of the total number of refugees, mainly from Iraq. Europe, on the other hand, hosted 16 per cent of the total refugee population, who mostly originated in Iraq, Serbia and Turkey. The Americas hosted the smallest number of refugees, mainly from Colombia. Due to renewed armed conflict and violations of human rights in the Republic of Congo and Somalia, a new wave of refugees moved to the Republic of Congo and Kenya (UNHCR, 2010).

A number of third countries run specific resettlement programs in cooperation with UNHCR. The largest programs are run by the United States, Canada and Australia. A number of European countries run smaller schemes; in 2004, the United Kingdom established its own system, known as the Gateway Protection Program, with an initial annual quota of 500. The quota rose to 750 in the financial year 2008–09 (Evans and Murray, 2009).

In September 2009, the European Commission unveiled plans for new Joint European Union (EU) Resettlement Program. The scheme would involve EU member states deciding together each year which refugees should be given priority. Member states would receive €4,000 from the European Refugee Fund per refugee resettled (BBC, 2009).

Between 1981 (when Japan ratified the UN Convention Relating to the Status of Refugees) and 2002, Japan recognized only 305 persons as refugees. According to the UNHCR, Japan accepted 26 refugees for resettlement in 2006 (*The Japan Times*, 2008).

Even in a supposedly 'post-conflict' environment, it is not a simple process for refugees to return home. The UN Pinheiro Principles are guided by the idea that people not only have the right to return to their home country but also to the same property. It seeks to return to the pre-conflict status quo and ensure that no one profits from the violence. Yet this is a very complex issue, and every situation is different. Conflict is a highly transformative force and the pre-war status quo can never be re-established completely, even if that were desirable (Pantuliano, 2009).

According to the most recent UNHCR report, there were 922,000 individual claims for asylum or refugee status registered in 2009. South Africa received the highest number of applications, followed by the United States and France. The highest number of asylum applications by unaccompanied and separated children (UASC) originated from Afghan and Somali children. More than 18,700 asylum applications were presented by UASC. The United Kingdom registered approximately 3,000 claims, followed by Norway, Sweden and Germany. Outside Europe, UASC applications were mostly received by Malaysia and Ecuador (UNHCR, 2010).

In 2000, a special UN Resolution instituted World Refugee Day, which falls on June 20, coinciding with the date on which African Refugee Day used to be commemorated in a number of African countries (FMO, undated).

In the United Kingdom, World Refugee Day is celebrated as part of Refugee Week, a nationwide festival featuring various cultural and educational events designed to promote understanding and to celebrate the cultural contributions of refugees (FMO, undated).

Education. Why and how?

Armed conflicts and the rise in number of refugees and IDPs has been a major obstacle in realizing the Education for All (EFA) goals that were set in 1990 at Jomtien, Thailand (Tawil, 2000). Ensuring that all children, without discrimination, have the right to education is crucial to children's development and future opportunities. Education is a basic human right and should be provided to all children with no exception. Article 26 of the Declaration of Human Rights states that:

> Education shall be directed to the full development of the human personality and to the strengthening of respect for human rights and fundamental freedoms. It shall promote understanding, tolerance and friendship among all nations, racial or religious groups, and shall further the activities of the United Nations for the maintenance of peace.
>
> (UNHCR, 1999, p. 8)

During conflict, displacement and refugee situations, education gets disrupted. In the case of camps hosting refugees or IDPs, there are no guaranteed means to start a system of education without humanitarian assistance from the host country or from other international organizations and NGOs. School buildings have been destroyed, there is a lack of administration, teaching materials are no longer available, there is a shortage of qualified teachers, funds are lacking, schools are used as shelters, there is the risk of landmines around school premises, and students lack the motivation to study. For refugees, asylum seekers and IDPs, education acts as a source of psychosocial support and helps reduce the children's exposure to threats, violence, physical attack and – in the case of child soldiers – military recruitment. It also develops conflict resolution and peace building skills and leads the populations towards reconstruction and social and economic development (Sinclair, 2002). Nicolai (2003) claims that education plays an important role in the care of disadvantaged groups such as girls, ethnic minorities and children with disabilities, especially when the crisis situation leads to further vulnerability among children. The *Guidelines on Protection and Care* established by the UNHCR tackle some significant issues in education worth considering while planning refugee education (UNHCR, 1994).

Various agreements related to the provision of education to refugees and children affected by armed conflicts have elaborated on education rights. According to the 1989 Convention on the Rights of the Child (CRC), it is each state's responsibility to provide children with the right to education. Article 28 of the CRC emphasizes the right to education stating, 'Each child has the right to education. The goal is free and compulsory primary education, secondary education (general or vocational) available to all, and higher education "on the basis of capacity"' (UNHCR, 1994, p. 109).

The CRC has become highly important to refugee children because all signatory governments have agreed to its standards. These standards become strong means of protecting children, including refugees, in any country. The CRC has also become the guiding principle of the UNHCR work in refugee protection, and, in the case of a state not being a signatory, the CRC may be used as a basis for the protection of refugee children (UNHCR, 1994, p. 109). For the benefit of all refugee children, UNHCR supports the implementation of the CRC standards by all states and by international organizations and NGOs. According to Article 22 of the CRC, a child who is either seeking refugee status or is already considered a refugee should receive 'appropriate protection and humanitarian assistance in the enjoyment of applicable rights set forth in the present convention and in other international human right or humanitarian instruments to which the said States are Parties' (UN, 1989, Article 22, p. 1). In other words, child refugees and asylum seekers are entitled to the same rights as any other child living in his country of origin.

Moreover, the goals set by the 1990 World Summit for Children were significant in setting standards that states could implement in developing national plans of action for 'children in especially difficult circumstances' (UN, 1989, Article 22, p. 20). The World Declaration on Education for All highlights the significance of 'active' commitment in order to provide equal educational opportunities even to 'those displaced by war' (Mooney and Wyndham, 2010, p. 254). The UN Committee monitoring implementation of the International Convention on Economic, Social and Cultural Rights points out availability, accessibility, acceptability and adaptability as the four significant elements that education must include (Mooney and Wyndham, 2010, p. 254).

The Inter-Agency Network for Education in Emergencies (INEE), established in Geneva in November 2000, provides support to professionals in the field of education in emergencies. INEE's main achievement has been the publication of *Minimum Standards for Education in Emergencies, Chronic Crises, and Early Reconstruction* (Davies and Talbot, 2008).[3] INEE's aim is to 'promote access to and completion of education of high quality for all persons affected by emergencies, crises or chronic instability' (Nicolai and Triplehorn, 2003, p. 13). Its objectives are:

- to share knowledge and experience
- to promote greater donor understanding of education in emergencies
- to advocate for education to be included in emergency response
- to make teaching and learning responses as widely available as possible
- to ensure attention is paid to gender issues in emergency education initiatives
- to document and disseminate best practices in the field
- to move towards consensual guidelines on education in emergencies (Nicolai and Triplehorn, 2003, p. 14)

In the last decade there has been a considerable research on the importance of education in conflict and emergencies. The Organization for Economic Cooperation and Development (OECD), the EFA Fast Track Initiative, as well as many individual governments and organizations have devoted significant attention to analyse the relationship between high-quality education and the abatement of state fragility. It is significant to acknowledge the importance of education, educational institutions and post-conflict reconstruction in the case of fragile states (Davies and Talbot, 2008).

According to Sinclair (2002), complex humanitarian emergencies refer to the displacement of people across borders of their own country, forcing them to become refugees. The term also refers to continuous conflict and insecurity within countries leading to the collapse of central governments. In general, all the programmes initiated for refugees, displaced people and disaster victims are identified as 'emergency' programmes.

Nicolai defines education in emergencies as a 'set of linked project activities that enable structured learning to continue in times of acute crisis of long-term instability' (2003, p. 11). The term *emergency education* used by various agencies and organizations refers to education in situations where children do not follow the national curriculum of their own country due to natural disasters or human-made crises (Sinclair, 2002, p. 4).

The United Nations Educational, Scientific and Cultural Organization (UNESCO) defines emergency education as 'a crisis situation created by conflicts or disasters which have destabilized, disorganized or destroyed the education system . . . requir[ing] an integrated process of crisis and post-crisis response' (UNESCO, 1999 in UNHCR, 2001, p. 4). Emergencies as defined by UNESCO include natural and human-made disasters. On the other hand, UNHCR sends emergency teams for a short period of time to the locations where crises exist until new posts dealing with a continuing emergency are created (Sinclair, 2002). The educational assistance provided by UNHCR is summarized in Table 1.1.

The educational response provides education for the internally displaced, refugee and repatriating children. It can be delivered by qualified teachers, trained volunteers, youth workers or children's peers with the involvement of local government, NGOs and the communities themselves (Nicolai, 2003). Education is crucial for the development of children. Save the Children explains the importance of education for children affected by emergencies: '[Education] protects the well-being, fosters learning opportunities, and nurtures the overall development . . . of children affected by

Table 1.1 The Educational Assistance Provided by UNHCR

Educational goals	Standards	Planning	Monitor	Assistance
Primary education	Gender	Community participation	Monitoring indicators	Construction/maintenance of schools
Post-primary education	Access	Plan of action		Equipment/materials/ supplies
Non-formal education	Quality	Expertise		Teacher training
Timing	Curriculum	Refugee teachers		Educational curriculum and training materials development
	Relevance	Parents' committees		Provision of school fees
	Peace Education			Transportation
	Language			School uniforms
				Teachers' salaries

UNHCR, 1994, pp. 110–18.

conflicts and disasters' (Save the Children Alliance Education Group in Sinclair, 2002, p. 23).

Emergency education can take place in various locations depending on the availability of premises such as schools, community buildings and tents. Indeed, emergency education can occur anywhere depending on the availability of students and space. It can take place as an after-school activity, in shifts or during regular school hours (Sinclair, 2002, p. 23).

The *Guidelines on Protection and Care of Refugee Children* emphasize that the disruption and insecurity in certain refugee situations can harm children's physical, intellectual, psychosocial and cultural development. Therefore, organizing and supporting educational activities helps to lessen the impact of trauma and protect at-risk groups. Integrated educational programmes enhancing the well-being of refugee children have been successfully implemented in places such as Rwanda, Yugoslavia, Somalia, Liberia and southern Sudan. UNICEF and UNESCO responded to the crisis in Rwanda by restoring schools and training teachers to understand the needs of children affected by trauma. Despite the immediate response to crisis situations, there are many obstacles to overcome to successfully provide education to all refugee children. When host governments are unable to support the provision of primary education due to inadequate resources and a lack of infrastructure and professionally trained teachers, refugee students have a greater risk of basic educational rights being restricted (UNHCR, 1994). Due to the status of the host country, the quality of education may be poor, with only a few hours of instruction per day and with limited instructional materials. Under such conditions, it is the host country's responsibility to collaborate with various governmental and non-governmental organizations to ensure compulsory primary education for all (UNHCR, 1994). The *Guidelines for Educational Assistance to Refugees* call attention to the rapid educational response necessary for refugees as they first establish in a host country, especially when they find themselves in inhabited areas of a developing country. UNICEF, UNESCO and UNHCR emphasize three phases in the process of developing temporary schools to meet the educational needs of the refugee population: the recreational/preparatory stage is known as phase one; the second phase relates to the establishment of non-formal schooling; the third phase is recognized as the 'near-normalcy' stage, including restoration of curriculum and introduction of mixed curricula (Retamal and Aedo-Richmond, 1998). In all three phases, teachers should provide familiar education using a familiar language. The 'introduction of mixed curricula' includes elements of the host country's educational system in addition to that of the country of origin and can be implemented in case of delayed solution of repatriation (Retamal and Aedo-Richmond, 1998).[4]

The 1990 World Summit for Children targeted 'universal access to basic education and completion of primary education by at least 80 percent of primary age children' (UNHCR, 1994, p. 110). Refugee children were also targeted in the above goal in light of the belief that they should not miss the opportunity of education due to the trauma of displacement. Specific attention is given to gender parity as far as refugee education is concerned. The *Guidelines on Protection and Care* emphasize the need to design and implement educational programmes involving the participation of both boys and girls equally. In 2000, the World Education Forum in Dakar adopted a framework for action targeting the objective of education for all. The framework was significant due to its recognition of the need for education in emergency situations: 'meet the needs of education systems affected by conflict, natural calamities and instability[5] and conduct educational programmes in ways that promote mutual understanding, peace and tolerance, and that help to prevent violence and conflict' (World Education Forum in Sinclair, 2002, p. 21).

Host governments should also provide equal educational opportunities for nationals and refugee children either by giving the refugees access to existing schools or by establishing schools for them. This is important for governments in order to abide by Article 28 of the CRC. 'Every effort should be made to ensure that all refugee children of primary school age have access to some type of formal or non-formal educational programme' (UNHCR, 1994, p. 112). Article 22 of the *Guidelines for Refugees* emphasizes that contracting states should treat the refugees in the same way as they treat their nationals (OHCHR, 1950).

Educational response in refugee emergencies

Education offers many short- and long-term solutions to various problems communities face. Education is particularly beneficial for traumatized children. Once children get back to the routine of schooling, their psychosocial needs are met and they enjoy the therapeutic value of education. Emergency education programmes such as vocational education and training are crucial in helping young people and child soldiers stay away from additional violence. Such programmes also facilitate the in-service training of teachers by improving the quality of education provided to the population in crisis. Educational responses in refugee emergencies are significantly important for nation-building and overall development. In addition, democratic values and attitudes are reinforced through extracurricular activities such as plays, dance and songs (Retamal et al., 1998). Following its mandate, UNESCO initiated the Programme for Education for Emergencies and Reconstruction (PEER) in January 1993 in Mogadishu. In cases of emergencies, especially in East Africa, PEER has proved to be very successful in providing education to refugees. The reintroduction of a standardized curriculum, the preparation of teacher guides and textbooks, the training of teachers, and the introduction of landmine awareness and health education are just a few of the achievements of PEER (Retamal et al., 1998).

Despite the programme mentioned above (implemented in Somalia, Rwanda and other regions), there cannot be specific guidelines to support refugee education because each refugee situation is unique in its own ways. For instance, the case of Palestinian refugees, due to their unique history and the lack of a durable solution to their problem, cannot be compared with that of refugees worldwide. Palestinians have been living in refugee camps in host countries for more than half a century. Programmes in refugee education are not implemented by the UNHCR; it is the responsibility of UNRWA to provide education, relief and health services to the Palestinian refugees residing in host countries. The considerable literature on 'refugee education' that has developed overlooks the case of Palestinian refugees in host countries.

In cases of possible voluntary repatriation of refugees, the children follow the curriculum of their country of origin so that the process of reintegration becomes easier in the future. UNHCR tries to provide textbooks from the country of origin. If that is impossible, the textbooks of the host countries are modified to the needs of the refugee population (UNHCR, 1994). In addition, it is essential that the education delivered to the refugees is relevant to their own needs. Language is another vital element in the provision of refugee education. Hence, UNHCR recommends that the medium of instruction for refugee children be their mother tongue, at least during the early grades. Learning a second language becomes necessary when there is a need of integration into the community of the host country. In refugee situations it is important to grant educated refugees opportunities to work as teachers or social workers (Sinclair, 2002). It is interesting to look at cases of refugees of the same group living in two different host countries, one where the provision of education is geared towards assimilation, the other towards repatriation. According to a comparative case study conducted by Smawfield (1993), the provision of education to Mozambican refugees in Zambia allowed assimilation, whereas the provision of education to Mozambican refugees in Malawi promoted repatriation. Mozambican refugees in Zambia followed the national curriculum and were taught in English by local teachers (and in Portuguese by refugee teachers). In Malawi, however, schools followed the Mozambican national curriculum, and students were taught only in Portuguese by refugee teachers of Mozambican origin. Moreover, Malawi had a school policy of open enrolment, and schools were intended to accept only refugee students. Zambia restricted its enrolment based on capacity, but was open to both refugee and Zambian students. Interestingly, enrolment rates among refugee students were higher in Zambia than in Malawi.

The importance of a child's early years should not be overlooked during emergency situations. The years from birth until the child is expected to begin school are very important for the psychosocial, physical and intellectual development of the child. Unfortunately, in emergencies families are under extreme pressure which may have negative impacts on children. Engaging young children in play and exploration ensures that children are in a safe environment where their needs are met (Nicolai, 2003).

Finally, the role of NGOs is highly valued in crises situations. NGOs and their partners often meet the needs for education for out-of-school children, young people and adults. Sophisticated cooperation between NGOs and local governments is very important in achieving the educational goals and supporting the communities in need (Sinclair, 2002).

In order to ensure access to education for refugees, UNHCR should promote equal educational rights for all children by establishing refugee education coordination committees and contributing resources to encourage the efforts of refugees, host governments and other organizations. In emergency and refugee situations, special care should also be given to the education and training of disabled refugees because employment opportunities may be limited for them. Facilities in the learning environment should be accessible to disabled children so that they can study in a comfortable setting without feeling excluded. Moreover, teachers, parents and communities should be aware of the special needs of children with disabilities; teachers should be trained to use special teaching methods to assist the children, whereas parents should be trained to encourage and enhance the self-esteem and independence of their disabled children (Revised [1995] *Guidelines for Educational Assistance to Refugees*).

The psychological impact of trauma and loss

Apart from physical wounds or starvation, a large percentage of refugees develop symptoms of post-traumatic stress disorder (PTSD), depression or survivor's guilt. These long-term mental problems can severely impede the person's functioning in everyday situations; they make matters even worse for displaced persons (particularly those at a high risk for suicide) who are confronted with a new environment and challenging situations. Among other symptoms, post-traumatic stress disorder involves anxiety, over-alertness, sleeplessness, chronic fatigue syndrome, motor difficulties, failing short-term memory, amnesia, nightmares and sleep paralysis. There have also been cases of refugee children experiencing a 'survivor's guilt'. A vast amount of literature discusses the negative impact of traumatic experiences on children's academic and cognitive development, in addition to the long-term effects of war. Refugee children are at risk of having mental health problems due to their experiences; therefore, it is crucial that schools and other health services provide appropriate help, consultations and guidance (Yule, 2000). Often, these children are suspicious of authority figures as a result of their former experiences at home, or in camps. The school environment can be very influential on the well-being of war-affected children who need a secure and predictable atmosphere in order to develop trusting relationships (Yule, 2000).

Frater-Mathieson (2004) explains PTSD as the diagnosis given to a series of distressing symptoms which are the result of an individual's experiences of life-threatening events. PTSD is classified as an anxiety disorder in formal psychiatric diagnostic schemes, described as 'a normal reaction to an abnormal situation' (O'Donohue and Eliot, 1992 in Yule, 2000, p. 696). Hence, it is debated whether it should be considered a psychiatric disorder at all. PTSD is composed of four clusters: affective indicators such as depression, anxiety, guilt, grief and detachment; physical indicators which include nightmares, somatic complaints, headaches and fatigue; cognitive distortions such as negative perceptions, self-blame, loss of interest and poor concentration; and, finally, behavioural indicators including regressive behaviours such as withdrawal, agitation, isolation and others (Frater-Mathieson, 2004).

PTSD has been diagnosed in 34.1 per cent of Palestinian children, most of whom were refugees, males and working. The participants were one thousand children aged 12–16 from governmental, private and UNRWA schools in East Jerusalem and various governorates in the West Bank (Khamis, 2005). Moreover, a study by the Department of Pediatrics and Emergency Medicine at the Boston University School of Medicine demonstrated that 20 per cent of Sudanese refugee minors living in the United States had a PTSD diagnosis. They were also more likely to have worse scores on all the Child Health Questionnaire subscales (Geltman et al., 2008). A further study showed that 28.3 per cent of Bosnian refugee women had symptoms of PTSD three or four years after their arrival in Sweden. These women also had significantly higher risks of depression, anxiety and psychological distress than Swedish-born women. For depression, the odds ratio was 9.50 among Bosnian women (Sundquist et al., 2005).

Many more studies illustrate the problem. A meta-study conducted by the psychiatry department of Oxford University analysed 20 surveys providing results for 6,743 adult refugees from seven countries. In the larger studies, 9 per cent were diagnosed with PTSD and 5 per cent with major depression, with evidence of much psychiatric co-morbidity. Five surveys of 260 refugee children from three countries yielded a prevalence of 11 per cent for PTSD. According to the same study, refugees resettled in Western countries could be about ten times more likely to have PTSD than age-matched general populations in those countries. Worldwide, tens of thousands of refugees and former refugees resettled in Western countries probably have PTSD (Fazel et al., 2005).

Refugee populations consist of people who are terrified and are away from familiar surroundings. There can also be instances of exploitation at the hands of enforcement officials or citizens of the host country. Instances of human rights violations, child labour, mental and physical trauma or torture, violence-related trauma and sexual exploitation – especially of children – are not entirely uncommon.

Terr (1991, cited in Frater-Mathieson, 2004, p. 15) studied the behaviour of school children and concluded that the behavioural changes among children vary based on their age. For instance, for younger school-age refugee children, common behaviours include performance decline, low self-esteem, obsessive talking and discrepancy in mood. Older school-age children show acting-out behaviours, have low self-esteem and can be highly self-critical. According to a longitudinal study by Ahearn and Athey of resettled refugees (1991, cited in Frater-Mathieson, 2004), the child's age at the time of the traumatic event seems directly related to the particular symptoms exhibited. According to Yule (2000), regressive, antisocial, aggressive and destructive behaviours are very common among children of preschool age. Most preschool children express their emotions by drawing and playing around themes characterizing the trauma they experienced.

Refugees who have been uprooted from their homes share the feeling of displacement which is considered one of the most crucial losses faced during the refugee experience. Fullilove (1996, cited in Frater-Mathieson, 2004, p. 12) refers to the 'psychology of place' in regards to the individual's need to create a sense of belonging to a place. The sense of belonging is the result of the needs of attachment, familiarity and identity. Once uprooted, refugees lack the significant foundation of safety or security in order to develop emotionally, psychologically and cognitively. Hence, many young refugee children suffer a great deal when they arrive in a host country and become active in the academic life there. Frater-Mathieson (2004) discusses the three stages of migration affecting the psychological development of refugee children. It is understood that *pre-migration* experiences differ among refugee children, depending on the events they witnessed and the circumstances under which they were uprooted. Culture, cognitive development, emotional experiences and parental support are also key factors affecting a young child's ability to cope with traumatic experiences and feeling of loss, as well as adjust to a new environment. Usually, children have two ways of coping with loss. The first way is identified as 'loss-oriented behaviour' in which the child faces the loss followed by grief. The 'restoration-oriented' behaviour occurs when the individual tries to find ways to deal with the new reality, even if that requires changing or finding new roles and identities (Stroebe and Schutt, cited in Silverman, 2000; Frater-Mathieson, 2004, p. 27).

Trans-migration factors may have positive or negative effects on the life of a refugee child depending on the amount of time spent in transition – most commonly in a refugee camp. *The post-migration* stage refers to the adaptation of a new country and culture, often very stressful due to culture shock, changes in family roles, lack of educational experience and familiar language of instruction, and financial problems (Frater-Mathieson, 2004).

The school environment can help enhance the adaptation of refugee children both culturally and socially. Unfortunately, fleeing from one's country distracts the process of socialization, in addition to halting the learning of new information and skills. Hence, schools should act as a major catalyst in building a safe and supportive environment for the refugees and asylum-seeking children. The school administration, teachers and peers should ensure a positive learning environment for students who have experienced trauma and loss and who are unfamiliar with the culture (Frater-Mathieson, 2004).

The process of adaptation is an interactive process of various systems involving the individual, the family and other social structures such as schools and institutions. During the adaptation stage, the roles of family members usually change, creating a new and often challenging atmosphere within the family setting. In many instances, the husband who had been the one supporting the family now has to stay home and take care of the children, whereas the wife finds a job outside the house and becomes the wage earner. In other instances, refugee children easily learn the language of the host country and the parents depend on the children to complete everyday tasks, such as paying bills, communicating with their surrounding and learning the traditions of the new culture (Frater-Mathieson, 2004).

Refugees and asylum seekers are vulnerable due to their past experiences in their home country. It is usually assumed that children are most vulnerable, followed by women, and then men. However, in reality, children are the ones best able to adapt to their new environment by learning the language of the host country (if different than their mother language), the rules and the customs; by dealing with all practical details of everyday life; and by making use of opportunities provided to them. Children have a great survival instinct and are much more optimistic than adults (Hieronymi, 2009). Of course, one should not disregard the effect of traumatic experiences on children. Even though children adapt well to a new environment, they still need psychosocial support to overcome their fears and feelings of loss. A key question in relation to the future of refugee children is: 'To what extent are the interests and the preferences of the children taken into account when decisions are made about repatriation, resettlement or integration and assimilation?' (Hieronymi, 2009, p.13).

Former child soldiers-education

Former child soldiers should not be excluded from educational opportunities provided to children affected by crises. Betancourt et al. (2008) examined the reintegration of former child soldiers to academic institutions after the end of the civil war in Sierra Leone. According to UN figures, approximately 250,000 child soldiers were victims of more than 50 conflicts in 2005 (UN, 2005 in Betancourt et al., 2008). According to the first global survey of child soldiers, over the past decade, more than half a million children have been abducted or conscripted into government forces and armed groups in 87 countries (UN, 2005 in Betancourt et al., 2008). UNICEF defines a child soldier as

> any person under 18 years of age who is part of any kind of regular or irregular armed force or armed group in any capacity, including but not limited to cooks, porters, messengers and anyone accompanying such groups, other than family members. The definition includes girls recruited for sexual purposes and for forced marriage. It does not, therefore, only refer to a child who is carrying or has carried arms. (UNICEF, 1997)

Child soldiers, similar to refugee- and asylum-seeking children, become victims of traumatic experiences and extreme violence that disrupts their psychological well-being. The loss of educational opportunities is a threat to long-term stability in the case of child soldiers. Research conducted in northern Uganda by Annan and Blattman (2006, in Betancourt et al., 2008, p. 566) showed that the longer children were in captivity of rebel groups, the larger the gap in educational outcomes. Moreover, children abducted at a younger age were less likely to return to school. However, further research suggests that adequate educational opportunities provided to former child soldiers can positively impact their lives. After the end of the civil war in Sierra Leone, numerous NGOs and community-based organizations, together with UNICEF's Community Education Investment Programme (CEIP), facilitated the school attendance of former child soldiers. Even though barriers in education existed when these programmes came to an end, the benefits of education in the reintegration of former child soldiers were significant. Research shows the relationship between literacy and vocational skills and economic security and stability for former child soldiers. Attending school and other training programmes provides youth affected by war with a sense of normalcy, as well as safety (Betancourt et al., 2008). The opportunity to learn certain skills and tasks enhances children's confidence and provides them with a sense of purpose. Being engaged in learning can also act as a coping mechanism. Kline and Mone (2003, in Betancourt et al., 2008) studied Sierra Leonean refugees in a Liberian camp and found that the group of war-affected children who were coping well with their experiences during war were those who highly valued education. It is important to emphasize that the opportunities of both educational and vocational programmes provide means of normalizing the lives of returning child soldiers, helping them develop a sense of self-worth. The provision of educational opportunities to former child soldiers was considered extremely important in improving social cohesion and reversing the moral destruction the youth had experienced. Moreover, education provided peer support, especially for child soldiers who had experienced loss of friendship and peer networks due to migration or death (ibid.).

Challenges in school settings

Academic and social learning

Winthrop and Kirk (2008) analyse children's social and academic learning by referring to data collected by the International Rescue Committee's (IRC) Healing Classrooms Initiative, launched in 2003. The shared experiences of Eritrean refugee children in Ethiopia, Afghan students in Afghanistan and Liberian refugee students in Sierra Leone were categorized between social and academic learning – both important for the psychosocial well-being of children affected by crises. Children from all three countries stated the importance of schooling as a hope for a bright future, consistently believing that being engaged in a learning process provides better future opportunities. Eritrean refugees in Ethiopia identified literacy and communication skills as fundamental to their educational experience. Students also talked of the importance of friendship, especially of how their friends helped and encouraged their own learning. In Afghanistan, students emphasized the significance of social learning – such as proper manners – as a means for a bright future. Children correlated going to school with being good and felt rewarded when they followed proper social codes. Liberian refugee children in Sierra Leone responded similarly to Eritrean students; they valued the academic skills such as reading and writing, as well as speaking English. They believed these skills would enable them to assist their families and communities. However, in all three countries, students' distress in school was also mentioned with varying significance. Relationships with teachers and peers did not always positively impact students. Abuse, exploitation, corporal punishment, harsh treatment, teasing and bullying in the schools were perceived as sources of distress (Winthrop and Kirk, 2008). In order to plan and implement refugee education in conflict zones, it is crucial to understand the culture of children and their understanding of learning.

Adaptation in a new school system

One of the main challenges for refugee children is adapting to a new school setting and to an unfamiliar environment. In order to overcome their fear and trauma, refugee children have to develop socialization skills in their new setting with the help of school administration, teachers, peers and parents. Schools have the responsibility of providing a safe environment for the newcomers, as well as introducing new learning experiences in the school curriculum that enhance the adaptation process and make refugee students feel welcome. Schools have to support refugee students by understanding their background and making the transition phase as smooth as possible. Teachers should be well trained and familiar with various cultures in order to help the students feel protected and develop a sense of belonging.

As mentioned above, while in the adaptation stage, children carry premigration, trans-migration and post-migration experiences which either facilitate or interfere with their adaptation to the new environment. It is challenging to prepare students and teachers in an already-existing school for the changes that accepting refugee students in their classrooms will bring. According to Bronfenbrenner (in Hamilton, 2004), the child is embedded within layered systems such as schools, community, family, helping services and the society. The interaction of these layers affects the child's development. The school and the family have an important role; hence, the interaction between the academic institution and the family is crucial in managing a well-balanced adaptation stage in the life of a refugee child.

Hieronymi (2009) identifies refugee or IDP children as 'passive learners' (p. 11) due to the fact that parents or caregivers make the decision to leave or to stay in one's country. Depending on the circumstances of the family, children are often sent ahead to ensure safety or to join other members of the family who had fled earlier. It is true that people who flee accept becoming refugees and experiencing life's uncertainties, but one should not doubt that the same people have high hopes of a better future which makes their decision of fleeing more comforting. Nations should not ignore the fact that refugees have as much hope for a better future as do migrants in a given country. In other words, the potential of refugees should be well used by host countries as opposed to being wasted (Hieronymi, 2009, p. 11).

A successful refugee experience is one which provides a better future than the past. Safety, security, economic conditions and living standards are some of the factors that determine a successful refugee experience (Hieronymi, 2009, p. 11).

School environment: integration into a new setting

The literature on refugee education greatly emphasizes the need for best national policy practices by host governments in order to integrate the refugee students into the new school system successfully. Administrators should work on ensuring that teachers in local schools have the appropriate understanding of various cultures and student backgrounds and are able to reach the needs of newcomers, making them feel accepted and secure in their new environment. Teachers should be responsible for providing a diverse classroom environment that is comfortable and familiar to both local and refugee students. Acceptance of cultural differences and implementation of cross-cultural activities is of great importance in engaging refugee students in the new setting. In order to avoid the negative outcomes of acculturation, there should be vital changes at the levels of national policy and the local school (Hamilton and Moore, 2004). Refugee students usually feel isolated in the new school setting. They have difficulties making new friends and many of them face language problems either due to interrupted schooling or limited knowledge of English. Competency in English is critical; most refugee children acquire self-confidence and develop social interaction as soon as they feel comfortable speaking the language of the mainstream (Candappa, 2000).

Teachers and administrators should facilitate ways to keep refugee students in school. In case of refugee students in US schools, antisocial behaviour and rejection by mainstream students, lack of psychological and academic preparation before entering schools, unsafe school conditions, dissonant acculturation, poverty and unfriendly social environments were seen as main reasons for dropping out (McBrien, 2005). Stereotypes, prejudice and discrimination adversely affect the social and academic development of refugee students. According to interviews conducted in Maryland (Birman et al., 2001, in McBrien, 2005), Somali students did not feel welcomed in US schools. Interviewees mentioned difficulties understanding subjects due to their refugee experience, inability to make friends and feelings of discrimination by their peers. On the other hand, US teachers reported their dissatisfaction concerning the lack of involvement by Somali parents. In order to best assist refugees and avoid any tension between the newcomers and the mainstream group, schools should adopt new policies.

Some suggestions for best practices include:

1. Develop policies to eliminate bullying and racism within the school setting.
2. Introduce cross-curricular topics in the curriculum and encouraging projects within schools with the goal of enhancing values of cultural understanding, acceptance and respect.
3. Appoint a mentor such as a teacher or a counsellor in order to assist the students in need, in this case, the refugees.
4. Encourage local students to participate in programmes that help them expand their knowledge of different cultures, diversity and human rights.
5. Implement programmes that help students increase their self-esteem and develop social skills.
6. Provide professional development by policymakers, supporting schools and teachers to gain the necessary skills to focus on refugees while implementing inclusive educational practices.
7. Foster cooperation between schools and policymakers in order to develop a curriculum that meets the needs of refugees and tackles issues of human rights and cultural diversity. (Hamilton and Moore, 2004)

Schools are usually in need of new instructional methods and assessment materials to help non-voluntary migrant groups learn the host country's language. It is equally important to identify bilingual workers who can help teachers communicate with refugee students (Hamilton and Moore, 2004). A country's national policy should be flexible enough in order to collaborate with other service providers outside the school setting, such as health care providers, counselling services, language training for adults, and others.

The classroom environment and instruction methods significantly affect the achievement of refugee students, especially when these students have gone through traumatic experiences. The students' and teachers' expectations vary based on the cultural background of each. Cheng (in McBrien, 2005) has identified cultural differences such as short responses, embarrassment at being praised and sudden non-verbal expressions that teachers misinterpreted as deficiencies. Dealing with traumatized children may also require specific experience and knowledge; therefore, teachers should be well trained in dealing with various situations in the classroom and ensuring that the curriculum enhances positive experiences and is relevant to the new students. Teachers should be prepared to deal with traumatized children and be aware of ways to boost the students' self-esteem and confidence. Hamilton and Moore (2004) suggest some ways for ensuring the best classroom environment and instruction:

1. Include refugee students in mainstream classes in order to increase their exposure to English-speaking students and decrease stigmatization.
2. Develop a peer tutoring system.
3. Offer chances for refugee students to raise issues that are important to them in order to make them feel that their culture and their first language are respected.
4. Encourage group activities in the classroom to create a tight bond between host students and refugees.

According to McBrien (2005), language acquisition is often affected by traumatic experiences as well as the availability of parental and social support. It is important that schools use cultural elements from the students' home countries to facilitate language acquisition and integration into the classroom. Moreover, because refugee students are not familiar with the new culture, student assessment should be broad-based as opposed to standardized. Teachers and counsellors should be aware that students who seem to have adjusted well and are high achievers might still need psychosocial support (McBrien, 2005). According to studies conducted with ESL students in Canada and the United States (Hakuta et al., 2000 in Brown et al., 2006) students need more than one year to acquire the necessary skills of writing, speaking and catching up with their peers who already have a developed competency in language skills. In ideal situations it takes three to five years to become proficient in oral language and four to seven years to gain academic English proficiency. For disadvantaged children, these timeframes are much longer. Furthermore, students with interrupted schooling lack specific vocabularies of academic subjects as well as cultural knowledge to develop understanding. Teaching and learning approaches may vary among the mainstream and the refugee groups. For example, in a regular Australian classroom, the use of multimedia and group work resulted in difficulties among refugee students who had trouble watching a video and taking notes or were hesitant to participate in group work due to their language limitation or unfamiliarity with the approach (Brown et al., 2006). While bringing refugee students closer to the mainstream and ensuring the growth of friendship and development of language skills (through their peers) may benefit the refugee student, teachers and administrators need to be aware of the drawbacks of such approaches.

Matthews (2008) expresses concern about the education of African and Middle Eastern refugee students in Australia because little is known there about the historical and cultural backgrounds of these refugees, or their experiences of trauma, loss, acculturation and resilience. Australian schools had been accustomed to newcomers from Asia and Europe; now is the time for them to develop new strategies and implement teaching methods suitable to the needs of these new refugees.

English as a Second Language (ESL) methods in Australian schools focus on Asian and European students; in the case of refugee students, assessment tools are needed to monitor progress as opposed to measuring summative achievement (Rutter, 2006 in Matthews, 2008). Immigrant and refugee students currently enrolled in the educational system of Australia face a lot of challenges while trying to adjust to the mainstream curriculum and the language. Sudanese students constitute the largest group of refugee arrivals to Australia. Though they have great expectations and aspirations, they struggle with adjusting to the new school system, the English language, and the new social environment (Brown et al., 2006).

One should not forget the fact that a group of refugees who have come from different regions of the same country may have different cultural values and beliefs, as well as diverse linguistic and religious experiences. Mainstream teachers and students should be aware of these differences. For example, Sudanese refugees currently finding refuge in Australia are usually from South Sudan. The majority of them are Christians and they speak diverse languages such as Dinka, Zande and Bari. Even though Arabic is the official language of Sudan, it is only in North Sudan, where the population is predominantly Muslim, that Arabic is used as the first language (Brown et al., 2006). Due to interruptive schooling over the years many of the Sudanese refugees have little to no literacy in their first or second language upon arrival in Australia. Moreover, interruptive schooling has also left the refugee students with little, if any, knowledge of school routine. These challenges, in addition to the traumatic experiences of living in refugee camps, losing a loved person or trying to adjust to new conditions, must be dealt with when refugee students are integrated into the mainstream school system (Brown et al., 2006).

Interviews conducted with refugee students in secondary schools in Canada indicated that students were unhappy. Most refugee students did not 'fit' in the new community, or they had difficulty learning English as a second language. Spanish-speaking students of refugee families – primarily from Honduras, El Salvador, Nicaragua and Guatemala – found English-only curriculum difficult, thus putting them at risk educationally. Vietnamese students who entered Canada as refugees also had problems learning English; they had linguistic problems that appear due to the different tones and pitches of one's native language. The majority of the Vietnamese students had to attend ESL classes for a longer term than other students of immigrant groups. Other than the language problems, the students faces socio-emotional and socio-economic problems. Many Vietnamese refugees reported being victims of racism and discrimination. (Gunderson, 2007).

Home to school communication

In a normal school setting, parental involvement has had a positive impact on the students' achievements. The more parents are involved at school, the better the children's academic records. Parental involvement is equally important for refugee children in a new school setting. However, it is much harder for refugee parents to participate in school programmes, volunteer in schools or help their children with homework. Often, the parents' lack of fluency in the new language, their own traumatic experiences, limited provision of emotional support to parents, and finally, their expectations about school and teachers become obstacles to parental involvement (McBrien, 2005). Ascher (1998 in McBrien, 2005) explains that refugee students usually misbehaved in school settings due to adjustment problems, survival behaviour adopted in the camps and in reaction to prejudice of US-born students. A study on Southeast Asian refugee parents in the United States showed that parents usually viewed the teachers as experts and therefore had no expectations of being involved in their children's education. Hmong parents, who expected a controlled school environment where learning takes place through memorization, seemed to be confused about the system of learning in the United States (Timm, 1994 in McBrien, 2005). Hence, schools are required to reinforce programmes supporting parental involvement by meeting the needs of refugee parents. Lee et al. (1993, cited in Hamilton, 2004, p. 86) suggested some ways of enhancing parental involvement: introducing parent education programmes by training parents in becoming better educators at home, enhancing second-language acquisition and parental understanding of the school curriculum, developing functional communities around the schools to encourage participation of parents from specific communities and, lastly, developing effective parent–school partnerships.

As previously mentioned, in order to encourage parental involvement, schools have to create healthy communication channels between home and school. Lopez et al. (2001, in Hamilton, 2004, p. 92) suggest that it is critical to meet the parental needs before considering involvement issues. It should be clear that refugee parents of various backgrounds will have different levels of involvement compared to the mass parent population of a specific school. Mediators play an important role in creating healthy communication between school and home. Mediators should have a thorough understanding of both cultures and act as a bridge between the child, school and parents (Hamilton, 2004). Mediation has proved to play a crucial role in facilitating the transition phase from one culture to the other. Parents should be regularly called for meetings, especially at the beginning of the student's school experience, to build strong ties between the school and the family.

Various case studies of refugee students have demonstrated the significance of strong communication between home and school, such as the case studies conducted by Jones (1998, cited in Hamilton, 2004, p. 90) in Greenwich, England. In Jones's study, the lack of communication was adversely affecting students' academic progress.

It is equally important to consider the ways in which students are welcomed in a new school setting – often known as the 'induction process'. Assigning a 'buddy' to the refugee student (Richman, 1998 in Hamilton, 2004, p. 90), assists the student's transition. More importantly, a social and educational assessment should be conducted to obtain information on various affecting factors, such as the language spoken at home; the child's previous education, academic achievements and current English language abilities; the parents' education and literacy level; and academic support at the home level.

Hamilton and Moore (2004) discuss the benefits of engaging members of the refugee community as teacher aides (if bilingual) and in refugee-helping services to build trust between the existing communities and the newcomers. It is equally important to include the refugee parents in the school's process of decision-making.

Opportunities of vocational and higher education

Refugee education does not end at the school level. Attention must also be given to tertiary refugee education. Refugee students are not considered locals; therefore, it is difficult for them to continue their education at universities and colleges, when paying tuition comes into play. However, university education is crucial to the future of refugees who want to find employment and contribute to the sustainable development of their community in either the host country or the country of their origin (Morland and Watson, 2007). Moreover, pursuing higher education gives a sense of self-accomplishment and confidence, especially for first-generation refugees. They have the urge to succeed and accomplish what their parents were not able to do because of their resettlement experiences.

The Annual Programme offers a limited number of scholarships for vocational education to secondary school graduates. The *Guidelines for Educational Assistance to Refugees* suggest that such scholarships be for short, job-oriented 'para-professional' courses preparing students for administrative, supervisory and technician levels of employment (Retamal et al., 1998). Additionally, UNHCR can support courses in language and management skills to enhance the employability of secondary school graduates in refugee camps or settlements. Moreover, UNHCR should help refugee communities organize non-formal educational and other training activities, in addition to providing training opportunities to vulnerable groups such as the disabled or female-headed households (Retamal et al., 1998).

The Albert Einstein Academic Refugee Initiative (DAFI) Programme (in German, *Deutsche Akademische Fluchtlingsinitiative Albert Einstein*) provides scholarships to refugees to study in polytechnic institutions, colleges and universities. This programme, inspired by the fact that Einstein himself was a refugee, is the only one that ensures higher education for refugees and is considered a significant component of the UNHCR mandate. By financing the annual DAFI in 1992, the German government responded to the call of various international declarations that reinforced the notion that education is a basic human right. DAFI provides refugees with the necessary qualifications for entering the workplace and contributing to the stability, reconstruction and development of their home country and the region. The main strategic objectives of DAFI are:

1. Help the sponsored student and his/her family achieve self-reliance through gainful employment.
2. Develop qualified human resources in order to contribute to the reconstruction of the country of origin upon repatriation.
3. Contribute to the refugee community pending a durable solution or repatriation.
4. Facilitate integration, temporary or permanent, and contribute skills to the host country if repatriation is not or not yet possible.
5. Serve as a role model for other refugee students to further their education, particularly female students to promote girls' education. (Morlang and Watson, 2007, p. 2)

Even though the number of DAFI scholars is limited, their contribution is great. Most scholars return to their country of origin and find employment in NGOs and other UN agencies.

Institutions assisting refugees and asylum seekers

Numerous organizations and institutions, along with the main UN bodies, work for and with refugees and asylum seekers worldwide. The International Institute for Educational Planning (IIEP), founded by UNESCO in 1963, aims to establish access, equity and quality in education and to develop leadership skills, analysing, evaluating and planning educational interventions as well as introducing capacity development strategies in developing countries. As part of its emergency response, the World Food Programme organizes school feeding programmes in developing countries aiming at increasing girls' enrolment (Nicolai and Triplehorn, 2003). The International Committee of the Red Cross, an independent organization founded in 1863 (whose mandate is similar to the 1949 Geneva Conventions), provides assistance to people affected by conflict and violence while promoting the laws protecting war victims (ICRC, 2010). The World University Service of Canada, composed of individuals and post-secondary institutions, established the Student Refugee Program in the 1950s to provide opportunities to people to continue their education once interrupted due to armed conflicts or persecution.[6] The Scholar Rescue Fund, launched as an initiative of the Institute of International Education, provides fellowships to scholars whose lives are threatened in their home countries due to their academic work. Through those fellowships, scholars find (temporary) refuge worldwide in colleges and universities where they can work without fear. Furthermore, the Iraq Scholar Rescue Project grants opportunities to Iraqi scholars to hold temporary academic positions in universities, colleges and institutions established in the Middle East and North Africa (IIE, Scholar Rescue Fund). Norwegian People's Aid, Save the Children, the European Council on Refugees and Exiles (ECRE), the US Committee for Refugees and Immigrants, the Sphere Project, Amnesty International, the Christian Children's Fund, the International Rescue Committee (IRC) and the Jesuit Refugee Service constitute a few of the main organizations working towards ensuring and protecting the education, health and employment of refugees, asylum seekers and IDPs.

The volume's content

This current volume on *Education, Refugees and Asylum Seekers* is composed of in-depth case studies conducted by professionals in the field of education. Issues of primary, secondary and non-formal educational opportunities – in relation to refugees and asylum seekers residing in the United Kingdom, the United States, Lebanon, Thailand and Korea – are discussed in the following chapters. The authors highlight the problems and challenges, both on the local and governmental levels, of providing education to refugees and asylum seekers. Education is one of the main components of humanitarian response during and after emergencies, hence it is the responsibility of policymakers, governmental organizations and NGOs to pay special attention to the challenges and drawbacks of providing education during and after human-made or natural disasters that result in the flow of thousands of refugees in various regions of the world (Asia, Africa, the Middle East or South America).

In Chapter 1, Candice Kay Lee examines the educational life histories of 25 North Korean defector university students in South Korea and looks in-depth at their formal, non-formal and informal educational experiences in North Korea. While much has been written on North Korean defectors, little is known about the implications that various educational events have on resultant learner values, attitudes, behaviours and other patterns of learning. By using the lens of educational transition the study contributes greater cultural understanding of the specific learning processes that individual North Korean defectors have experienced in largely foreign systems of education.

Chapter 2 discusses how the refugee community and international and non-governmental organizations (NGOs) attempt to reconcile their notions of the purpose of education – nation-building, livelihoods, the promotion of peace and conflict-prevention – in the seven predominantly Karen camps given the restrictions imposed by the Thai authorities and the ambiguity surrounding their future.

Su-Ann Oh analyses the education provided in the refugee camps in Thailand, highlighting that it is a product of dialogue between different sets of actors with distinct interests, as they negotiate the break in the links between education and the nation-state, education and livelihoods, and education and protection and peace.

In Chapter 3, Lala Demirdjian examines the challenges the NGOs and the UNRWA schools face in their attempt to provide formal and non-formal education to Palestinian refugees in Lebanon. This case study focuses on the relevance of educational content to refugee education. The harsh living conditions of Palestinian refugees in Lebanon compared to those in the rest of the host countries raises an interest in exploring the current situation in schools and among the youth of the Palestinian community.

In Chapter 4, Shriberg, Downs-Karkos and Weisberg discuss the attempts to introduce non-formal educational programs to the resettled refugee communities in the United States. The school-based and community approaches to reaching the needs of refugees (children, youth and adults) are discussed through the case studies of the WorkStyles and the International KidSuccess programmes introduced at the Spring Institute for Intercultural Learning and the Jewish Family Services in Denver, Colorado.

Chapter 5 examines the case of refugees established in Kent in England. James Dada highlights the interaction of the refugee population with the local community, as well as the community's response towards the flow of refugees in the region. Attention is given to the experiences of refugees from Europe, Africa, Asia and the Americas, as well as to the implementation of special projects such as the Finding Your Feet project and the Sunlight Centre.

Finally, in Chapter 6, McCorriston explores the provision of inclusive education for refugees and asylum seekers in secondary schools in England based on the new legal mandate that schools promote community cohesion. The provision of education pays great attention to the curriculum, instruction and extended school services. The case studies indicate a positive experience with implementing inclusion programs through which schools can promote social cohesion for refugee students.

Notes

1 Information available from the Columbia Electronic Encyclopedia (2007) at www.infoplease.com/ce6/history/A0850078.html.

2 Palestinian refugees living in host countries (Lebanon, Syria and Jordan) are under the protection of the United Nations Relief and Works Agency for Palestine Refugees in the Near East (UNRWA). UNRWA also operates in Gaza and the West Bank and is responsible for providing relief, health and education services to Palestinian refugees who are not under the UNHCR mandate.

3 For more information about INEE, visit www.ineesite.org.

4 For detailed information on the 'Revised (1995) Guidelines for Educational Assistance to Refugees' refer to Annexe 1 in Retamal, G., and Aedo-Richmond, R. (1998), *Education as a Humanitarian Response*, 289–359.

5 Emphasis added.

6 For more information on the WUSC, visit www.sfuwusc.ca.

References

BBC News (2 September 2009), 'EU plans to admit more refugees'. Available from http://news.bbc.co.uk/2/hi/europe/8233187.stm (last accessed 26 October 2010).

Betancourt, T., Simmons, S., Borisova, I., Brewer, S., Iweala, U. and De La Soudiere, M., (2008), 'High hopes, grim reality: Reintegration and the education of former child soldiers in Sierra Leone'. *Comparative Education Review*, 52(4), 565–87.

Bocker, A. et al. (eds) (1998), *Regulation of Migration: International Experiences*. Amsterdam: Het Spinhuis.

Brown, J., Miller, J. and Mitchell, J. (2006), 'Interrupted Schooling and the Acquisition of Literacy: Experiences of Sudanese Refugees in Victorian Secondary Schools'. *Australian Journal of Language and Literacy*, 29(2), 150–62.

Candappa, M. (2000), 'The Right to Education and an Adequate Standard of Living: Refugee Children in the uk'. *The International Journal of Children's Rights*, 8(3), 261–70.

Clark, B. (2006), *Twice a Stranger: The Mass Expulsions that Forged Modern Greece and Turkey*. Cambridge, MA: Harvard University Press.

Davies, L. and Talbot, C. (2008), 'Learning in Conflict and Postconflict Contexts'. *Comparative Education Review*, 52(4), 509–17.

Elliott, M. (1973), 'The United States and Forced Repatriation of Soviet Citizens, 1944–47'. *Political Science Quarterly*, 88(2), 253–75. The Academy of Political Science.

Evans, A. and Murray, R. (2009), 'The Gateway Protection Programme: an evaluation. An overview of Immigration research and Statistics (IRS) research exploring the integration of refugees resettled under the UK's Gateway Protection Programme in Sheffield, Bolton, Hull and Rochdale'. Home Office Research Report 12. Available from http://rds.homeoffice.gov.uk/rds/pdfs09/horr12c.pdf (last accessed 8 November 2010).

Fazel, M., Wheeler, J. and Danesh, J. (2005), 'Prevalence of Serious Mental Disorder in 7000 Refugees Resettled in Western Countries: A Systematic Review'. *The Lancet*, 365(9467), 1309–14.

FMO (undated), 'World Refugee Day and Refugee Week'. Available from http://www.forcedmigration.org/browse/thematic/refugeeweek.htm (last accessed 8 November 2010).

Frater-Mathieson, K. (2004), 'Refugee Trauma, Loss and Grief: Implications for Intervention', in Hamilton, R. and Moore, D. (eds), *Educational Intervention for Refugee Children: Theoretical Perspectives and Implementing Best Practice*. London, New York: RoutledgeFalmer, pp. 12–34.

Geltman et al. (2008), 'The "Lost Boys" of Sudan: Use of Health Services and Functional Health Outcomes of Unaccompanied Refugee Minors Resettled in the u.s.'. *Journal of Immigrant and Minority Health*, 10, 389–96 (Springer).

Goodwin-Gill, S. G. and McAdam, J. (2007), *The Refugee in International Law* (3rd edn). Oxford: Oxford University Press.

Gunderson, L. (2007), *English-Only Instruction and Immigrant Students in Secondary Schools: a Critical Examination*. Mahwah, NJ: Lawrence Erlbaum Associates.

Hamilton, R. and Moore, D. (2004), in Hamilton, R. and Moore, D. (eds), *Educational Intervention for Refugee Children: Theoretical Perspectives and Implementing Best Practice*. London, New York: RoutledgeFalmer, pp. 106–16.

Hamilton, R. (2004), 'Schools, Teachers and Education of Refugee Children', in Hamilton, R. and Moore, D. (eds), *Educational Intervention for Refugee Children: Theoretical Perspectives and Implementing Best Practice*. London, New York: RoutledgeFalmer, pp. 83–96.

Hassell, J. E. (1991), Russian Refugees in France and the United States Between the World Wars (Transactions of the American Philosophical Society). American Philosophical Society. Philadelphia.

Hieronymi, O. (2009), 'Refugee Children and Their Future'. *Refugee Survey Quarterly*, 27(4), 6–25.

Horakova, P. (2003), 'Forced displacement of Czech population under Nazis in 1938 and 1943'. Available from http://www.radio.cz/en/section/talking/forced-displacement-of-czech-population-under-nazis-in-1938-and-1943 (last accessed 8 November 2010).

Hornberger, J. G. (April 1995), 'Repatriation – The Dark Side of World War II', Part 3. Freedom Daily. The Future of Freedom Foundation. Available from http://www.fff.org/freedom/0495a.asp (last accessed 3 November 2010).

ICRC (2010), 'About the International Committee of the Red Cross'. Available from http://www.icrc.org/eng/who-we-are/overview-who-we-are.htm (last accessed 11 November 2010).

Institute of International Education, Scholar Rescue Fund (undated), 'About Us'. Available from http://www.scholarfund.org/pages/aboutus.php (Last accessed 11 November 2010).

The Japan Times (editorial) (12 October 2008), 'Refugees in Japan'. Available from http://search.japantimes.co.jp/cgi-bin/ed20081012a2.html (last accessed 23 October 2010).

Khamis, V. (January 2005), 'Post-Traumatic Stress Disorder Among School Age Palestinian Children'. *Child Abuse and Neglect*, 29(1), 81–95. Pergamon.

League of Nations (1936), 'Provisional Arrangement of 4th 1936 concerning the Status of Refugees Coming from Germany'. League of Nations Treaty Series, vol. 171 (3952). Available from http://www.unhcr.org/refworld/pdfid/3dd8d0ae4.pdf (last accessed 8 November 2010).

Marek, M. (2005), Deutsche Welle, 'Final Compensation Pending for Former Nazi Forced Laborers'. Available from http://www.dw-world.de/dw/article/0,,1757323,00.html (last accessed 8 November 2010).

Matthews, J. (2008), 'Schooling and Settlement: Refugee Education in Australia', *International Studies in Sociology of Education*, 18(1), 31–45.

McBrien, J. L. (2005), 'Educational Needs and Barriers of Refugee Students in the United States: A Review of the Literature'. *Review of Educational Research*, 75(3), 329–64.

Mooney, E. and Wyndham, J. (2010), 'The Right to Education in Situations of Internal Displacement', in Kalin, W. et al. (eds), *Incorporating the Guiding Principles on Internal Displacement into Domestic Law: Issues and Challenges*, Studies in Transnational Legal Policy, No. 41, pp. 247–90. Brookings-Bern Project on Internal Displacement, the American Society of International Law.

Morlang, C. and Watson, S., (2007), 'Tertiary Refugee Education: Impacts and Achievements 15 years of DAFI'. Technical Support Section, Division of Operation Services, UNHCR, Geneva.

Nansen International Office for Refugees. The Nobel Peace Prize 1938 'History of Organization'. Available from http://nobelprize.org/nobel_prizes/peace/laureates/1938/nansen-history.html (last accessed 8 November 2010).

Nicolai, S. (2003), *Education in Emergencies: a Tool Kit for Starting and Managing Education in Emergencies*. London: Save the Children.

Nicolai, S. and Triplehorn, C. (2003), *The Role of Education in Protecting Children in Conflict*, Network Paper 42. London: Humanitarian Practice Network.

North, J. (2006), 'Soviet Prisoners of War: Forgotten Nazi Victims of World War II' (originally appeared in the January–February 2006 issue of *World War II* magazine). Available from http://www.historynet.com/soviet-prisoners-of-war-forgotten-nazi-victims-of-world-war-ii.htm/2 (last accessed 3 November 2010).

OHCHR (1950), 'Convention relating to the Status of Refugees'. Available from http://www.unhchr.ch/html/menu3/b/o_c_ref.htm (last accessed 12 August 2007).

Pantuliano, S. (ed.) (2009), *Uncharted Territory: Land, Conflict and Humanitarian Action*. Warwickshire, UK: Practical Action Publishing.

Retamal, G. and Aedo-Richmond, R. (eds) (1998), *Education as a Humanitarian Response*. International Bureau of Education, London: Cassell.

Rigsby, Kent J. (1996), *Asylia: Territorial Inviolability in the Hellenistic World*. Berkeley: University of California Press.

Sinclair, M. (2002), *Planning Education In and After Emergencies*. UNESCO.

Sinclair, M. (1998). 'Refugee Education in the Mid-1990s', in Retamal, G. and Aedo-Richmond, R. (eds), *Education as a Humanitarian Response*. International Bureau of Education, Cassell, London, pp. 262–70.

Smawfield, D. (1993), 'A comparative study of the primary education for Mozambican refugees in Malawi and Zambia'. *Journal of Refugee Studies*, 6(3), 286–95 (Oxford University Press).

Sundquist, K., Johansson, L. M., DeMarinis, V., Johansson, S. E. and Sundquist, J. (2005), 'Posttraumatic Stress Disorder and Psychiatric Co-Morbidity: Symptoms in a Random Sample of Female Bosnian Refugees'. *European Psychiatry: The Journal of the Association of European Psychiatrists*, 20(2), 158–64.

Tawil, S. (2000), 'International Humanitarian Law and Basic Education'. *International Review of the Red Cross*, 839, 581–99.

The Columbia Electronic Encyclopedia (2007), 'United Nations Relief and Rehabilitation Administration'. New York: Columbia University Press (6th edn). Available from http://www.infoplease.com/ce6/history/A0850078.html (last accessed 8 November 2010).

Time (1979), 'Refugees: Save Us! Save Us!'. Available from http://www.time.com/time/magazine/article/0,9171,920455-5,00.html (last accessed 8 November 2010).

Tolstoy, N. (1988), 'Forced Repatriation in the Soviet Union: The Secret Betrayal'. Available from http://www.hillsdale.edu/news/imprimis/archive/issue.asp?year=1988&month=12 (last accessed 5 November 2010).

UNHCR (1994), *Refugee Children: Guidelines on Protection and Care*. Geneva: UNHCR.

UNHCR (1999), *The United Nations Decade for Human Rights Education (1995–2004)*. Geneva: United Nations.

UNHCR (2001), *Learning for a Future: Refugee Education in Developing Countries*. Geneva: UNHCR.

UNHCR Core Group on Durable Solutions (2003), 'Framework for durable solutions for refugees and persons of concern'. UNHCR: Geneva. Available from http://www.unhcr.org/partners/PARTNERS/3f1408764.pdf (last accessed 3 November 2010).

UNHCR (2009), 'Protecting Refugees and the Role of UNHCR'. Available from http://www.unhcr.org/refworld/topic,4565c2251d,459e770f2,49f1d3e92,0.html (last accessed 10 November 2010).

UNHCR Division of Programme Support and Management (2010), *2009 Global Trends: Refugees, Asylum-Seekers, Returnees, Internally Displaced and Stateless Persons*. Geneva: UNHCR. Available from www.unhcr.org/statistics (last accessed 2 October 2010).

UNHCR (2010), 'Convention and protocol relating to the status of refugees'. Geneva. Available from http:www.unhcr.org/3b66c2aa10.html (last accessed July 5, 2011).

UNICEF (1997), 'Who is a child soldier?', *Cape Town Principles and Best Practices on the Recruitment of Children into the Armed Forces and on Demobilization and Social Reintegration of Child Soldiers in Africa. Cape Town, 27–30 April 1997. Available from* http://www.unicef.org/emerg/index_childsoldiers.html.

US Department of State, Office of the Historian, 'Milestones: 1921–1936: The Immigration Act of 1924 (The Johnson-Reed Act)'. Available from http://history.state.gov/milestones/1921-1936/ImmigrationAct (last accessed on 7 November 2010).

Winthrop, R. and Kirk, J. (2008), 'Learning for a bright future: schooling, armed conflict, and children's well-being', *Comparative Education Review*, 52(4), 639–61.

Yule, W. (2000), 'Emanuel Miller Lecture; From Progroms to "Ethnic Cleansing": Meeting the needs of war affected children', *Journal of Child Psychology and Psychiatry*, 41(6), 695–702.

Zurcher, E. J. (2003), 'Greek and Turkish Refugees and Deportees 1912–1924'. Turkology Update Leiden Project (TULP) working papers archive department of Turkish studies, Universiteit Leiden. Available from http://www.transanatolie.com/english/Turkey/Turks/Ottomans/ejz18.pdf (last accessed 29 October 2010).

1

The Educational Life Histories of a Group of North Korean Defector University Students in South Korea

Candice Kay Lee

Chapter Outline

Introduction

The economic decline of North Korea over the past 20 years has severely damaged the national education system that nurtures the ideologically rigid socialist state. As images of an ideal nation, crafted carefully over the past half century, begin to give way to a new reality, many North Koreans have experienced dramatic shifts in their perceptions of their so-called worker's paradise. This is evident from the numerous defector testimonies captured in human rights reports, academic research and journalistic accounts, most recently popularized in Barbara Demick's seminal work entitled 'Nothing to Envy' (Demick, 2010). The rapid rise in the number of refugees fleeing the country creates a problem for governments affected by an increasing number of immigrants seeking inclusion in many educational systems around the world, particularly that of South Korea.

The South Korean government, with its geographical and historical proximity to North Korea, is most significantly affected, facing the challenge of how to accommodate most of the North Korean defectors, who usually enter its border via other countries. From the end of the Korean War in July 1953 until 2009, an estimated 18,000 defectors have entered South Korea, a number which is almost certain to surpass 20,000 by the end of 2010 (North Korean Economy Watch, 2009). While these figures are still relatively low, the Bank of Korea estimates that if reunification were to occur, the total number of North Koreans in what is now South Korea would exceed three million (Ko et al., 2004).

Thus, as migration of North Koreans continues to increase, it is necessary to better understand the defector population. Little is known currently about the North Korean refugee experience that would help host nations better understand and therefore better accommodate the educational adaptation needs of North Koreans. This lack of understanding justifies an in-depth study of individual North Korean refugees' historical and current processes of educational change and the impact that various formal, non-formal and informal learning events encountered during transition have for their lives as students in South Korea.

But a major hindrance to such understanding is the prevailing climate surrounding North Korean studies – often one of speculation and fascination. Like Burma, Cuba and many other closed societies in the world, North Korea is often portrayed as a country shrouded in mystery. Sensational and biased media coverage perpetuates this stereotype. There also exists the threat posed by some academic studies that promote a narrow right-wing agenda, confirming preconceptions about the so-called hermit kingdom. For example, seminal works by leading North Koreanists in the United States such as Victor D. Cha, Marcus Noland, Stephen Haggard and other members of the Council of Foreign Relations are written mainly for an international security audience and thus fail to objectively perceive North Korea country issues from a depoliticized vantage point. This sometimes breeds cavalier liberal democratic attempts by mostly Western observers to universalize the rights and wrongs of the North Korean situation, especially within a post-communist geopolitical framework that is concerned largely with human rights, cultural relativism and self-determination issues. In effect, North Korean studies are approached by some Western researchers as if the proverbial slate of the Cold War has been wiped clean along with any genuine desire to render a thoughtful, respectful and informed depiction of its cultural heritage and the values of its people.

This general fascination also persists in North Korean defector research. If ever there were a 'popular' refugee group, according to a phrase coined by Gibney (1999), North Korean refugees would be it. As objects of foreign interest, they too often succumb to unwarranted scrutiny by outsiders, particularly the media, wishing to comment generally and in essentialist terms on North Korean defectors and their processes of migration and adaptation into the new South Korean landscape. One needs only to read a news article or view a documentary on the North Korean refugee crisis to get a sense of the ideological puritanism applied in such reporting. Throughout the duration of this study, I have received numerous requests from foreign journalists who were 'fascinated' by the chance to obtain a 'rare glimpse' into the everyday lives of defectors, hoping to document how they operate an ATM machine, shop at the local markets, and so on.

The basic premise of their inquiry is more often than not couched in somewhat patronizing logic: having been educated in a climate so thoroughly dominated by a monolithic worldview, scholars and experts wonder how refugees can cope with a radically different set of ideological circumstances. They wonder if transitioning from dictatorship to democracy creates a tug of war within the minds of the refugees – 'Who am I?', 'What is true?' and 'What can I rely on?' How do North Korean defectors cope with the culture shock of adapting to a new democratic society? How does a North Korean mind make the leap into the South Korean context, which is heavily influenced by modernization and the capitalist culture of the West? How effective is the indoctrination and how capable of change are defectors? Furthermore, what does their migration augur for the future regional stability and changing social landscape of the Korean Peninsula?

There is so much valuable cultural information to glean from North Korean defectors' educational journeys, if only to – according to one of the foremost thinkers in comparative international education, Sir Michael Sadler (1901) – 'be better fitted to understand our own' (Sadler, 1901, cited in Bereday, 1964 and Phillips, 2006). Therefore, while the subject matter concerns theoretical determinants of large-scale human migration, either forced or voluntary, this study is situated clearly within the field of international education and has been inspired by several comparative educationists such as Sir Michael Sadler (1908), Edmund King (1979), Brian Holmes (1981) and many others. This disciplinary focus is important as my research primarily aims at a better understanding of the educational life histories of North Korean immigrants, who struggle to reconcile their past and present lives. One way to acquire such understanding is to study the actual learning processes these individuals experience throughout transition, adaptation and integration into their new host societies.

Rationale

Three main dimensions– substantive, methodological and theoretical – of this study are considered to justify its value. First, the current study is in part justified by the dearth of research, in both English and Korean literature, on North Korean defector university students. This research gap poses a problem particularly for non-Korean speaking Western scholars wishing to conduct research on North Korean defector education. It is therefore hoped that the results of this study will benefit an anglophone research audience.

Further, there are methodological difficulties not only in overcoming the language barrier but also in geographical constraints for accessing defector populations located in China, South Korea and other third countries. As North Korea is arguably the most closed society in the world, it is almost impossible to obtain primary data or conduct observations, surveys and interviews from within the country. The reliability of any emerging data remains highly suspect due to the lack of transparency, adequate research cooperation and scholarly exchanges between North Korea and the rest of the world. Because state officials have been consistently known to act in ways and express views contradictory to their official propaganda, it is difficult to verify the data due to the lack of empirical evidence to support claims. Thus, it is advised that materials, official data, statistics and policies of the North Korean government are never to be taken at face value. To overcome this dilemma, proximity research with defectors is often undertaken by South Korean researchers who look upon defectors as a proxy for large-scale system integration. While relying on defector interviews is not ideal, it has been a valuable source of information for those interested in gaining new policy insights on the issue of rapprochement between the two Koreas.

A third problem is that essentialist frameworks are often applied to North Korean research. Thus, analysis of defector education and migration from communism into the larger world of vastly different ideological reference points is constructed around rigid ideological classifications. As a result, there remains 'a scarcity of empirical data on this [which] prevents us from any in-depth analysis. Only some scattered evidence may be introduced' (Kim and Lee, 2003, p. 303).

> Even the relatively limited social analyses have not been too keen about approaching the study of North Korea from a perspective of the sociology of development and modernization. In other words, the difficulty of even simply depicting what the society is like has overwhelmed social analysis to the extent that few have dared to formulate a decent theoretical framework for the study of North Korean society. (Kim and Lee, 2003, p. 2)

This portrays a visible bias operating in several previous research attempts. I have observed the stigma attached to South Koreans wishing to conduct research with North Korean defectors, who may be looked upon as odd – a familiar experience that I encountered not only from strangers but also from relatives living in South Korea. Reasons for this stem from decades of learned prejudice that South Koreans apparently still harbour against North Koreans. Thus, this study's findings may help the educational researcher who hopes to comment more generally on North Korean issues pertaining to a larger philosophical dimension in the unification debate: the challenges, problems and processes of bringing together the minds of peoples from two very different Korean cultures. In aiming to gather information on individual defector learning processes and their impact on learner values, I hope to deepen existing theoretical frameworks within which we understand integration of North Korea and North Koreans into a more globalized world.

Life history

To explore these learning processes, this study examines the life histories of a number of North Korean defector university students currently living in South Korea and the impact that various formal, non-formal and informal educational experiences have had on them. The study addresses the following overarching research question: what are the educational experiences of North Korean defector university students throughout multiple learning landscapes and what influences do these have upon their resultant learner values, attitudes, behaviours and other patterns of learning?

The aim is to arrive at new understandings of North Korean defectors' past and current educational experiences and the potential dilemmas arising from them, as well as the possibility of overcoming these adaptation challenges. By gathering defector biographical educational information and analysing the implications of various dilemmas arising from processes of transition and adaptation throughout multiple learning landscapes – North Korea, China, South Korea and other transition countries – it is hoped that these data may contribute new knowledge on a group of learners about whom the world knows very little.

Collecting life histories is important for gaining a full account of defector formal, non-formal and informal educational experiences throughout transition across multiple geographical and social landscapes. The method by which historians attempt to make sense of the thick and oftentimes 'messy' qualitative data they gather is useful for the current research. Faraday and Plummer (1979) argue that the life history technique 'is at its best when it is being used in an exploratory fashion for generating many concepts, hunches and ideas, both at the local and situational level and on a historical structural level' (p. 785). Thus, the life history method used in the main study extended the exploratory study and was useful for gaining a 'broad general *exploratory* [emphasis mine] understanding' (Faraday and Plummer, p. 782) of the primary research question and subquestions. This approach 'contemporarily [pursues a] hermeneutics [that] is concerned with ways to explain, translate, and interpret perceived reality . . . recounting accurately the meanings, which research participants give to the reality around them' (LeCompte and Preissle, 1993, p. 30).

In order to meet this a posteriori goal for facilitating the hermeneutic process of elicitation and explanation of emerging themes and concepts, the research design also used ethnography, in which the main concern is with the 'graphia' aspect for its use, 'which is writing or representing in a specified field [about the] ethnos, or race, people, or cultural group' (LeCompte and Preissle, 1993, p. 1).

Despite the various labels given to life history, among which are 'life story', 'oral history', 'biography' and 'lived experience', all share in common 'two essential characteristics, its historicity and subjectivity' (Bertaux, 1981, p. 20). Historicity 'throws light upon historical changes which have occurred in the wider world during that person's lifetime' (Faraday and Plummer, 1979, p. 780). Researching the individual must take into account the provenance or historical background of his/her learning biography, wherein

> the main characteristics of this 'formal' life history are the emphasis on long-term continuities in individual experience, rather than on broadly based thematic and comparative topics . . . because of this it can lead us to a fuller understanding of the stages and critical periods in the process of his development (Burgess, 1984, p. 34).

Subjectivity, on the other hand, focuses the analysis upon individual experiences rather than a broad set of collective 'thematic and comparative topics'. The life historian aims 'to understand how larger concepts get defined and worked out by one individual' (Hatch and Wisniewski, 1995, p. 119). Subjectivity helps to explore the inner life of the defector and 'how' they respond to and draw relationships with various features of their sociocultural processes of education, transition and adaptation. In sum, historicity interacts with subjectivity by situating the individual within a broader personal, historical, social, institutional and/or political context.

In sum, life history was considered an important approach for exploring in depth the educational past and present of the defectors. The analysis examines learning dilemmas arising from these experiences that take place across various transition points and/or phases. The critical judgements and educational decisions individuals make at these life stages consequently form their characters or what may be considered their learning personalities.

Conceptualization of the study

In order to understand the research aims, it is important to explain what is meant by education and associated patterns of learning and learner values. Education is often thought of as a primary social institution that transmits core cultural and political values to its citizens, manufacturing a nation's ethos generation after generation (Althusser, 1971; Bowles and Gintis, 1976; Gramsci 1971). Every nation's education system has its own political aims and pedagogy, shaping the worldviews and value orientations of its citizens – be they in a liberal or Marxist framework – such as in North Korea where education and the ruling state ideology are one and the same. But more than being a mere conduit for national attitudes, values and behaviours, existentialists such as Greene (1978) and Oakeshott (1933, 1989) would argue that education is not a series of fixed events, but rather acts as a powerful socializing agent resulting in 'praxis', 'wide-awakeness', self-change and self-discovery, or what Kneller (1958), remembering Kierkegaard's homage to Socrates' states, called a human being's 'implied subjectivity' (p. 133). Therefore, in this study, education is perceived to be a process that drives the transformation in learner values, attitudes and behaviours, occurring across several stages of development such that no two learners' experiences are exactly alike.

By directing the educational investigation around defectors' changing values, attitudes and behaviours, I hope to reveal individual understandings about self and self-change taking place throughout transition, as well as how learner personalities are formed and transformed by select educational experiences. This embodies another important idea, that of education as being essentially an experience. Put another way, every experience of an individual has the potential to be educational. According to Dewey (1916), education is a process that allows one to 'learn from experience', making 'a backward and forward connection between and facilitating our process' of the way we see 'that a certain way of acting and a certain consequence are connected' (pp. 140–5). Just as past and present educational events are connected, so are the experiences of social relation to that existing reality. It is this romantic confrontation with the outside world or one's sociocultural environs that may give rise to a Byronesque set of conflicts and dilemmas faced by each individual.

A broad definition of education does not aim to pit communist North and liberal democratic South Korean ideals against one another, as is often the case, but rather seeks to understand the 'changes' and 'processes' that occur as learners journey from one learning context to another. It is not merely a process of replacing old values with new ones, or in this case communist values derived from a North Korean socialist education system to one defined by liberal, Western values. Rather, education is understood as a process of enculturation, the gradual acquisition and acceptance of the ideas, beliefs, roles, motives and thought patterns of a particular culture, whether through formal or non-formal systems. The process of education becomes a reinvention of culture oriented around the creation of new learner values and the abandonment, preservation and reshaping of old ones. According to theorists such as Bruner (1986, 1990, 1996), education is inextricably bound up in culture.

> The culturalist approaches education in a very different way. Culturalism takes as its first premise that education is not an island, but part of the continent of culture. It asks first what function 'education' serves in the culture and what role it plays in the lives of those who operate within it . . . education is a major embodiment of a culture's way of life. (Bruner, 1996, pp. 11–13)

Stenhouse (1967) similarly argues that its role in the curriculum is 'as culture rather than knowledge' (p. 88).

Thus, education acts as an important cultural mediating tool for the refugees as they navigate their way through multiple learning landscapes. The variety of educational experiences they encounter must be seen as occurring within larger sociocultural processes, shaping past and current patterns of learning. Focusing the educational investigation about these cultural reference points helps our understanding of changing values throughout defector adjustment processes and the meanings defector learners give to the various educational experiences in the 'complex pursuit of fitting a culture to the[ir] needs . . . and of fitting [themselves] and their ways of knowing to the needs of the culture' (Bruner, 1996, p. 43).

Investigating individual learning processes, according to Spence (2007), helps to deepen our own cultural understanding of a people about whom we know very little. I am very interested in what occurs during transition and the extent to which aspects of traditional educational cultures are retained. It is hoped that a conceptual understanding of historical and theoretical determinants of defector learning processes may help us to analyze the impact that formal, non-formal, and educational experiences have upon their changing lives. By acknowledging a variety of past and current educational circumstances and the values they impart, I hope to build a composite picture of who 'they' are. And here I want to make clear that this study is not about the North Korean 'collectivity', living in a society dubbed 'the hermit kingdom' and virtually shut off from the rest of the world; these are exactly the sort of stereotypes this study takes aim at. Rather, the focus is on 'individual' North Korean defectors whose educational life histories in many respects – especially since defection – are very different from those still living in the North.

Theoretical framework

While utilizing historical information helps to capture the nuances of refugees' educational circumstances and learner values during transition, a theoretical framework must take account of their entire journey from beginning to end. Transition models are drawn from the fields of comparative and international education, and to a lesser extent from refugee studies. They serve the purpose of ordering defector educational experiences by conceptualizing processes of transition as not chaotic, but describable through various transition points and phases. Identifying key transition points shows how external educational changes affect an individual's internal value changes and learning processes.

Educational thinkers such as Dewey (1934, 1938) have often used the idea of experience to describe an individual's encounter with moments of chance, choice and change. Existentialists, as indicated above, might apply this thought to education by conceiving of it as a process towards greater awareness and self-discovery leading to the formation of a person's consciousness and character. So too is the concept of 'educational experiences' used in this study as a framework for describing these personal value changes by pinpointing specific transition points throughout defector learning processes, suggesting how life may indeed be experienced as a series of events throughout one's educational life history as well as the sociocultural significance that various educational settings have for defector learner values. Hence, by its very nature as an 'ideographic method', life history utilizes 'existing theory [that] can be used as a basis for formulating the questions directed at the . . . subject' (Faraday, 1979, p. 782).

Hence, educational transition theories and models are drawn upon to reinforce this concept and help to facilitate our ability to structure, organize and describe complex educational journeys and the experiences taking place at various transition points, to show how larger meta-narratives and sociocultural processes of adaptation interact with defectors' personal experiences of education in ways that significantly impact upon their various learner values, attitudes, behaviours and other patterns of learning.

Theories have been used in educational research to describe processes of transition of former communist countries such as those in Eastern Europe and the former Soviet Union (Birzea, 1994, 1996; Broadfoot, 2000; Broadfoot et al., 1981; Offe, 1996). Reflecting on large-scale transitions in these regions, Griffin (2002) claims that national education systems and the institutions that comprise them must be a cornerstone of such transitions and indeed 'part of a greater societal change, which involves paradigm shifts in a country's culture, economics and societal relationships' (p. 13). Other researchers elaborate upon this by using socio-anthropological models and transition theories to describe processes of adaptation or adjustment (Calhoun, 1991; Giddens, 1982; Habermas, 1988).

Birzea (1994; 1996) has developed an educational transition sequence that borrows ideas from other education specialists and behavioural models. He identifies: (a) a pre-transition phase of ideological collapse; (b) uncertainty about future development, during which time new laws may be adopted, in particular those to reinstate culure; (c) introducing more formal political reforms; (d) purging the unnecessary such as histories, philosophies; (e) seeking stabilization/formalization of the education system and structure; (f) implementing further educational reforms, legislations, revitilizations, along with economic growth and firming up of legal educational framework.

Similarly, McLeish and Phillips (1998) employ a 'pebble in the pond' metaphor to potray the increasing complexity that these societies in transition experience, culminating in a vast array of problems (economic globalization, educational resources and efficiency). They recognize that a significant limitation of system-level transition practices is that they fail to take into account how government policy will affect single educational institutions and individuals (students, parents, teachers) who are involved in the process of education and whose roles are largely left out of their statecraft strategems.

Thus, while such macro models depict widespread educational reforms occuring at the state leve;, transition models must also address the increasing complexity for individuals who are affected by system-level educational reforms. In his research on the processes of educational transition occuring in the countries of post-Cold War Europe, Birzea alludes to the notion of cultural transitions occuring as part of larger systematic institutional changes in the individual's outer world. This supports the idea of education (put forth in the introduction) as being a process of enculturation affected significantly by external sociocultural factors. Although some values are strengthened during this process – such as citizenship and values associated with nationhood, rediscovery of religion and so on – others have the possibility of being misunderstood, misinterpreted and rejected by the participating individual.

Writing mainly for an educational policy audience seeking guidelines for new forms of citizenship, Birzea argues that in order to achieve civic and political socialization of peoples from these various regions, a paradigm shift must be made away from a focus on institutional transitions (i.e. political pluralism, the rule of law and a market economy) to cultural transitions and at the level of the individual, by which he means 'the changing of mentalities, attitudes, values and social relations,' which is an altogether more 'delicate matter' (Birzea, 1996, p. 674). He implies that large-scale educational aims ought to be transferable to the individual's experience of transition, such as the more universal humanist values of democracy and democratization. Thus, while some changes take place at the systems level, such as at educational establishments, this study looks more closely at the individual level, portraying a psychosocial dimension of post-communist mental transitions.

A more useful position to this individualist concern on changing values may be found in Hopson's (1984) psychosocial model of transition, which examines various internal phases and dimensions of change. Hopson's conceptualization of transition focuses on a more learner-oriented, behavioural psychosocial model to analyse processes of social adaptation and integration, and contains several stages that correspond to phases indicated in other transition theories. His model elegantly portrays the idea that every transition, 'as a rule', consists of eight phases:

> a) the initial shock due to political and ideological upheaval; b) underestimation of success of change; c) depression once reality is accurately perceived; d) habituation to the new situation; e) understanding of the meaning of that change; f) the search for solutions to overcome the crisis; g) the end of transition. (Hopson, 1984 cited in Birzea, 1994, p. 139)

In the first phase of Hopson's model, initial or culture shock has been described as the loss of the sense of direction individuals experience when they find that they come into contact with fundamentally different cultures and can no longer act according to the norms familiar to them (Henslin, 1995). It builds a relationship with theories proposed in immigration studies, where it has been noted that the sociological development of the outsider's critical mind in this way is nothing new.

> Schutz (1964) notes how, in the weeks and months following an immigrant's arrival in a host society, what he or she previously took for granted as knowledge about that society turns out to be unreliable, if not obviously false . . . In the process of learning how to participate in the host society, the stranger gradually acquires an inside knowledge of it, which supplants his or her previous 'external' knowledge. (Crossley et al., 2007, p. 8)

Hopson's model then integrates a key Durkheimian concept on *anomie,* occurring at stage 3 or transition point 3. Birzea acknowledges the importance of the anomie phase in transition that each individual experiences, which he defines as a state of insecurity, uncertainty, apathy, existential reckoning and moral disorientation. Gaining an understanding of these said internalization processes are central to a deeper understanding of defector educational experiences.

The next and most important stage, according to Hopson, is habituation. A better way of understanding this transition phase within a post-communist framework may be achieved by translating system-level terms of 'glasnost' (openness) and 'perestroika' (realization of reforms) into a more micro context. A form of 'mental' glasnost, or receptivity to new external reforms and experiences, marks the point at which defectors begin internalizing various dilemmas. Internalization processes eventually result in the externalization of those dilemmas through a form of 'learning' (perestroika), or educational outcomes. This highlights the usefulness of acquiring personal defector perspectives on transition. Employing these two metaphors of learning processes taking place at the level of the individual by emphasizing mental and personal transformations and their interaction with certain external sociocultural forces helps to capture a more psychosocial dimension of learning.

In sum, whereas the macro model helps to more accurately describe the effects that important sociocultural processes have upon the educational lives of defectors the psychosocial model helps to answer the question, 'What do their complex educational journeys tell us about them?' Together, the theoretical and conceptual lenses adopted for this study help to evaluate learner-oriented perspectives of North Korean defectors' experiences of educational transition and the value changes taking place at the level of individuals and occurring along a sociocultural historical continuum of events, such that the more micro, psychosocial transition model represents.

Sample population, data collection and ethical considerations

The main study involved a total of 25 participants, consisting of North Korean defector students studying at four universities in Seoul (Yonsei, Sogang, Hankuk and Chungang), where a large North Korean student group already exists on campus. During the time the main study was conducted, the total number of North Korean defectors attending either a two- or four-year university in Seoul increased from 222 in the 2006 academic year to an estimated

380 in the 2007 academic year, resulting in greater on-campus support for the student population.

Characteristics of the sample

A total of 25 North Korean defectors currently attending a South Korean university at the start of the study participated in the main study: 10 women and 15 men with ages ranging between 22 and 34. The majority (22) came from North or South Hamkyung province, and two from Pyongyang. All belonged to what is known as the same 'transition cohort generation' (Miller, 2000, p. 32), implying that all students participating in this study had a common set of shared historical experiences over a similar time period as well as basic background characteristics associated with transition.

They shared similar educational backgrounds in terms of level of schooling achieved in North Korea. Out of 25 students, 24 had attended middle-high school (MHS) in North Korea, though 9 did not graduate and 9 others had attended university or a two-year technical or teacher's college in North Korea (though may not have graduated). These nine students also appear to have fled North Korea on average four to five years later, perhaps an indication of the better circumstances in North Korea that presumably allowed them to achieve higher levels of education before defection.

Most had spent an average of three to four years in China and had been living in South Korea for an average of three to four years. This is highly significant as it helps to justify the need to examine defectors' time in China as an equally major part of their educational journeys. Also significant is the average period of three years from entry into South Korea to enrolment at university. The time lapse indicated preparing for university entrance, working due to financial difficulties or suffering from emotional hardships – circumstances of which are less severe for those with a greater number of family members in South Korea.

Data collection

The primary data were generated from defector learner biographies collected through the use of life history interviews. Individual, semi-structured, in-depth interviews were used as the data collection tool. Two semi-structured in-depth interviews were carried out with each of the 25 informants with follow-up interviews when the need arose. Normally, follow-up interviews would take place with those students who spoke at greater length during the interviews and/or with whom the researcher had built up less rapport. 'Phase One' took place from June to September 2007 while 'Phase Two' lasted from December 2007 to March 2008. Although the iterative and comparative nature of interviews allowed them to simultaneously form a part of the data analysis, the main formal analysis did not begin until completion of both data collection periods.

Preliminary meetings were used to introduce the research project to the participants, sign the consent form and complete the basic information sheet, both of which were translated into Korean. The majority of these meetings took place on campus, usually at the conclusion of the *dongari*; however, I aimed to arrange some of these preliminary sessions at my place of residence in Seoul for the purposes of increasing the students' familiarity with the main interview setting as early as possible. It was important to ensure that personal interviews were conducted where the interviewees preferred. Although students did request to meet at campus cafes and classrooms, a majority of the students asked to return to my residence for the interviews, which in any case turned out to be the most practical location for voice-recording purposes and matters of privacy that defectors were concerned about.

All interviews from the two sessions with each student were conducted in a mix of English and Korean and were digitally recorded. Each of the two semi-structured in-depth interviews lasted between one and a half to two hours, not including the time spent building trust into each individual researcher–informant relationship before the interview session as such commenced. Semi-structured in-depth interview questions included personal and historical educational queries, along with questions about various dimensions of their university experience such as social, psychological, scholastic and financial difficulties as suggested by previous studies. The questions were developed from previous research carried out on similar groups and findings from the exploratory study. I developed main questions, probes, prompts and follow-up questions in the interviews in order to draw out in-depth explanations of responses (Rubin and Rubin, 1995). The flexibility in asking more questions helped to maintain the conversational tone of the interviews, allowing free exchange of opinions between the interviewer and interviewee if needed, thereby increasing the naturalism throughout the data collection process. Thus, there is not total uniformity among all interviews.

The life history biographical data were further supplemented by background material. These included material on the North Korean education system, findings from previous studies on the North Korean defector educational experience and notes from informal interviews based upon ethnographic participation during the exploratory study. These materials were referred to continuously so that any new or unique information arising from the data could be noted.

Several difficulties arose during the interviews. First, conducting the preliminary meetings and two interview sessions meant scheduling over 75 individual meetings. Conflicts in scheduling challenged the time frame constraints inherent in the field research. Missed meetings or last-minute cancellations were a common occurrence, which perhaps reflects the psychological duress refugees experience throughout adaptation. Second, there was a delay between each interview session in some instances because data collection occurred in two phases with a three-month time gap between them. For example, by the time I had returned to the field for our second interview, one student had disappeared. As it was necessary to gain a full rather than half profile of each participant, extra time was needed to seek an appropriate replacement who could commit to the two interview sessions. Another student who had served as a key informant in the research had personal health issues, which became fatal after three months, and this introduced another set of ethical concerns.

Ethical considerations

The rationale behind the use of two interviews with each participant responds to the need for an ethical development in the interview process that respects the sensitivity in broaching 'difficult-to-discuss' topics for defectors. It helped that a degree of trust had already been established with all new informants through introductions made by our mutual North Korean defector acquaintances. While a degree of trust was built up during preliminary and all other informal meetings, it was hoped that a deeper acceptance would gradually develop throughout the course of two interview sessions. This was accomplished by organizing the interview schedule in a specific sequence, beginning with general questions and moving on to more specific and personal questions out of respect for the traumatic and difficult-to-discuss portions of their narrative lives. Ultimately, the two-part interview schedule proved a fitting tool for capturing the richness of defector narratives by allowing participants sufficient time to reflect on their personal life histories between each session. In these ways, maintenance of trust and the ethics of the research were centrally incorporated into the overall design of the interview schedule.

To this end, I followed the BERA Revised Ethical Guidelines for Educational Research (2004) and gained ethical approval from the University Research Ethics Committee (CUREC). Ethical and legal responsibilities I bore to my participants included preserving their anonymity, using informed consent procedures for all interviews and remaining sensitive to past trauma suffered by many of the participants. In devising the methodology, part of the intention was to create an ethically responsible and empathetic research design to maximize the overarching consideration of 'trust between the researcher and subjects implicit in the life history method' (Du Boulay and Williams, 1984, p. 256). Thus, it was an essential aim of this study to remain focused on conducting sympathetic and humane research throughout the use of the life history method.

Particular consideration was given to psychosocial wellness issues of North Korean defectors due to the trauma they may have experienced in North Korea and upon fleeing the North and experiencing harsh treatment in China and other third countries. North Korean defectors often suffer from depression, anxiety and stress after their traumatic experiences – expressed in post-traumatic stress disorder (PTSD) or somatization of psychological symptoms. Therefore, I attempted to familiarize myself with these psychological concerns by volunteering with the NGO *Jayoutuh*, as well as by maintaining close contact with one of the few working medical experts on North Korean defector psychological rehabilitation located at Hanawon. I also abided by ethical standards of what Langness (1965) argues must be the 'taking of life histories [which] should be left until relatively late in the fieldwork period' (p. 35) when a sufficient degree of sincerity and familiarity have been assessed by both the interviewee and interviewer so that 'courtesy status' is established.

A final ethical consideration relates to issues of reflexivity and the need for me to remain aware of my role as a researcher in order to maximize the responsibilities to the participants. Throughout the study, the researcher must focus on knowing the relative statuses of the interviewee to gauge the effects that outside influences might have upon how the interviewee frames his/her responses. To reduce 'reactivity' (Landau and Jacobsen, 2003) the I needed to be aware of my own actions, biases and beliefs that were changing dynamically throughout the exploratory study – the learning curve was steep. At times, I found myself wanting to portray the participants positively the longer

I spent working with them in the field. It was important that my researcher's role was distinct from my role as a 'friend' and that the latter not interfere with the outcome of the interview process. Thus, there was a personal need to maintain emotional distance from the participants' personal lives.

Park (1996) describes the need to 'empathise with North-Korean decision-makers' by undertaking a 'phenomenological approach in the sense that North Korean perceptions constitute the reality and that these perceptions must be articulated from the standpoint of the perceiver' (p. 3). However, this research is ideologically opposed to the purity of such phenomenological pursuits and rather aims to strike a balance between both insider and outsider perspectives. But remaining detached and objective proved difficult as relationships with the students deepened over time. This involved an ethical awareness of a certain 'do-gooder' attitude in refugee assistance that I gradually learned to balance. Although some students expressed satisfaction in discussing their own identity concerns throughout the data collection process, according to Miller (2000), it would be naïve to think that this was a wholly therapeutic event.

Analysis

The analytic aim was to seek broader contextual concepts in the life histories of North Korean defectors by drawing relationships between the educational experiences and the patterns of learning as revealed by the 25 participants.

To begin, all interviews were rewritten into storied narrative forms or 'portraits' enhancing the chronological flow and coherence of each life history, best understood in a literary sense by constructing a coherent and linear plot development of defector educational experiences. This process involved developing plots around the facts of their life biographies and placing them into a chronologically ordered format or timeline of historical educational events. This was carried out with the understanding that 'narrative as a way of knowing' is important to life history research (Bruner, 1986, p. 126).

After creating the narrative historical sequence of life events through portraiture, each life history portrait was read multiple times with the intent of deconstructing interviews 'ad hoc' into 'pragmatic categories' (Miller, 2000).

Here I was interested in discovering how the subject relays and relates to these historical events that occured in North Korea, and in what ways they impact North Korean defector patterns of learning.

This process is based on an important research principle in the field of cultural-historical and activity theory, namely, that the individual cannot be treated separately as a unit of analysis without taking into account the institutional function and social and cultural context which they inhabit. 'The dialectic between human individual function and social and cultural context is paramount' (Wertsch, 1991).

The use of the Constant Comparative Method (CCM) facilitated the analysis by helping to draw thematic relationships between formal, non-formal and informal educational experiences and events occurring within these two larger sociocultural processes – North Korean schooling and economic/ideological collapse – that correspond to the initial phases of Hopson's (1984) model and serve the purpose of periodization, or ordering defector educational experiences. Identifying key transition points and phases shows how external educational changes affect an individual's internal value changes and learning processes. They help to facilitate our ability to structure, organize and describe complex educational journeys, to show how larger meta-narratives and sociocultural processes of adaptation interact with defectors' personal experiences of education in ways that significantly impact upon their various learner values, attitudes, behaviours and other patterns of learning.

The data generated from individual historical learning biographies gave me a better understanding of the impact that these past educational events have had upon defectors' orientations and attitudes towards learning. It revealed individual dilemmas and personal transformations arising from defector educational life histories and occurring at various transition points.

Findings

The findings present information on the historical, primary context of North Korean defector learners and describes how formal, non-formal and informal educational experiences in North Korea significantly shape their resultant values, attitudes, behaviours and other patterns of learning. Two overarching meta-narratives are used to examine these historical experiences and the dilemmas that transition poses for North Korean defectors – the North Korean schooling system and the period of economic decline – which correspond to the initial stages of both educational transition models laid out above. This section begins with a review of the historical context of the North Korean education system, to help illustrate a more accurate account of defectors' changing mentalities and newly emerging value systems at the beginning stages of their educational journeys.

North Korean Schooling

With the loss of over 20 per cent of the population and its capital city razed, post-war reconstruction of the North Korean state began in 1958, led by its Soviet-backed leader Kim Il-Sung, who inherited socialist methods and principles for state building and reform from its strongest wartime ally. But unlike the Marxism–Leninism that swept through parts of Asia, Africa, Eastern Europe, the former Soviet Union and China, North Korea's desire for national sovereignty led it to abandon its ideological roots and develop and solidify its own particular brand of communism, calling this new ideology *juche*.[1] Generally translated as self-reliance, juche was enshrined in the Democratic People's Republic of Korea (DPRK) constitution in 1972 and emphasizes three main principles that constitute the country's national identity: '*chaju* (independence) in politics, *charip* (self-sufficiency) in economic capability, and *chawi* (self-defense) in military capability' (Suh, 1998, p. 302). Juche serves as the guiding principle of politics, economics, the military – indeed, all of life – exhibited by totalitarian control of the working masses through political socialization and revolutionization of the entire society into a labour class. It shares with Marxism-Leninism the materialist viewpoint that there is no greater thing than Man who is at the centre of the universe and who is master of all creation. According to Kim Il-Sung (1973), 'the basic theory of the juche idea is that a man is master of himself and that he is the one who decides everything . . . for human beings, independence is life. If one loses independence in society, his life is no different from that of an animal' (p. 273).

In another North Korean publication on the 'Juche Theory and Application', the word *independence* occurs 23 times across two consecutive pages to explain its central objective (Ajami, 1978, pp. 51–2).

But there was a fundamental way in which the juche theory departed from Marx's and Engels' universal call to unite all workers of the world, which was in its desire for DPRK state independence and sovereignty from other communist nations. 'The idea of the initiative of self-reliance stressed that the revolution of Korea had to be carried out to the last *by* the [Korean] people's own efforts and through *their own* responsibility' (*Dictionary of History*, 1971, p. 126).

In choosing to abandon notions of solidarity with other socialist nations for the single-minded, independent pursuit of self-reliance, the state isolated itself. While some scholars assert that at the core of the juche philosophy lies the national historical legacy of a formerly united Korean resistance to the

Japanese occupation from 1910 to 1945 (Kim, 1973), what remains largely undisputed is the fact that the rise of North Korean nationalism during this period created a state eager to assert its nationalist form of independence and claim autonomy from the Soviet Union, in contrast to what it saw as the colonial takeover of the South by United States forces.

Several Koreanists have identified various interpretations and characterizations of juche as synonymous with nationalism (Cumings, 1984, 2007; Hassig and Oh, 2000; Martin, 2006; Park, 1996). Just as Maoism was Marxism-Leninism adapted for China, so too may juche be construed as North Korean-style socialism, also known as *Kimilsungism*, and later *Kimchongilism*, as it was exported abroad to other communist countries. By transforming the practice of Soviet-style socialism to fit the unique context of North Korean culture and politics, juchian independence, or 'self-reliance' as it is more commonly referred to, began forming a distinctively nationalist character, powerfully cultish in its worship of Kim Il-Sung and the later ruler Kim Jong-Il.

To this end, state-sponsored institutions and activities played an important role in fostering and disseminating the personality cult of the Great and Dear Leaders, a key feature of the juche philosophy. Many public rhetorical spaces were used, especially the media. In her thesis on 'The Juche Ideology of North Korea: Socio-Political Roots of Ideological Change,' Kim (1991) conducted an in-depth analysis of narratives on juche as they appeared in North Korean news dailies like *Nodong Sinmun*:

> Starting with the juche manufacturing, the ideograph juche was vehemently applied in every possible area. There were the juche education, the juche science, the juche medical science, the juche philosophy, the juche architecture, the juche farming method, the juche pomiculture, the juche poultry, the juche fisheries, the juche art, the juche movies, the juche literature, the juche gymnastics, and the juche athletics. There were even the juche cotton, the juche table tennis, and the juche soccer. (Kim, 1991, pp. 123–4)

Quite literally, North Korea became involved in a process of 'dyeing the whole society with the *juche* ideology' (Kim, 1991), exemplifying just how integrated it was in the daily lives and activities of North Korean citizens.

Another way in which the state promoted its ideas throughout the reconstruction period was through the adoption of new cultural policies to eradicate

> the last traces of pre-revolutionary thinking and acting in order to create a new type of man – unselfish, nationalistic and dedicated to the achievement of a

> socialist paradise on earth [where citizens were to be reared as] new communist human beings . . . under the warm care of the Comrade Kim Il-Sung. (Martin, 2006, p. 171)

A rare cultural policy document written by North Korean officials and published by UNESCO in 1980 helps illustrate this point. It discusses the country's history and heritage, describing in detail how all literature, art works, museum holdings, public shrines, festivals and other activities would be 'socialist in content, national in form . . . sustained by the government's juche principles . . . extol[ing] the working masses and the struggle against imperialism' (Chai and Hyon, 1980, p. 23). Mass culture, however, was often enforced, and sometimes even forged, with an iron fist. One defector writes that Kim Il-Sung organized a group of palace writers named the '4.15 Creation Group', made up of writers, composers and dramatists who were commissioned to write both fictional and non-fictional 'immortal classic works' about their Great Leader, but dated 40 years prior to their actual publication dates (Lim, 1982).

However, the most notable post-war reconstruction efforts were directed towards successive reforms in the field of education, critical for disseminating the state ideology. Juche succeeded in blending political, economic and social policy goals together, nurtured by its inextricable link with the nationalist schooling system. The fundamental aim of the North Korean education system lies in remolding students into loyal and obedient revolutionaries, proletarians and communists based upon values and norms grounded in the juche ideology (Kim, 1977). In 1973, the state integrated the juche philosophy, purpose and methods into its communist education system. Then, in 1975, the North Korean Supreme People's Assembly formally established the 11-year compulsory, uniform, free and universal education system that is currently in use in North Korea, thereby maintaining the educational structure and administration of the Soviet Union.

Schooling begins in the crèche or nursery school, which intentionally liberates parents – especially mothers – to participate in the economic, social and political life of the country. This is followed by one year of kindergarten, four years of primary school and six years of middle school before joining the military . Select students graduate to university or post-compulsory education known as SWYWS (study-while-you-work-system), which offers them more opportunities for higher education in order to meet the state's commitment to 'intellectualize' the entire society (Han, 2005; Lee, 2003). Like the education systems of other socialist states, the most significant features of the

North Korean system are its high level of centralization, bureaucratic control and ideological orientation (Tomiak, 1972).

Juche began emphasizing nationalism as part and parcel of its fundamental state identity inculcated heavily upon its citizenry. In his 1977 '*Theses on Socialist Education*', Kim Il-Sung outlines the philosophy, purpose and method of North Korean education. He develops systematic themes and principles, pedagogy, content and policies. The qualities that constitute the highly nationalist, socialist personality are:

> first, a dedicated party and working-class spirit; second, a love for learning about their language, culture, history, and the revolutionary traditions; third, that they remain in love with revolutionary practice, for theory without practice is meaningless, and theory alone cannot meet real needs satisfactorily in carrying out revolution. (Kim, 1977, p. 17)

According to another North Korean government document, these educational aims were implemented to 'accelerate socialist construction' of all that was 'backwards in all fields of the economy, culture, ideology and morality' (Juche 87, 1998, p. 6). This form of 'politico-ideological indoctrination in communist morality' begins as soon as a child enters the educational system (Grinker, 1998).

North Korea claims remarkable past- having developed faster than the South, in the 1970s, and continued growth in its education system. Researchers generally acknowledge North Korea's high rate of literacy and accept its assertion 'that some 2.3 million people in the North were illiterate at the time of the Korean liberation in 1945, and that only 35 percent of school age children attended school' (Yang, 1994, p. 767). Other figures display a most exemplary case of North Korea's development in education through the continuous growth of nurseries and kindergartens throughout the 1960s after universal primary education was established in 1956. By 1970, it is estimated that '1.12 million children were attending 6,800 kindergartens' (Scalapino and Lee, 1972, p. 105). Adult evening workshops and Korean alphabet schools were set up all over the country so that by the 1980s the North claimed that there was virtually no illiteracy and that all school-age children were attending school (Choi, 1968). According to a UNESCO report issued in 1995, by that year North Korea had 142 college students per 10,000 individuals, which represented a high level among less-developed countries (Radi, 2005).

Indeed, North Korea still boasts that it is a 'country of education and learning' where 'every citizen can learn anytime and anywhere' (Han, 2005, citing *Education Weekly*, 1 April 2004). It is significant that during the decade 1974–83, the DPRK participated in 317 meetings, of which 141 were UNESCO-related (Chung, 1986). North Korea will continue to use nationalistic schooling practices and a curriculum steeped in a somewhat inaccurate account of historical facts built around octogenarian cult worship of one leader to exert a powerful influence over students' habits, values, beliefs, thinking patterns and behaviours. But despite these professed educational advances in North Korea during this period, particularly in eradicating illiteracy, there is evidence that the education system has deteriorated significantly since the late 1980s, when the Soviet Union collapsed. Experts argue that far from providing a liberal civics education as some Western democracies do, North Korea's juche-led schooling system produces a rather false consciousness among its citizens that betrays its intended Marxist outcomes.

North Korea is one of the last remaining bastions of communism, and thus of communist schooling practices in the world. North Korean ideologues use schools as a dominant tool of socialisation for achieving nationalistic ends, with the particular educational intent of modelling students into loyal and obedient communists. This ideological context of schooling has the potential to shape and modify learners' attitudes, values and beliefs via select pedagogical processes in an educational system that is unique and one we know very little about.

Its thoroughgoing delivery of collective state values is made possible by rigid schooling structures and ritualised forms of educational participation, instilling in learners particular attitudes and behaviours centred about *juche* ideals of patriotism and collectivism.

Nearly all defectors, as if rehearsed, began their narratives by describing the highly regimented North Korean nationalistic schooling system and certain values it imparts such as collectivism, patriotism and filial duty to their Leaders. Defector narratives described its method and delivery in widely similar terms, focusing on two major features of the schooling system, its rigidity and ritualization. While there was some narrative variation in the cohort sample, which may be attributed to regional differences and by year of defection, the majority of narratives tended to yield more similarities than differences. This is perhaps due to the uniformity of North Korea's 11-year free and universal education system across all regions through which the highly nationalistic *juche* ideology and the personality cult of the two Kims imbued students with stringent ethics of patriotic obedience, filial duty and service to their nation and leaders.

All narratives began by emphasising the most important patriotic contents of the compulsory curriculum. Students listed verbatim, as if by mandate, two critical courses of study for every North Korean, that of '*Kim Il-Sung and Kim Jong-Il's Childhood and Revolutionary History*' and '*Communist Morality*' lessons beginning from year 1 in elementary school. These courses included studies of the 'respectable Father', Kim Il-Sung, revolutionary records of the 'beloved Leader', General Kim Jong-Il and other prominent figures in North Korean history. After listing the 11 required subjects such as '*geography, chemistry, music . . .*' Lisa displayed absolute shock at having forgotten to list the most important foundational subjects: '*. . .oh, oh no, and the most basic, most important classes on the Kims' revolutionary history, of course! If you do well in all your other subjects it wouldn't matter as long as you receive poor grades in these subjects.*'

High grades on these topics in entrance exams are required of students if applying for better placements in the elite middle-high schools as well as determining whether they will advance onto further education where study of these compulsory subjects continues.

Studying their histories was akin to worshipping a deity as all were taught that they were descendants of Kim Il-Sung and Kim Jong-Il.

> *While I was in elementary school there was a campaign called the 200 day struggle for the purpose of carrying out the 7-year plan, but it wasn't proving successful. So, in order to make the plan successful in 200 days the students were motivated to solve 200 questions. The students' motivation was a political motivation. What the teachers taught the students was that we are not learning because we want to become intelligent persons. Rather, it was to honor the Great Father and become his honorable sons and daughters. That was the motivation for learning things* (Cassie).

Such educational activities designed by the State to transmit and inculcate cultural and political values and beliefs cast an aura of the divine around the two Kims' cult of personality and the *juche* belief system.

Memories also depicted a schooling atmosphere of 'collectivism' that several students recalled fondly. Narratives alluded to their general acceptance of 'group' interests infused with a strong sense of 'unity' and were placed higher than those of the individual. These important cultural values were reinforced by the military, a crucial aspect of the North Korean national education and training system. After graduating from middle-high school students typically served 10 years in the army before advancing to university where indoctrination of nationalistic and militaristic *juche* principles continues. Male students in particular attributed positive connotations to the military. The military represents a common form of collectivism consisting of over 1 million students who have been trained and educated for war and infused with a deep sense of nationalism that shapes their single-minded, self-sacrificing pursuit of becoming a hero and bringing honor to their family.

> *I wanted to become a good military man. We North Koreans are willing to die for our country. That's patriotism, which is a problem for South Korea if we are to have a war because we are trained not to have any attachment to our lives. The society pushes people to enter the army and they educate them that this is a holy thing to do and that it's our duty. Before I went to the military I was kind of fantacizing about what it would be like, thinking it was an ideal place, that I could become a hero and bring honor to my family* (John).

John assumed a great deal of pride in his military service to the state that outweighed more academic goals or pursuits. Or according to Dylan, '*There simply was no desire other than to go to the military after middle-high school, it was an honor and a trend in North Korean society to do so.*' Thus, for both male and female students, the military marked an important period in their educational life histories, helping to shape their moral-political values around the military first ideology and revolutionary spirit of the North Korean state and develop their loyalty and patriotism to the country, key traits of the juche man and woman.

But state promotion of the Kims' cult of personality was not limited to the formal curriculum. Students repeatedly recalled experiences of group membership in special youth collectives in elementary school, middle-high school and university. These compulsory non-formal schooling activities were composed of marching, dancing and anthem singing all in honour and celebration of the Great and Dear Leaders. The most commonly discussed events were the tri-annual celebrations taking place on three significant dates in North Korean history: Kim Jong-Il's birthday on 16 February, Kim Il-Sung's birthday on 15 April, and Foundation Day of the State and the WPK (North Korean Worker's Party) on 6 June. For six to eight months, students must forgo normal schooling lessons in order to practice and partake in these national celebrations and military parades. According to Gordon (2001) who documented the awesome spectacle of the 6 June 'torchlight processions' and 'mass games', more than ten thousand university students participate in the event.

Another schooling ritual that the North Korean state relied heavily upon for disseminating its political and ideological lessons and activities was the mandatory self-criticism course called saenghoalchongwha. It is literally translated as a feeling that increases worship of the leader. According to students, these self and collective criticism sessions generally took place one to two times per month after school, though they varied by year and occurred less frequently during the peak famine years between 1994-1998. Students were educated in these collectives to point out their own mistakes and shortcomings, as well as that of their peers, within the past month that could have disrupted '*the party's life of total harmony*". For example, if they ever expressed dissatisfaction with the government or its policies, they were told to come up with problems and solutions themselves and to '*study harder*,' instead of blaming Kim Il-Sung or the regime.

> *During chongwha sessions, the class president usually makes a report about who has been good or bad during the month. For example, my school was in the city where there was a statue of Kim Il-Sung right there in the middle of the city. A part of showing loyalty and patriotism was to clean the statue every morning, a required activity. So the attendance rate for this activity, together with the grades we received in class, were all added up, evaluated, written up by the class president, approved by the board, and presented at chongwha where students were either praised for being good or criticised for being bad. Then, individuals would come up to the front of the class and report on their own monthly activities whether they had been good or bad. After the self-evaluation, another student would be selected and accused. For example, if I cleaned the statue every day I would choose a student who I thought was not doing a good job. So it's not just about looking back on my own life for that month but chongwha was also about accusing others and making them behave better the next time* (Lisa).

Although defectors did not regard *saenghoalchonghwa* sessions as having been wholly negative experiences, some students expressed how they were unaware at the time that such activities were '*unnecessary*", and perhaps even '*wrong*".

North Korean defector students acquired values, beliefs, norms and behaviours that resulted from formal and non-formal nationalistic schooling practices forming the basic personality of the learner. This begins to create interest in the potential conflicts that may arise when parts of their taught *juche* infused patterns of learning and state inspired behaviors are challenged during the next stages of transition, when sociocultural factors during the period of economic decline of the North Korean state collide with these ideologically derived learner values.

Economic Decline

Under a functioning North Korean system most memories of educational experiences, with few exceptions, are recalled with fondness, as childhood memories often are. However, the period of economic decline in North Korea marked a clear and decisive moment when narrative recollections of students' past formal educational experiences dramatically change.

After the fall of communism, the ideology proved too weak to be self-sustaining, and state goals began giving way to the grim reality of their so-called worker's paradise. By the 1980s, North Korea had become a state characterized by problems of increasing political instability, structural imbalances in the economy and foreign policy, and ideological rigidity, having a profound effect on its citizens.

The situation reached a climax when, in 1995, North Korea entered a period generally referred to by researchers as 'The Great Famine'. The widespread effects of the famine were exacerbated by the devastating floods of 1996, which resulted in an estimated three million deaths and sent hundreds of thousands of its citizens fleeing across the Sino-Korean border. Although North Korean propaganda blamed the 'unique' floods for the famine, some researchers have suggested that the famine was not the direct result of these natural disasters, but rather the consequence of Kim Jong-Il's rigid politics and isolationist stance, which prevented national and international governmental mechanisms from responding appropriately to the crisis. Amartya Sen (1999) supports this theory by noting the remarkable fact that no substantial famine has ever occurred in any country with a democratic form of government. Furthermore, the fact that North Korea's Public Distribution System was malfunctioning even before the Great Flood supports the argument that links countrywide famine with authoritarianism.[2] Thus, we can conclude that North Korea suffers from what Sen describes as 'extreme (or absolute) poverty', that is, lacking basic material needs such as clothes, food and shelter. The consequences of this are evident in the ongoing North Korean humanitarian and refugee crisis.

This period corresponded to the stage of ideological collapse in the transition models where informal educational experiences functioned as powerful socialising agents of change. Although the North Korean education system had a strong influence on defector learning patterns, original values were greatly moderated by a series of shocking educational events during the period of economic decline. The weakened political system greatly diminished the effectiveness of nationalistic and ideological practices, creating a wide disparity between the reality students experience in society and what was taught in the classroom.

After Kim Il-Sung's death in 1994, the public distribution system collapsed revealing several weaknesses in the education system. Negative schooling experiences during this period included increased incidences of teacher and student truancy, insufficient classroom materials, decreased quality in school textbooks and poor classroom infrastructure, especially during the winter season. Other criticisms included over-emphasis on political ideology lessons and intensified labor duties particularly after 1997 when, after a brief 3-year period of loosening controls, Kim Jong-Il took power and began tightening his grip. This return to ideological control over students through schools to instil regime loyalty instigated the changing values of some students. Jackie expressed his growing antipathy towards the North Korean state during this time:

> *I changed my mind in the 2nd year of middle high school and began to really hate the ideology, especially saenghoalchonghwa. I remember really hating it when people ordered me around. Also, I was beginning puberty whilst the country was bearing down on us hard with ideology so you can imagine my problems.*

Other students levelled similar criticisms against increases in patriotic activities outside of class such as mandated organisational activities in *saenghoalchonghwa* (self-criticism), labour during *sochohoaldong* (after-school activity), and other educational measures for controlling the masses.

After seeing the lack of importance that educational and extracurricular services bore to their lives, this led to the inability of some students to revert back to formal ideological lessons thereby contributing to their changed values and mental dispositions towards schooling. Students believed these circumstances detracted from the more academic course-work at school and more importantly prevented them from providing for their own basic needs for survival.

Newly emerging social realities over their changed ideological circumstances were significantly impacted by the growing inequalities at school. Although students recognised that inequality in the classrooms existed before the 1994 food crisis, it was then only a minor 'open secret", exacerbated after the economic collapse when it became obvious that a better quality of education was provided only for children of elite families. Problems endemic in the North Korean economy began to manifest themselves in the growing social divisions at school between the rich and poor students exposing larger social divisions in society. This situation supports Marxist educationists view of education as an ideological tool of a governmental elite for the purposes of benefiting some classes more than others.

Increased classroom inequalities had a significant impact upon students' changing values of North Korean education and society. Teachers often displayed favoritism towards students from more elite backgrounds, defined as well to do families of good political standing with the ruling regime. Children of elite families or those earning a comparable government salary were able to afford bribes. These monies were used to change test scores, secure university lottery tickets as well as exempt students from military service and compulsory labor practices, which the government increased to compensate for stalled farming activities. These unfair schooling practices diminished their standing in the eyes of some students.

Crumbling educational conditions revealing a new changed reality was the precursor to students' internal ideological collapse, significantly reshaping many students' *juche* inspired socialist ideals of equity and integrity in the North Korean schooling system and society generally.

> *At first it was hard to accept this new reality because I was a teacher at the time and part of the group educating society about North Korea being a good country. It was a truly hard experience to go through as I was realising that North Korean society is in fact not as ideal as what I had been taught and what I had to teach my students* (Cassie).

Those who went onto the military gained a stronger sense of the increasingly defunct North Korean ideology.

> *When I was in the military I had opportunities to visit other villages and saw how the situation was worsening. I was trained to think that I was doing the right thing and understood that the sanctions from America were to blame and not our government. I accepted those facts but then as time went by and as I was trying to encourage myself that things were going to get better, and they weren't, I really came to feel like I was doing all of this for nothing. I was supposed to be guarding the country and that's my job but then the society wasn't what it was supposed*

> *to be so over time my thoughts changed and I didn't feel like I was doing the right thing and that it wasn't worth my time* (John).

For Cassie, John and many other students, no longer was the *juche* philosophy of 'I am the owner of my own destiny' a valid one as it became increasingly obvious that in fact *suryeongwan* or 'the leader guides you' was what really dictated their lives. John therefore surmised that, '*if destiny was not in* [his] *own hands then what was the point of education after all.*' Another student echoes this impression:

> *I think juche is fundamentally a good ideology – I am the owner of my life. But I grew to realise that the way it is used in North Korea is not good. If I am the owner of my own life then I choose and decide things but we cannot do so because we don't have that freedom to choose those things that we desire. I changed my mind about age 13, and I began to really hate the ideology, especially saenghoal-chonghwa lessons* (Harold).

Students complained that the government did not take the necessary actions to connect the *juche* ideal with reality, or as Martin puts it, '*socialism is good in theory but our juche ideology is not achieving that. There is no equality. Everything just goes to the Kims.*' Students faulted *juche* for what proved to be the biggest contradiction in its *raison d'etre* which was that man is not free, he is in fact not the owner of his own destiny.

Such open, direct and fundamental ideological questioning of *juche* teachings led several students to de-emphasise the role of schooling in their lives.

> *I did not really feel the need to be educated in North Korea. I didn't see the point (. . .) if by my own pure effort I would never be able to achieve whatever I desired no matter how hard I studied* (Dylan).

> *There was the question of why students must study in North Korea because teachers began to care more about students who could do good labor or who could pay for their labor not those who could study well* (Harold).

Students failed to see how *juche* and the overall North Korean education 'ideal' had any bearing upon the circumstances of their 'real' material lives. Ideological confusion and tension concerning their resultant learner values and newly emerging educational realities led many students to redirect the focus of their lives from the classroom to the workplace.

With the ideological function of schools greatly debilitated and hunger and survival now students' number one goal, work was elevated as a more significant socialising agent of change with implications for their changing minds. Work was an important informal learning context portraying 'a hidden curriculum' of values different from what is consciously taught. Transitions from school to work reflected processes of re-socialisation toward new understandings of defectors' growing reality that lay in opposition to state professed ideals. On an ideological level, defectors learned about emerging grass-root market forces and other signs of modern forms of trade and a private economy. As newly acquired realisations of market activity and capitalism were becoming a fact of life, students quickly began losing faith in the government while gaining faith in markets. The transition from school to what was often illegal work in the North Korean markets constituted an important set of informal educational experiences. It ignited more radical shifts in their thought processes about the educational worth of schools as students began relying more on developing their economic capabilities to support oneself rather than pursuing education to attain a political rank. In short, more education did not mean more food.

Market forces influenced the changing perceptions of several defectors about the worth of an education and the state ideological values it imparted. Narratives described how newly acquired purchasing powers created new selfhoods of individualist tastes and tendencies apart from the homogenising state collective values. Students began learning that it did not pay to be merely a good student, loyal worker or party member if schools were unable to prepare them for a world of work. These circumstances revealed to students a world of schooling and service without rewards and a North Korean education system they began struggling to see the point in.

It is a fact that grass-root market forces and other signs of modern forms of trade and a private economy are emerging in North Korean society. But because remaining a fait accompli and occurring within the black market, the current Kim Jong-Il regime, though aware of this recent market trend, chooses to formally declare that nothing is amiss in its socialist engine.

> *They kept telling people that it would get better and that we would win and get victory in our hands, but then I realised that this was not happening. The society was getting worse and many people were starving. I stared building up a curiosity about other countries which North Korea kept on stating were not good countries* (Sara).

But through engaging in commercial activities, the students were given for the first time the opportunity to meet other people and see the harsh conditions taking place in other North Korean regions.

> *My eyes were open to the wider world, curiosity was in full bloom and I realised that there was only a little strip of water separating heaven and hell and that I must leave North Korea* (Joy).
> *When I travelled to Pyongyang I was shocked to see that even in our capital there were so many homeless children lying dead on the street. Why is out country like this? I remember the trains were very slow. They didn't have seats or glass in the windows and ran on electricity not gas. If someone didn't have a ticket they would escape to the rooftop and sometime got electrocuted and in the winter they would get speared by icicle when going through tunnels. I remember thinking how people's lives were like a fly's* (Joe).

Further in his narrative, Joe displayed an inner conflict over his ideological indoctrination that he struggled to contend with.

> *While travelling I heard many good things about china (. . .) after observing and learning all of this I experienced great conflict and changed my mind – this is not the right way to live. But I was so brainwashed that even I didn't understand my own country. Even as I saw people dying, my own country perishing, I still thought about our juche and thought that I must clear my head and throw these thoughts away, telling myself, 'no you cannot go'.*

He expressed reluctance to accept immediate emerging realisations of the reality of his circumstances in North Korea despite the widespread trauma surrounding him, as many others do. Gradually, students began to understand better their relative isolation and the comparative reality of a more prosperous life that existed in China prompting the decision for many to escape.

In sum, defectors' informal learning experiences during this transition period of economic decline significantly reshaped their learner attitudes and behaviours towards school. Their educational values became reoriented around capitalistic thinking and actions for survival antithetical to all they had been inculcated to believe under *juche*. The revolutionary rhetoric of the North Korean *juche* ideology was weakened and eventually replaced by personal, pragmatic, and individualistic values. Students experienced dynamic polar shifts to individualism from collectivism, to a growing concept of private autonomy from socialism, to economic matters more than governmental loyalty, changing market values, new desires for ownership of private property, material possessions, combined with opportunity to travel were all factors that contributed to many of the students' final decision to escape.

Refugee reports state that hunger and economic hardship are the most common reasons for escape rather than political restrictions on basic freedom of thought, speech, religion, association, access to information and domestic and international travel (Amnesty International, 2004; Hawk, 2003). There are various reports that estimate a wide-ranging number of North Korean refugees scattered throughout parts of China, Mongolia, Russia, Thailand, Cambodia, Vietnam, Laos and Burma (Myanmar), and increasingly in the US, Japan, Germany, the UK and other European Union countries, numbering anywhere from 20,000 (Chang, 2006) to 400,000 (ICG, 2006). According to field workers working on Seoul Train (the underground network of North Korean refugee human rights activists), smaller populations are known to exist in Singapore and the Philippines ('Irene', personal communication, 3 January 2008).

Those who make the journey safely to South Korea still encounter problems of social adaptation and national integration that are complicated by struggles such as trauma and mental transitions between two vastly different worlds. Suh (1994) concludes, as others have done when commenting on transitions in the former Soviet Union and Eastern European societies, that these changes create a widening gap or 'dualization' in social values. Many researchers have used this notion of dualization to aid their thinking on defector adaptation processes into South Korea by juxtaposing the values of the two diametrically opposed national education systems (Lee, 1993; Lim, 2007; Yang, 1994). But it is not the aim of this study to preserve such essentialist thinking, to describe how one journeys from point *a* to *b* or North Korea to South Korea. Rather, this study sought historical information as a tool or way of seeing and anticipating much more complex issues dealing with the processes and value changes occurring within each individual through the lens of transition.

Conclusion

This study presented information on formal and non-formal educational experiences and the various dilemmas arising from them that defectors encounter throughout the initial stages of their transition. It found that a series of sociocultural events related to the beginning stages of educational transition models affected changes occurring in defectors' inherited learner values centred around their juche ideological teachings. These transition points included ideological collapse of the national education system and the struggles refugees face throughout escape, migration and adaptation into new educational systems. The historicity of these educational experiences, analysed as learning processes, will play an instrumental role in the dynamic transformations taking place in defectors' changing values and mentalities of what were, up until now, mostly uncontested and unconscious acceptance of dominant state-inherited ideals and principles of juche teachings.

These data reveal the beginnings of major dilemmas in replacing old knowledge with new ways of seeing reality, indeed, acquiring new patterns of learning. Overcoming these wide discrepancies initiated the process of refugees reconciling 'the disparity between the socialist ideal and cultural reality' (Hart, 2000). New learner dilemmas emerged as students began acknowledging their confusion, doubts, dissatisfaction and distrust of the communist ideology and party. Defectors' internal rebellion against previously accepted realities and inherited ideals led to their final decision to escape and created new learner values independent from the state.

Ideological dilemmas arising from the period of economic collapse constituted some of the major learning challenges defectors faced as they began their physical and mental transitions across the North Korean border into China.

Continued processes of internal ideological value changes may be revealed in further educational experiences occurring throughout migration via China and other third countries and transition into South Korea, where defectors will realize the vast differences between reality and their former vague notions of the outside world. Without any systematic or reliable method for learning about their changed circumstances, defectors experienced great difficulty in reconciling old teachings with new knowledge.

These dilemmas arising from initial shock will mark the beginning of a critical and comparative process of historical reconciliation of facts and ideological values. As illegal migrants with limited means for accessing support, some North Korean refugees will often find themselves caught in psychological and ideological limbo and lacking the tools to help them mediate between two cultures, two worlds where absolute certainty had been withdrawn. Thus, analysing non-formal educational experiences during migration, transition and adaptation into largely foreign systems of education may reveal significant transitions taking place for each learner 'as a historical character' from a North Korean learning environment so dominated by idolatrous worship of one leader, one history, one ideology to a new realization that so many parts of that education were in fact lies.

Finally, these findings highlight a need for the further understanding of defectors' educational life histories, as the current study could potentially be read as diasporic research. In posing the research question, I sought to address the wider South Korean public, who could benefit from obtaining greater cultural understandings of North Koreans in light of possible future coexistence. As a member of the overseas Korean American community, I am interested in the perspectives of defectors who are my ethnic counterparts, and challenging essentialist identifications of the 'other'. In doing so, we might be better able to explain and understand North Korean defectors' educational realities – what was, is, and could be the impact of transition and adaptation upon their lives.

Key Questions

1. How can studies of other migrations around the world assist the understanding of the North Korean refugees' case?
2. What can be done for the countries most affected by the North Korean refugees' issue, especially between nations in the 6-Party talks?
3. Consider what better methodologies could be considered for researching the North Korean refugees' case.
4. How can life history research of North Korean refugees' educational experiences contribute to better outcomes of their transition and adaptation processes from North Korea, into China, South Korea and other third countries?
5. How could arts education help North Korean refugees in their educational transition experiences and processes?

Notes

1 This study adopts the Revised Romanization of Korean, the official system of romanization for Korean words in South Korea replacing the older McCune-Reischauer system (1938). 'Ministry of Culture & Tourism: The Revised Romanization of Korean'. Available from http://www.korea.net/korea (accessed July 2000).

2 For more on famine, see Lautze, S. (1996), '06 June 1996 North Korea Food Aid Assessment'. US Agency for International Development; Lautze, S. (1997), 'The Famine in North Korea: Humanitarian Responses in Communist Nations.' Feinstein International Famine Center, School of Nutrition Science and Policy, Tufts University; Natsios, Andrew S. (2001), 'The Great North Korean Famine'. Washington, DC: United States Institute of Peace; Lee Suk (2005–06), The DPRK Famine of 1994–2000: Existence and Impact. Seoul: KINU.

Further reading

Demick,B. (2010), *Nothing to Envy*. New York: Speigel & Grau/Random House.

Human Rights Watch (2008), *Denied Status, Denied Education*. New York: Human Rights Watch.

Martin,B. K. (2004), *Under the Loving Care of the Fatherly Leader*. New York: St. Martin's Press.

References

Ajami,C. (1978), *Juche Theory and Application*. Pyongyang, North Korea: Foreign Languages Publishing House.

Althusser,L. (1971), *Lenin and Philosophy and Other Essays*, translated by Ben Brewster. New York: Monthly Review Press.

Amnesty International (2004), Starved of Rights: Human Rights and the Food Crisis in the Democratic People's Republic of Korea (North Korea). *New York: Amnesty International, ASA 24/003/2004, pp.* 1–41.

Bertaux, D. (ed.) (1981), *Biography and Society: The Life History Approach in the Social Sciences*. Sage Series in International Sociology, 23. Beverley Hills: Sage.

Birzea, C. (1994), *Educational Policies of the Countries in Transition*. Council of Europe Secondary Education for Europe. Strausbourg: Council of Europe Press.

Birzea,C. (1996), 'Education in a World in Transition: Between Post-Communism and Post-Modernism'. *Prospects*, 26(4), 673–81.

Bowles,S. and Gintis,H. (1976), *Capitalist Schooling in America: Educational Reform and the Consequences of Economic Life*. London: Routledge.

Broadfoot,P. (2000), *Culture, Learning and Comparison: Lawrence Stenhouse's vision of education for empowerment, BERA Stenhouse Lecture*. Southwell: British Educational Research Association.

Broadfoot,P., Brock, C. and Tulasiewicz, W. (1981), *Politics and Educational Change*. London: Croom Helm.

Bruner,J. S. (1986), *Actual Minds, Possible Worlds*. Cambridge, MA: Harvard University Press.

Bruner,J. S. (1990), *Acts of Meaning. Jerusalem Harvard Lectures*. Cambridge, MA: Harvard University Press.

Bruner,J. S. (1996), *The Culture of Education*. Cambridge, MA: Harvard University Press.

Burgess,R. (1984), *In the Field: An Introduction to Field Research*. London: Routledge.

Calhoun,C. (1991), 'Indirect Relationships and Imagined Communities: Large-Scale Social Integration and the Transformation of Everyday Life', in Bourdieu, P. and Coleman, J. S. (eds), *Social Theory for a Changing Society*. Boulder, CO: Westview Press, pp. 95–120.

Cha,V. D. and Kang,D. C. (2003), *Nuclear North Korea: A Debate on Engagement Strategies*. New York: Columbia University Press.

Chai, S. S. and Hyon, J. H. (1980), *Cultural Policy in the Democratic People's Republic of Korea*. UNESCO Studies series on 'Studies and documents on cultural policy'. Vendome: Imprimerie des Presses Universitaires de France.

Chang, C. (2006), 'Another Journey to Freedom'. Report prepared for the Asia-Pacific Human Rights Coalition, Inc.

Choi,K. S. (1968), *'Changing Process of Educational Politics and Administration in Communist North Korea', in Hernandez, J. M.* (ed.), *Education in North and South Korea.* Issued by the WACL (Secretariat of the World Anti-Communist League

Chung, Y.S. (1986) 'North Korea in a Regional and Global Context', in R.Scalpino and H.K. Lee (eds). Institute of East Asian Studies, University of California, CA Center for Korean Studies.

Claxton,G. (2002), 'Education for the Learning Age: a Sociocultural Approach to Learning to Learn', in Wells, G. and Claxton, G. (eds), *Learning for Life in the 21st Century.* Oxford: Blackwell Publishers, pp. 21–34.

Cumings,B. (2007), 'Division, War and Reunification', in Kim, H. R. and Song, B. (eds), *Modern Korean Society Its Development and Prospect.* Berkeley: Center for Korean Studies. In Korea Research Monograph. Institute of East Asian Studies. University of California.

Cumings, B. (1984), *The Two Koreas*, Foreign Policy Association Headline Series, No. 269. New York: Foreign Policy Association.

Dewey,J. (1916), *Democracy and Education.* New York: Free Press.

Dictionary of History (1971), Vol. 2. Pyongyang, North Korea: Foreign Languages Publishing House.

Du Boulay,J. and Williams,R. (1984), 'Collecting Life Histories', in Ellen, R. (ed.), *Ethnographic Research: A Guide to General Conduct (ASA Research Methods in Social Action 1).* London: Academic Press, pp. 247–57.

Faraday,A. and Plummer,K. (1979), 'Doing Life Histories'. *Sociological Review*, 27(4), 773–98.

Gibney, M. J. (1999), 'Kosovo and Beyond: Popular and Unpopular Refugees'. *Forced Migration Review*, August 28–30.

Giddens,A. (1982), *Sociology: A Brief but Critical Introduction.* London and Basingstoke: The Macmillan Press Ltd.

Gramsci,A. (1971), *Prison Notebooks.* New York: International Publishers, pp. 24–43.

Greene,M. (1978), *Landscapes of Learning.* New York: Teacher's College Press.

Griffin,R.(ed.)(2002), *Education in Transition: International Perspectives on the Politics and Processes of Change.* Oxford: Symposium Books.

Grinker,R. R. (1998), *Korea and Its Future: Unification and the Unfinished War.* New York: St. Martin's Press.

Habermas, J. (1988), *The Theory of Communicative Action*, Vol. 1. 'In the Reason and the Rationalization of Society series'. Boston: Bacon.

Han,M. G. (2005), 'Changes and Future Issues in DPRK's Education System', *International Symposium on Promoting International Cooperation for Educational Development in DPRK Proceedings.* Seoul: Korean Educational Development Institute, pp. 195–214.

Hart, D. (2000), 'Proclaiming Identity, Claiming the Past: National Identity and Modernity in North and South Korean Education'. *Asian Perspective*, 24(3), 135–58.

Hassig,R. C. and Oh,K. (2000), *North Korea through the Looking Glass.* Washington DC: Brookings Institution Press.

Hatch, J. A. and Wisniewski, R. (eds) (1995), *Qualitative Studies*, Series 1. London: The Falmer Press.

Hawk,D. (2003), *The Hidden Gulag: Exposing North Korea's Prison Camps Prisoners' Testimonies and Satellite Photographs*. Washington, DC: US Committee for Human Rights in North Korea.

Henslin,J. M. (1995), *Sociology: A Down-to-Earth Approach*. Boston: Allyn and Bacon.

International Crisis Group (2006), 'Perilous Journeys: The Plight of North Koreans in China and Beyond'. Asia Report No. 122, 26 October 2006.

Juche 87 (1998), *Kim Jong Il: Brief History*. Pyongyang, North Korea: Foreign Languages Publishing House.

Kim, I. S. (1973), 'Selections from the Writings of Kim II Sung', (6) Pyongyang, North Korea: Foreign Languages Publishing House.

Kim,I. S. (1977), *Theses on Socialist Education*. Pyongyang, North Korea: Foreign Languages Publishing House.

Kim, S. H. (1991), *The Juche Ideology of North Korea: Socio-Political Roots of Ideological Change*. Unpublished PhD Thesis. Athens, Georgia: University of Georgia.

Kim,K. D. and Lee,O. J. (2003), *Korean Studies Series: The Two Koreas – Social Change and National Integration*, Vol. 23. Seoul: Jimoondang.

Kneller,G. F. (1958), *Existentialism and Education*. New York: John Wiley & Sons.

Ko, S. H.Chung, K. and Yoo-Seok, Oh. (2004), 'North Korean Defectors: Their life and well-being after defection'. *Asian Perspective*, 28(2), 65–99. Seoul: Kyungnam University.

Landau, L. and Jacobsen, K. (2003), 'Researching refugees: Some methodological and ethical considerations in social science and forced migration'. *New issues in refugee research*, working paper no. 90, Switzerland, UNHCR.

Langness, L.L. (1965) Life History in Anthropological Science (Studies in Anthropological Method), New York: Holt, Rinehart & Winston.

LeCompte, M. D. and Preissle, J. (1993), *Ethnography and Qualitative Design in Educational Research* (2nd edn). London: Academic Press.

Lee,C.J. (2003), 'A Study on the Characteristics and Functions of Education in the DPRK', Pub.no.RR 2003–12, Seoul:KEDI.

Lim,S. H. (2007), *Value Changes of the North Korean New Generation and Prospects*, Vol. 1. Seoul: KINU.

Lim, U. (pen name) (1982), *The Founding of a Dynasty in North Korea: An Authentic Biogrpahy of Kim Il Sung*. Translated from 'A Secret History of the Founding of a North Korean Dynasty' (in Japanese). Jiyu-sha.

Martin,B. K. (2006), *Under the Loving Care of the Fatherly Leader: North Korea and the Kim Dynasty*. New York: St. Martin's Press.

McLeish,E. A and Phillips,D(eds) (1998), 'Processes of Transition in Education Systems'. *Oxford Studies in Comparative Education*, 8(2).

Miller, R.L. (2000), *Researching Life Stories and Family Histories*, London: Sage Publications.

Oakeshott,M. (1933), *Experience and Its Modes*. Cambridge: Cambridge University Press.

Oakeshott, M. (1989), *The Voice of Liberal Learning: Michael Oakeshott on Education*, ed. Timothy Fuller. New Haven: Yale University Press.

Offe,Claus. (1996), *Varieties of Transition: The East European and East German Experience*. Cambridge, MA: Polity Press.

Park, H. S. (ed.) (1996), *North Korea: Ideology, Politics, Economy*. Englewood Cliffs, New Jersey: Prentice Hall.

Radi,M. (2005), 'International Cooperation for the Education Development in DPRK', in *Promoting International Cooperation for Education Development in DPRK*. Seoul: Korean Educational Development Institute.

Rubin,H. J and Rubin,I. S. (1995), *Qualitative Interviewing: The Art of Hearing Data*. London: SAGE Publications.

Sadler,M. E. (ed.) (1908), *Moral Instruction and Training in Schools*. New York: Longmans, Green and Co.

Scalapino,R. A. and Lee,C. S. (1972), *Communism in Korea: Part I, The Movement*. Berkeley: University of California Press.

Sen,A. (1999), *Development as Freedom*. Oxford: Oxford University Press.

Spence, M. (2007), 'What space for new economic approaches?'. Speech delivered in the Launch of Oxford Poverty & Human Development Initiative. Oxford, May 31, 2007.

Stenhouse, L. (1967). *Culture and Education*. London: Nelson.

Suh,D. S. (1998), *Kim II Sung: The North Korean Leader*. New York: Columbia University Press.

Suh,J. J. (1994), *Changing Values of North Korean People: Comparisons in North Korean Society*. Seoul: National Unification Research Institute.

Tomiak,J.J. (1972), *The Soviet Union*. Newton Abbot: David & Charles.

Wertsch,J. V. (1991), *Voices of the Mind: a Sociocultural Approach to Mediated Action*. Cambridge: Harvard University Press.

Yang,S. C. (1994), *The North and South Korean Political Systems: A Comparative Analysis*. Seoul: Westview Press/Seoul Press.

2

Refugee Education in Thailand: Displacement, Dislocation and Disjuncture

Su-Ann Oh

Chapter Outline

Introduction

Refugee situations are characterized by spatial and temporal disjuncture. Refugee camps occupy politically, socially, legally, economically and emotionally ambiguous spaces. Geographically, they do not exist on a map. Along the border, they are a stone's throw away, but completely removed from the homeland; they are set apart from the host society by fences, inaccessible terrain, language, political boundaries and government restrictions. In a protracted context, refugee camp time does not exist in 'real' time: residents live in a 'present' that continues to stretch from year to year while they imagine a future that is always beyond their reach.

These dislocations in space and time are fully articulated and manifested in the dilemma over the purpose of education. The project of education grapples with these ruptures and ambiguities because formal education is often used to promulgate recognized ethnic, cultural and nationalist identities, and to prepare young people for a fairly certain employment future and for membership as citizens of a recognized nation–state. In a protracted refugee situation, these reasonably certain identities and futures – which permit education purpose to be fastened to space and time – are splintered in the currents of conflict, displacement and insecurity.

Since the 1960s, villagers from Burma[1] have been fleeing from armed conflict and structural violence to seek refuge in Thailand and other neighbouring countries. The nine official[2] refugee camps scattered along the Thai-Burmese border house more than 140,000 refugees (TBBC, 2010) and have been in existence, in one form or another, for more than 20 years. It is estimated that at least another half a million refugees live outside the camps (USCRI, 2009).

This chapter examines how the refugee community and international NGOs attempt to reconcile their notions of the purpose of education – nation-building, enhancing livelihoods and promoting peace– in the seven predominantly Karen[3] camps, given the restrictions imposed by the Thai authorities and the ambiguity surrounding the refugees' future. The cleavages that forced displacement creates in the links between education and the nation–state, between education and employment, form the analytical lens in this discussion.

Education in a protracted refugee context: dislocation from the 'nation–state'

A distinctive feature of education in refugee situations is that there is a disjuncture between education provision and the 'state'. This is because education has traditionally been situated within the purview of the nation–state and its sovereignty. Refugees and their educational endeavours are dislocated from their geographical, political, economic and social context, and are consigned to a place that is outside the recognized territory and sovereignty of the original nation–state.

At the same time, they are physically located in a nation–state that has sovereign power over them, but may or may not extend its benefits to them.

Unlike medical care, shelter and food, the content and outcomes of formal education are closely tied to the legitimacy and goals of national sovereignty (whether recognized or not), and these still remain within political and geographical borders.

In many instances – particularly initially – refugees, living in the hope that they will return to their homes, decide to use the educational structures and curricula of the country of origin. In other cases, where ethnic persecution was one of the reasons for their flight, refugees may choose to use their own language as the language of instruction and teach their own version of history. This is the case with the Karen in Thailand, for whom language, symbols of culture and a 'shared' history are tools for reconstructing and legitimizing notions of Karen identity (Oh, forthcoming b; Oh and Van Der Stouwe, 2008; Rajah, 1990; South, 2007). In other situations, refugees may not have a choice as to the form and content of education provision. Host governments may decide what type of schooling best serves their (the host governments') political and other interests.

Consequently, the refugee community and its leadership do not have ultimate control over the form, content and implementation of education in the camps, what Waters and LeBlanc (2005) refer to as 'mass public schooling without a nation-state'. The authority accorded to the 'state' is often superseded by the host government and 'shared' with other actors, such as humanitarian organizations.

Host governments in developing countries often recognize refugee rights to basic education on humanitarian grounds. However, they do have certain domestic and foreign interests that guide their stance on the provision of refugee education. Domestically, it would appear politically inappropriate for governments to permit refugee education to surpass the quality and quantity provided for the local population. At the foreign policy level, governments are reluctant to provide education and other services to refugees in border locations for fear of creating the impression of the permanence of camps, which may encourage more people from the other side of the border to claim refugee status in order to take advantage of such services and may aggravate diplomatic relations with the neighbouring state (Preston, 1988). This is indeed the case regarding refugees from Burma in Thailand.

Of course, the geopolitics of the region and the political climate of the epoch play a considerable role in determining the strategic interests and role of the host government, and how education would serve those interests. In the mid-1970s, Thailand permitted Indochinese refugees to reside along its eastern border, using the refugee camps as a buffer against the communists and as a base to arm Khmer resistance groups (Loescher, 1994). The Thai curriculum was taught in schools in the camps even though the Thai authorities had no intention of allowing the refugees to integrate into Thai society (LeBlanc and Waters, 2005).

In general, it is the United Nations High Commissioner for Refugees (UNHCR) and the United Nations Relief Works Agency (UNRWA) – in the case of Palestinian refugees – that coordinate the provision of services to refugees. This was the case for the Indochinese refugees in Thailand. However, Thailand's experience with the UNHCR-led relief effort overshadows and informs its approach to the Burmese refugees.

In the provision of education, international NGOs and multilateral organizations may also act as 'pseudo nation-states' (Waters and LeBlanc, 2005). For example, the UNRWA provides education for Palestinians in the occupied territories, Lebanon, Syria and Jordan. In doing so, they may inadvertently undermine the national or host government's capacity to educate its citizens, by offering higher salaries for employees and demonstrating their ability to provide basic services that the national or host government is unable to supply (Sommers, 2000). While they operate ostensibly with a humanitarian agenda, their perspective and approach are influenced by the discourse on refugees, forced migration and education embedded within the broader rhetoric of the international refugee regime. In addition, their funding is derived from donors who have particular interests and concerns. These organizations generally subscribe to the beliefs that:

- Conflict has a negative impact on education (Bensalah et al., 2001; Machel, 1996; Retamal and Aedo-Richmond, 1998; Sinclair, 2001).
- Education is a protective factor in emergency and relief situations (Aguilar and Retamal, 1998; Bensalah et al., 2001; Boyden and Ryder, 1996; Machel, 1996; Nicolai and Triplehorn, 2003; Preston, 1991; Retamal and Aedo-Richmond, 1998; Sinclair, 2001; Sommers, 1999; Triplehorn, 2001), through the promotion of normalcy and through the introduction of programmes specific to the 'refugee experience', such as psychosocial interventions (Ahearn et al., 1999; Boothby, 1996; Boyden and Gibbs, 1997; McCallin, 2001; Save the Children Alliance, 1996; Summerfield, 1996; Tefferi, 1999; Tolfree, 1996).
- Education should address and redress violence and conflict in the refugee experience – peace, peace-building, conflict resolution, conflict prevention (Baxter, 2001; Bush and Saltarelli, 2000; Fountain, 1999; Sommers, 2001).

- Education can add to the transformation and reconstruction of communities and nations (Buckland, 2005; Davies, 2004; Pigozzi, 1999).

Undoubtedly, these purposes are important, vital to restoring a sense of continuity and stability to communities that have fled from conflict and violence. However, it must also be pointed out that framing education in this way embeds it in a discourse that seeks to persuade host governments, donors and international NGOs to provide education materials, resources, infrastructure and training to people affected by political and social upheaval brought about by war and conflict (Sommers, 2002).This may not necessarily coincide with refugees' own interpretations of what is important in education.

While education has many positive functions in circumstances of conflict, it may also play a negative role during conflict (Bush and Saltarelli, 2000; Coulby and Jones, 2001; Seitz, 2004; Smith and Vaux, 2003) and in producing conflict (Davies, 2004). Thus, it cannot be assumed that education is always a good thing in these circumstances (Davies, 2005).

The impact of forced displacement on education derives from the dislocation of education from the nation–state, or the authority recognized as the nation–state. The result is that the purposes that are traditionally assigned to education no longer align themselves neatly with nation-building, employment, livelihoods and so on. The situation is further complicated by the introduction of distinct sets of actors with different and often contradictory interests. This means that the purpose and role of education are constantly being shaped and negotiated by these actors and by ever-changing external circumstances. While there are many examples of disjuncture between education and the nation–state in protracted refugee situations, this chapter focuses on education as related to nation-building, employment, livelihoods, and the promotion of peace and reconciliation.

Education, identity formation and nation-building

There is no doubt that education is characteristically used to promulgate and reproduce certain notions of identity to serve the enterprise of nation-building. In refugee communities, ethnic, nationalist and cultural identities often become highly valued features of individual and collective identity, buoys in the face of indignity and the loss of a homeland. Refugees, host governments and international NGOs are well aware that '[s]chools reflect, and have the potential to influence, the processes of collective memory transmission and transformation' (Freedman et al., 2008, p. 684). This is manifested in language choice and the curriculum followed (particularly the teaching of history) in formal schooling.

The appropriation of and control over education and its content ensures the political and cultural reproduction and legitimization of certain values as held by dominant groups. Refugee communities do not always have the ultimate say as to what type of identity should be transmitted through education, much less whether they can be allowed to even have schools. The host government controls this, and the international community – through multilateral organizations and NGOs – has some influence. Here, it is evident that the link between territoriality, sovereignty and belonging is broken with respect to the refugee communities; they must grapple with reconciling that to their own agenda for education.

Education and livelihoods

> A livelihood comprises the capabilities, assets (stores, resources, claims and access) and activities required for a means of living. A livelihood is sustainable when it can cope with and recover from stress and shocks, maintain or enhance its capabilities and assets, and provide sustainable livelihood opportunities for the next generation (Chambers and Conway, 1991, p. 6).

One of the most debilitating consequences of displacement is the loss of livelihood. This is the reality for Karen refugees displaced in Burma (KHRG, 2008). In refugee situations in developing countries, it is common for the host government to prohibit refugees from obtaining certain types of paid employment. For example, Palestinian refugees in Lebanon are barred from more than 75 professions and jobs (Oh and Roberts, 2006).

The link between education, employment and livelihoods is broken when host governments limit the movement and employment opportunities of refugees. In such circumstances, the role that education plays in preparing children and young people for employment and acquiring a livelihood despite their present circumstances is gravely undermined. Besides individual livelihoods, the break between education and employment also has an impact on the sustainability of education within a refugee community. Physical and human resources are needed to sustain community education. When individual livelihoods are lacking, the community is unable to generate its own resources for education. Added to this are the ongoing inflows and outflows of refugees resulting from intermittent waves of conflict and resettlement programmes.

Education and certification

For refugees, international recognition of their educational outcomes is critical to ensuring that the years spent in school in refugee camps are recognized (for further education and employment) when they move to another country or context (Kirk, 2009). When learning experiences are not recognized, frustration and disappointment result, and the promise of a better future through education is shattered. For example, the UNHCR/UNICEF sixth-grade graduation certificates earned by Rwandan refugees in Tanzania in the mid-1990s were not recognized by the Rwandan government when the refugees returned (Bird, 2003).

While the education in the refugee camps in Thailand is of a higher quality (KHRG, 2008) than in Burma, it only holds currency in the refugee context (Sawade, 2008). The challenges of gaining accredited learning is a concrete indicator of the broken link between education and the nation–state and has serious implications for the future of refugees, whether that comes in the form of resettlement, repatriation or integration into the host community.

Education for protection and peace

The predominant approach that the UNHCR uses in reference to children is that of protection (UNICEF, 2005). In refugee situations, much of this has been manifested as a focus on providing psychosocial intervention to large-scale refugee displacements as part of the humanitarian agenda so as to counteract the traumatic effects of conflict and displacement (Eyber, 2002).

In addition, there has been an emphasis on the use of education to promote peace and conflict resolution. Bush and Saltarelli (2000) describe education as a means of:

- dampening the impact of conflict through educational opportunity
- nurturing and sustaining an ethnically tolerant climate
- denying education as a weapon of war
- stimulating linguistic tolerance
- cultivating inclusive citizenship

- disarming history
- introducing education for peace programmes
- using educational practice as an explicit response to state repression

At the same time, they acknowledge that education in emergencies and conflict can also be used to perpetuate or create negative practices, such as

- distributing education unevenly
- using education as a weapon in cultural repression
- manipulating history for political purposes
- manipulating textbooks
- influencing self-worth and hating others

There are countless programmes and documents on peace education, and these have been critically evaluated (Sommers, 2001). However, refugee communities do not always agree that peace education should be included in the curriculum. This is often the agenda of multilateral organizations and international NGOs, whose funding affords them leverage in implementing these programmes.

Karen refugees in Thailand: disjuncture between the 'nation–state' and the provision of formal schooling

Between the 1960s and 1984, Karen villagers crossed the border into Thailand seeking temporary refuge from incursions by the Burmese military. After each campaign, they would return to their villages. It became apparent after 1984 that the refugees would not be able to return to their homes. As a result, the Thai authorities permitted semi-permanent camps or 'temporary shelters' (the term used by the Thai authorities) to be set up, with the understanding that the refugees would return home as soon as they were able to. These camps functioned like open villages (Bowles, 1998) and the refugees set up their own churches, hospitals and schools, using the village structures that they had employed in the Karen State (Lang, 2002). Residents were able to enter and leave the camps and to forage in the nearby forests.

The Karen were proactive in setting up schools and the accompanying administrative structures; they also obtained assistance from NGOs for educational resources and materials. There had already been a system of school management in the Karen state that was under the Karen National Union (KNU). The KNU represents the state authority of the Karen 'nation' and it has always regarded education as a priority. Schooling and language have been used by the KNU – in its territories and in the refugee camps in Thailand – to facilitate social reproduction and identity formation so as to cultivate a certain form of Karen national consciousness (Rajah, 1990). To this end, the Karen Education Department (KED) – the education wing of the KNU – was tasked with the responsibility for managing education in the camps and in the Karen state.

Until 1995, the KNU controlled much of the border, enabling the refugee community to maintain a degree of integration with Karen communities in Burma and good access to resources (Brooks, 2004). This ensured the continued control of education by the 'nation–state' as represented by the KNU. However, in January 1995, with the assistance of the Democratic Karen Buddhist Association (DKBA), the Burmese army overran Manerplaw, the headquarters of the KNU. The KNU's hold on its territory was drastically reduced. At the same time, as a result of cross-border attacks on the camps, the Thai government, with the help of the UNHCR, moved and amalgamated camps to locations which were further away from the border (Brooks, 2004). It was only in 1996 that the Thai government officially permitted international NGOs to provide educational support in the camps. Tightened restrictions on refugee camp populations by the Thai government brought about increased dependence on international aid. This meant that decision-making about education in the camps had to be increasingly 'shared' with international NGOs.

The KED was responsible for education in the camps and in the Karen state until April 2009. However, its ability to do its job in the camps was severely hampered by its illegal status in Thailand and its lack of funding. This restricted its ability to travel to the camps and its capacity to implement, monitor and control education in the camps. Further, the KED had little ability to negotiate with the Thai authorities. This meant that it was subject to direct and indirect influence from international NGOs.

While the KED attempted valiantly to play the role of the authority in the 'nation–state', it was all too apparent in the camps and to other actors that it did not have the political and economic clout or the actual capacity to do so. This, coupled with donor concerns about funding a 'political' organization, brought about the establishment in April 2009 of the Karen Refugee

Committee Education Entity (KRCEE) under the Karen Refugee Committee (KRC). The task of the KRCEE was to take over the management of education in the camps.

In its work, the KRCEE collaborates with NGOs and community-based organizations (CBOs). The 70 schools in the seven predominantly Karen camps are staffed by approximately 80 headteachers and 1,600 teachers. Along with building caretakers, they ensure that the schools function on a day-to-day basis, supporting the learning of approximately 34,000 students (in 2009–10). Each school is overseen by a school committee which is made up of different members of the community. The committee determines school policy. Nursery school, general education, post-secondary schooling and vocational and adult learning programmes are also available in the camps.

With the change in authority, there has been a formal decoupling of the management of education from the KNU. This means that the education system in the camps is officially no longer being managed by the 'exiled state authorities', as represented by the KNU. Instead, education in the camps is now being run by a separate camp-based organization (the KED continues to oversee education in the Karen state).

The links between education management and the 'Karen state authorities' are not completely broken, though; some of the staff members in the KRCEE also represent the KNU and/or the KED and/or have affiliations with these bodies. So, although, there has been a formal decoupling, there are still clear links with the KNU and education is still being managed by the refugee community.

As this section has described, the exigencies of refugee life, civil war and the unrecognized status of the Karen state have created a disjuncture between state authority and the provision of education. The scope of the KNU/KED and KRCEE in managing education and determining policy on the content and form of education are firmly circumscribed by Thai government policies regarding refugees and the funding and programme priorities of the international NGOs and their donors.

While the Royal Thai Government (RTG) is not a signatory to the 1951 Convention Relating to the Status of Refugees or the 1967 Protocol Relating to the Status of Refugees, it does provide some form of sanctuary to the refugees and allows local and international NGOs to provide resources for shelter, food rations, security, health services, and education and training. Under Thai migration laws, refugees or 'displaced persons' occupy a particular administrative status, which only applies if they stay within the camps. Thus, these services are only available to them within the refugee camps. As such, the majority of refugee children are confined to schooling opportunities in the camps.

The RTG permits the refugees to run their own schools and allows international NGOs to fund infrastructure; provide teacher training, school materials and resources; develop the capacity of education staff; and establish systems for providing education services. For the most part, it has left these affairs to the camp committees, CBOs and international NGOs, and has taken the stance that its commitment to the humanitarian enterprise is temporary and minimal (Lang, 2002). It has imposed general restrictions on refugee movement and livelihoods and specific restrictions[4] on education in the camps. These are:

1. NGO personnel are allowed to work as advisors to teachers, but not as teachers.
2. No permanent school buildings may be constructed. This has been amended recently and it is now possible to construct semi-permanent buildings; iron poles, small wooden poles and steel roofs can now be used in place of leaves and bamboo poles. Concrete cannot be used.
3. The area designated for school buildings cannot be expanded.
4. Publications distributed in schools may not contain political ideas, attitudes or values.

These are the parameters within which the refugee community, with the assistance of international NGOs, carries out its educational endeavours. The result is that there are limitations to staff capacity, poor infrastructure and facilities, and limited resources.

The other actors with a say in how education is run are the international NGOs working along the border. Unlike other refugee situations, in this case the UNHCR does not run the camps nor implement education programmes. This is because the Thai authorities were concerned about the presence of the UNHCR attracting other people from Burma, as it did during the Indochinese relief effort. Thus, the government restricted the UNHCR's role to that of observer. In fact, it was only in 1998 that formal acceptance and a permanent role for the UNHCR on the Burmese border was permitted (Lang, 2002).

The management and administration of services (including education) to the refugee population was designated to a group of NGOs. In 1984, the Ministry Of Interior (MOI) invited the Coordinating Committee for

Services to Displaced Persons in Thailand (CCSDPT), a group of voluntary agencies working with the Indochinese refugees at the time, to oversee the relief effort for the Burmese refugee population. As a result, a small consortium of NGOs, now named the Thailand Burma Border Consortium (TBBC), was formed under the CCSDPT (Lang, 2002). The layout of the camps, the communal infrastructure (hospitals, schools and so on), and the organizational and administrative structures had already been put in place by the refugees. The NGOs worked in coordination with the refugee community structures for food and aid distribution, engendering a high level of trust and cooperation (Bowles, 1997). Thus, education services have always been coordinated and financially supported by NGOs in cooperation with the refugee community.

At present, the CCSDPT and the TBBC oversee the relief effort in coordination with the UNHCR. The UNHCR takes as its mandate the protection of refugees, not provision of education, and only provides funding for adult English and Thai language lessons in the camps.[5]

Over the years, many NGOs have provided education services in the camps, as coordinated by the TBBC and the CCSDPT. However, most of the current funding for primary and secondary schools in the seven predominantly Karen camps is provided by ZOA Refugee Care Thailand (ZOA), an international NGO with headquarters in the Netherlands. ZOA funds building materials, staff salaries, teacher training, teaching materials and resources (including textbooks), and stationery.[6] Other international NGOs, charitable organizations from other parts of the world (including faith-based institutions) and contributions from parents and the community provide the rest of the funding.

Donor agendas and the interests of the host government greatly influence the management of education in the camps. Both the refugee community and the NGOs work under the ultimate authority of the Thai government, but the international NGOs have much more leeway to negotiate with the Thai government and to influence policy on education. The refugee community relies on both the funding and the influence of the NGOs.

The different agendas of the refugees (even within its own community) and the international NGO community mean that the present content and form of education are the result of negotiation between the groups, particularly since the refugee community leadership has very clear reasons for providing formal schooling. This is explored in more detail in the next section.

Schooling without a nation–state

One of the most important functions of education, as perceived by the refugees in the camps, is the formation of political, social, cultural and ethnic identity. The leadership, in particular, places immense stock in the role of formal schooling in reproducing nationalist identity, in the service of nation-building and self-determination (Oh, forthcoming b; Oh and Van der Stouwe, 2008; Rajah, 1990; South, 2007). Within the ambiguity and uncertainty of forced displacement, this purpose transcends the limits set by education for repatriation, integration, resettlement or prolonged residence in camps.

According to Rajah (2002), Karen 'narrations of nation' drew upon symbolic and cultural resources, such as accounts of descent and origins recorded and 'adjusted' by missionaries, supported by the creation of a literate tradition through the introduction of writing and the establishment of schools and churches. These 'wrought a transformation in modes of consciousness so that educated Karen were not merely able to envision a shared or common descent for all Karennic-speaking peoples, but also how to *organize* the Karen trans-locally' (Rajah, 2002, p. 527). He argued that 'Karen identity, as it is made out by the KNU is an *invention*, rather different from the way that Karen in village communities identify themselves, and that the Karen "nation–state" is, to use Anderson's term (1983, p. 15), an "imagined political community . . . imagined as both inherently limited and sovereign"' (Rajah, 1990, p. 121).

The destruction of Manerplaw in 1995 and counter-insurgency operations resulted in 'profound' consequences for the 'reproduction of Karen narrations of nation and, thus Karen ethno-nationalism and nationalism. Their re-telling has been significantly influenced by the conditions in which they are reproduced; no longer in the Karen quasi-nation-state of Kawthoolei, which manifested an almost palpable local autonomy, but the severely circumscribed conditions of life in refugee camps' (Rajah, 2002, p. 532). At that time (2001), this 'reproduction of Karen narration' varied from camp to camp, as reported by Rajah.

In the camps, the emphasis on formal schooling as a tool in nationalist identity formation is manifested in the following ways. First, the language of instruction in the seven camps is Skaw Karen. Burmese and English are taught as subjects and Pwo Karen, a related language which is spoken by many Karen, is not included. Second, the history taught at the secondary level includes world history, Burmese history (compiled from different textbooks and other resources from Burma), Karen revolution history, origins of the Karen and

Karen hardships. Very little history of other ethnic groups is included. The third element is the standardization of school, staff and educational policy across all seven camps, formerly carried out by the KED and now by the KRCEE.

Using formal schooling to promote certain forms of nationalist identity is not unique to the Karen from Burma. This practice occurs in all formal education systems in the world. In itself, this is not a 'bad' thing. There are considerations in the Karen camps for those who do not subscribe to Karen nationalism. For example, Karen nationalist festivals are observed in the camps but not imposed upon schools. Further, other forms of identity, which are not solely nationalist in nature, are also being cultivated in schools. For example, children are schooled on the importance of community service and observance of social norms valued by the community. Various groups in the community, including the leadership, see education as a tool for inculcating certain notions of Karen cultural and social identity and forging solidarity through an understanding of shared oppression (Oh, forthcoming b).

However, an unintended effect of their policies on the language of instruction and the valorizing of Karen history over that of other ethnic groups is the systematic exclusion of non-Karen speaking students (Oh, forthcoming b; Oh and Van der Stouwe, 2008). This has significant implications for the non-Karen residing in the camps, made up of the Karenni, Shan, Mon, Burman, Rakhine, Chin and so on. They do not necessarily subscribe to Karen notions of identity and nationalism, and the language of instruction can pose challenges to their participation and achievement in school, particularly at the secondary level.

The Karen have much more control over the educational enterprise than the other groups living in the camps for two reasons: they were the first refugees who crossed the border and they set up the schools when they began living in the refugee camps. NGOs have been unintentionally complicit in this state of affairs. Commentators have observed that when the NGOs began working in the camps in Thailand, they accepted the existing power structures without question (Bowles, 1997; South, 2007). These structures were set up with the help of the CCSDPT, using the village structure that had existed in the Karen state (Lang, 2002).

Consequently, the NGOs did not question assumptions about language, history standardization and leadership structures. In the past few years, some NGOs have worked to change the nature of their involvement in these structures and to encourage power sharing among those who have fewer political resources, in the interest of expanding access and promoting educational equity. For example, NGOs have implemented programmes and initiatives that promote inclusion in education, such as special education (world education) and inclusion awareness and practices, in an attempt to embed inclusion at all levels and in all aspects of education provision and management (ZOA Refugee Care Thailand). This process has engendered awareness of inclusion and exclusion among camp education management staff and school staff.

Schooling for unemployment

The link between education, skills and employment is so deeply embedded in the conventional wisdom of modern societies that it is difficult to imagine otherwise. In the refugee camps, this link is broken – employment is the exception rather than the rule.

By law, the refugees are not allowed to obtain employment in Thailand outside the camps. They do, however, find employment illegally. In a sample of more than 2,400 respondents (this number excludes school personnel) in the seven predominantly Karen camps, 9.3 per cent of the respondents reported 'day labour outside camp' as their main occupation. This was the second largest proportion, after 'unpaid housework', which slightly more than half the sample reported. The third highest proportion was 'work in an NGO or community-based organization (CBO)', at 6.8 per cent.

In the nine camps, it is estimated that there are 7,000 paid jobs, consisting of about 1,800 in camp management, roughly 2,000 in the health sector and 3,400 in the education sector (this includes figures for the two Karenni camps) (Banki and Lang, 2007). Given that between half and two-thirds of the camp population consists of adults, the total number of people available for work (including the elderly and the disabled) is many times the number of paid jobs available in camp.

Income levels reflect the lack of jobs. In the same survey, more than half of the sample reported earning nothing, and less than a fifth earned between US$0.03 and US$3 a month (Oh et al., forthcoming a). This is the figure for the general population.[7] School and educational staff, on the other hand, earn between US$15 and US$24 a month. Camp residents working for other NGOs earn similar or higher incomes. Earning some form of income has become even more crucial, as the refugees are no longer allowed to forage in the nearby forests.

Given that there are so few paid jobs available to the refugees, education and learning opportunities that prepare them for paid employment may seem superfluous. The vocational programmes offered in the camps (sewing, baking, smithing and so on) were designed with repatriation in mind. However, repatriation has not been an option so far, and the skills taught are not suitable to local market conditions (Brees, 2008). While the participants relish the opportunity to acquire new skills, trainees do feel frustrated at not being able to practice their newly acquired skills and to earn an income (Brees, 2008; Oh and Pakdeekhunthum, 2007; WCRCW, 2006).

In response, NGOs have set up practice sessions and small income-generating projects, and worked with CBOs to do the same. ZOA Refugee Care Thailand set up a livelihoods project which combines agricultural skills training and actual agricultural production. These do provide some productive outlets for the skills acquired, but they are limited in terms of income generation and livelihoods for the refugee community.

Putting aside paid employment, there are many unpaid positions in the camps, such as working with committees, CBOs and gardening inside the camp. The development of skills and knowledge for these positions is valued and welcomed in the community.

Despite the scarcity of paid employment opportunities, education is still seen as invaluable to preparation for work (paid and unpaid). In an education survey conducted in 2009 (Oh et al., 2010), parents placed great value on education's role in preparing students for work, although they were realistic about the actual number of jobs available in camp (Tables 2.1 and 2.2).

Students were more realistic than their parents about the break in the link between education and employment. However, they were aware that they were more likely to obtain a good job in the camp if they achieved high levels of education.

Struggling for sustainability

The education system in the camps is unsustainable for a variety of reasons. First, the scarcity of income and poor livelihoods means that the financial resources that can be allocated to education from the refugee community as a whole is low and the individual costs of education are high relative to income. Private contributions to schools come in the form of school and school-related fees. School fees per year range from US$0.15 to US$9.00 for primary and US$0.15 to US$21.50 for secondary schools. Some parents also contribute to the maintenance of school buildings by donating bamboo leaves. The majority (64 per cent) of primary students pay between US$1.20 and US$3.00, while their secondary counterparts pay between US$2.15 and US$3.70 per

Table 2.1 Parents' Attitudes towards Schooling and Employment

Schooling is needed to get a good job.	96.2% agreed or strongly agreed. 2.3% disagreed or strongly disagreed. 1.5% don't know. *n*=2380
Children who achieve high levels of education in school are more likely to get good jobs in camp.	88.3% parents agreed or strongly agreed. 8.9% disagreed or strongly disagreed. 2.8% don't know. *n*=2385
There is no work so why bother going to school.	86% disagreed or strongly disagreed. 10.1% agreed or strongly agreed. 3.9% don't know. *n*=2384
The education that children receive in school is not useful for getting a job in camp.	79.8% disagreed or strongly disagreed. 15.3% agreed or strongly agreed. 4.9% don't know. *n*=2395

n = number of respondents

Table 2.2 Students' Attitude towards Schooling and Employment

	Primary students	**Secondary students**
I don't understand why I have to go to school when I won't be able to get a job after that.	23.5% agree or strongly agree. 76.4% disagree or strongly disagree. *n*=425	30.2% agree or strongly agree. 68.4% disagree or strongly disagree. *n*=377
The education that I receive in school is not useful for getting a job in camp.	11.5% agree or strongly agree. 88.3% disagree or strongly disagree. *n*=436	8% agree or strongly agree. 92% disagree or strongly disagree. *n*=375
If I achieve high levels of education, I am more likely to get a good job in camp.	98.2% agree or strongly agree. 1.8% disagree or strongly disagree. *n*=435	93.9% agree or strongly agree. 6.1% disagree or strongly disagree. *n*=376

n = number of respondents.

year. Almost all parents reported being able to pay school fees, irrespective of reported income levels.

Figures for the total amount of camp education funding are not available. However, it is possible to use ZOA's funding figures as an approximation of the total amount, given that it provides the bulk of education funding in the seven camps. In 2009, ZOA received roughly US$1.5 million for general education; the average amount of funding for the years 2007–09 was US$1.26

million (ZOA, 2009). For 2009, the average expenditure per student per year was US$44, compared to the US$1,048 spent on each primary school student in Thailand by the Thai government in 1998 (OECD, 2001).

One of the major drawbacks refugees in protracted situations face is donor fatigue (Brown, 2001). Donors become tired of providing funding to a situation without a foreseeable conclusion. In fact, after 2012, ZOA Refugee Care Thailand will no longer work in the camps. It is in the process of phasing out its operations in Thailand and will be handing them over to other NGOs and a newly formed body, Usakhanae Foundation. ZOA Refugee Care headquarters will continue to support the general education programme which will fall under the responsibility of the foundation.[8] However, this funding stream is not guaranteed. Moreover, the general education programme is the largest education programme, requiring the most funds. This development underlines the lack of sustainability and the precariousness of NGO funding.

The second challenge to sustainability is the capacity and motivation of the management and teaching staff. Teachers earn about US$15.00 a month. Given the challenging conditions and long hours, many teachers are demoralized and tempted to accept higher-paying jobs offered by other NGOs (Oh et al., 2006; 2010).

The Thai government insists that expatriate staff members do not work as teachers in the camps. The unanticipated benefit of this policy is that there is a high degree of community ownership over the education system. However, this also means that teacher training is not as extensive and effective as it could be. ZOA's external teacher trainers travel to all seven camps throughout the year to train teachers and camp-based teacher trainers. However, this is not enough, given the high rates of teacher turnover and the low subject and skill bases of the newer teachers. Further, there are not enough qualified people in the camps to work as camp-based teacher trainers.

The other challenge that the education system faces, common in refugee situations, is the constant turnover of educational staff that resettlement to other countries entails. Since 2004, more than 50,000 refugees from the nine official camps have been resettled in other countries (UNHCR, 2009); this has affected the education sector disproportionately. Within each education level, personnel with higher education levels were more likely to express interest, submit an application, be accepted and depart for resettlement than those with no education. Second, the majority of those who are highly educated and have jobs are those in the education sector. Finally, the education sector employs the largest number of camp refugees by far (Banki and Lang,

2007). The consequences of resettlement are lack of qualified and experienced teachers, disruption of school schedules and a sense of frustration and futility among teacher trainers and headteachers (Oh et al., 2010). The system builds up staff capacity, but when teachers resettle, they take their skill sets with them. While this is a good opportunity for them, it does mean that headteachers and camp-based teacher trainers are confronted with the frustrating and demotivating task of recruiting and training teachers constantly (Oh et al., 2010).

Learning made invisible

For refugees, international recognition of their educational outcomes is critical to ensuring that the years spent in refugee camp schools are recognized when they are repatriated, resettled or integrated into the host society, so that their learning counts for something when they attempt to access further education and employment. At present, there is some progress towards certifying the learning in the camps. A Framework of Cooperation with the Office of the Vocational Education Commission (OVEC) under the Thai Ministry of Education (MOE) was signed a few years ago with certification as one of the objectives. In addition, work is being done to obtain MOE certification for some subjects in the general education curriculum, such as math, science and English. This was spearheaded in 2007 by ZOA Refugee Care in partnership with UNICEF (van der Stouwe and Oh, 2009).

The discussion surrounding certification has focused on the alignment of the camp-based curriculum with the Thai MOE curriculum. The Karen education leadership expressed concern about maintaining the Karen nature of their curriculum and it was agreed that history and other social science subjects would not be included in the certification process. This reflects the tension between a 'Karen' curriculum and an accredited Thai curriculum, which reflects a wider conflict between Karen nationalist and cultural identity formation and the globalization of Karen education. The former is of utmost importance to the Karen leadership, in the project of nation-building. In fact, the curriculum used by the Karen holds currency among the Karen in the Karen state as well as in Thailand (Sawade, 2008). Moreover, the Karen Refugee Committee Institute of Higher Education (KRCIHE) is going ahead with plans to launch a higher education programme in the camps which will offer bachelor's degrees, given that the refugees are not permitted to enrol in Thai universities. However, given the refugee status of the Karen, a curriculum which is accredited by a recognized nation-state body has more currency outside the Karen setting (in the Karen state and in the camps).

Incorporating protection and peace in education

While education for protection, peace and conflict prevention is often at the top of the list of priorities for international NGOs, it is not always so for refugee communities. Peace education in the camps in Thailand was initiated in 1999 by the organization Living Values Education. Teacher training was conducted in one camp, as a one-off training session, using experiential activities and practical methods to assist teachers and practitioners in helping children and young people explore and develop 12 personal and social values: peace, respect, love, cooperation, freedom, happiness, honesty, humility, responsibility, simplicity, tolerance and unity (Tilllman, 2001). The programme incorporated psychosocial techniques for dealing with war and conflict. What was significant was the report that a headteacher in the training session declared that if they were to learn about peace, they would have to surrender and be killed (Tillman, 2001). For the refugees, survival has meant fighting or fleeing; in this context, the teaching of peace and conflict-resolution techniques are counterintuitive and dangerous. The training facilitator replied to the headteacher by asking if the refugees would have the skills to create a peaceful society when they returned to Burma (Tillman, 2001).

This exchange reflects the nature of the refugee context: since there is no certainty about the future, the experiences of the past guide their thinking and actions in general and in education. International organizations bring with them the perspective that peace is a certainty in the future, which contradicts the refugee experience and mindset. This difference in perspective has been reconciled by incorporating parts of the peace education programme into citizenship education. The programme has since been adjusted and adopted by the education management in all camps and included in the formal education curriculum, but in a slightly different guise. The KED, with the support of ZOA and the programme Creating Opportunities for Psychosocial Enhancement (COPE), incorporated 'living values' in its formal education curriculum as a citizenship component. The aim is to teach young people about governance – to manage townships and villages and the environment. In addition, issues relating to health and religion were included. Peace values became embedded in constructions of Karen values, Karen society and what it means to be a good Karen citizen: peace, faithfulness, honesty, dignity, unity, respect for elders, knowledge of Karen culture and so on.

The curriculum was written up by a group of organizations, such as the Karen Youth Organization (KYO), the Karen Environment Group (Kesan), the international NGOs that work on health and other religious groups in the camps. This was the first time such an initiative was launched. The citizenship and history components of the curriculum do not include the history and values of other ethnic groups from Burma. As Metro (2006) found, the 'challenge that the ethnic nationality groups face in their collaboration is to come up with guidelines for a curriculum that will be acceptable to all groups without silencing anyone' (p. 5). This is a dilemma that the Karen refugee community (and other ethnic refugee community groups from Burma) faces and has so far been unable to overcome. The nationalist bent in the curriculum in the camps is particularly relevant to the Karen and their notions of self-determination and nation-building, but they have not reconciled that with the nationalist concerns of other ethnic groups (and vice versa) and the role of education in post-conflict reconstruction. This has implications for future peace and resolution among all the ethnic groups in Burma.[9]

Education and the dilemma of displacement

Education in the refugee camps is characterized by disjuncture: between the state (identity) and territory (belonging), the present (protracted refugee situation) and the future (repatriation, resettlement, integration), nowhere (camp) and everywhere (global, resettlement). It is within this maelstrom of ambiguity that refugee communities rebuild their schools and education systems, often with the assistance (or interference, depending on one's perspective) from international NGOs and within the political, economic and geographical space circumscribed by the host government.

The refugee camps along the Thai-Burmese border were set up as temporary shelters, later transitioning into semi-permanent camps and then transformed into established camps. Repatriation does not seem[10] to be an option at present, but the Thai authorities oppose integration into the host society. Resettlement is a 'durable' alternative for a minority; prolonged encampment seems to be the only option for the majority. Meanwhile, new refugees have entered the camps, replacing those who have resettled.

All along, the provision of education has had to accommodate these issues and changes.

The dislocation that has occurred within the sphere of education was examined in this chapter: identity formation and nation-building outside a recognized 'nation–state', education for scarce employment, an education system that has difficulties sustaining itself, the limits of certification and the incorporation of peace values into notions of citizenship.

The Karen refugee community has considerable control over the formal education system in the camps, but its funding is dependent on the NGOs. This subtle balance is replicated in the relationship between NGOs and the Thai authorities. While the Thai government ministries have ultimate decision-making power over policies relating to education, the NGOs (which often act as intermediaries between the government and the refugees) play a role in that process. Fortunately, there continues to be space for NGOs to negotiate with the Thai authorities, enabling them and the refugees to pursue avenues for better educational quality.

This chapter has also highlighted cases in which the outcomes of different agendas among the actors have been negotiated:

- Between competing groups within the community. At some point, international NGOs were co-opted into the agenda of dominant refugee groups (Skaw Karen as the language of instruction and Karen history in the curriculum), unwittingly accepting the power dynamics that already exist in the community.
- Non-governmental organizations made decisions on how education should be provided (inclusion). Although the NGOs have the clout that comes with funding, they do tread a fine line in wielding this power; consensus with the community is often sought.
- Negotiation between NGOs and the Thai government (certification).

Despite, or maybe because of the restrictions and procedures of the Thai government, the education system in the camps is Karen-centric and staff members are drawn entirely from the camp community. The outcome is a high level of commitment, motivation and community ownership over the education system.

The refugees have been able to create and sustain an education system that is highly valued internally, for nationalist and community reasons. For some, the value they place on this may override the breaks in the link between education, further education and employment. In addition, the refugees have been able to work around the limits of sovereign power of the Thai state, as well as the Burmese state: the camps provide a nationalist education that is unavailable in Burma (Decha, 2007).

These questions (see Key Questions) point to fundamental considerations in the practice and delivery of education in refugee settings and are significant not just during conditions of forced displacement but also during post-conflict reconstruction.

Key Questions

1. In a protracted refugee setting, what are the best ways to integrate identity formation and nation-building in education in a multi-ethnic setting?
2. What are the best ways of developing knowledge and skills in young people in refugee settings in ways which take into account their reduced livelihood opportunities and the unknown possibilities of repatriation, integration, resettlement or prolonged encampment?

Notes

1 I would like to thank the Institute of Southeast Asian Studies, Singapore for its support, and my colleagues there for their invaluable comments on my work. I am also indebted to ZOA Refugee Care Thailand for allowing me to use their database.

2 In 1989, the Burmese government re-named the country *Myanmar Naing-ngan*. In this paper, the term 'Burma' will be used to refer to the country, and Myanmar will be used where quoted by that name. 'Burmese' is used to refer to the nationality of the people.

3 Wieng Haeng camp in Chiangmai province is a Shan refugee resettlement site and is not counted as an official camp by the Thai authorities. There are also unofficial camps along the Thai border, and unofficial ones for IDPs on the Burmese side of the border.

4 'Karen' is used as an umbrella term for the myriad groups living in different parts of Burma and Thailand that speak related languages. It includes the Skaw, Pwo, Kayah (also known as the Karenni) and White Karen (Smith, 1991). The word 'Karen', as used by the Karen National Union (KNU), refers to Karen political and cultural identity. In this chapter, 'Karen' is used to refer to the Skaw and Pwo subgroups, as is commonly defined by the residents in the camps.

5 'Guidelines to ensure that the project implementation conforms with MOI regulations' issued by the MOI to NGOs from interview with Duangporn Saussay, Manager External Relations of ZOA Refugee Care Thailand on 5 July 2010.

6 Interview with Duangporn Saussay, Manager External Relations of ZOA Refugee Care Thailand, 5 July 2010.

7 Jesuit Refugee Service (JRS) provides equivalent services to the two Karenni camps in the north.

8 Respondents were asked to choose a nominal category for the income they earned per month: 0 Baht, 1–100 Baht, 101–500 Baht, 501–1000 Baht, 1001–2000 Baht, more than 2000 Baht. Thus, an average income for the sample cannot be calculated.

9 Interview with Duangporn Saussay, Manager External Relations of ZOA Refugee Care Thailand, 5 July 2010.

10 I would like to thank Moe Thuzar for this insight.

Further reading

Sommers, M. (2002), 'Children, Education and War: Reaching Education for All (EFA) Objectives in Countries Affected by Conflict'. *Conflict Prevention and Reconstruction Unit Working Papers*. Paper No. 1. The World Bank.

Waters, T. and LeBlanc, K. (2005), 'Refugees and Education: Mass Public Schooling without a Nation–State'. *Comparative Education Review*, 49(2), 129–47.

References

Aguilar, P. and Retamal, G. (1998), *Rapid Educational Response in Complex Emergencies: A Discussion Document*. Geneva: International Bureau of Education.

Ahearn, F., Loughry, M. and Ager, A. (1999), 'The Experience of Refugee Children', in A. Ager (ed.), *Refugees: Perspectives on the Experience of Forced Migration*. London and New York: Pinter, pp. 215–36.

Banki, S. and Lang, H. (2007), *Planning for the Future: The Impact of Resettlement on the Remaining Camp Population*. Thailand: CCSDPT.

Baxter, P. (2001), 'The UNHCR Peace Education Programme: Skills for Life'. *Forced Migration Review*, 11, 28–30.

Bensalah, K., Sinclair, M. and Nacer Hadj, F. (2001), *Education in Situations of Emergency and Crisis: Challenges for the New Century*. Paris: Swedish International Development Agency, UNESCO.

Bird, L. (2003), *Surviving School: Education for Refugee Children from Rwanda 1994–1996*. Paris: IIEP-UNESCO.

Bowles, E. (1997), *Assistance, Protection, and Policy in Refugee Camps on the Thailand-Burma Border: An Overview*. Oxford: Refugee Studies Programme, Queen Elizabeth House.

Bowles, E. (1998), 'From Village to Camp: Refugee Camp Life in Transition on the Thailand-Burma Border'. *Forced Migration Review*, 2, 11–14.

Boothby, N. (1996), 'Mobilising Communities to Meet the Psychosocial Needs of Children in War and Refugee Crises', in Apfel, R. and Simon, B. (eds), *Minefields in their Hearts: The Mental Health of Children in War and Communal Violence*. New Haven: Yale University Press, pp. 149–64.

Boyden, J. and Gibbs, S. (1997), *Children of War. Responses to Psycho-social Distress in Cambodia*. Geneva: United Nations Research Institute for Social Development.

Boyden, J. and Ryder, P. (1996), *The Provision of Education to Children Affected by Armed Conflict*. Oxford: Refugee Studies Centre, Oxford University. (unpublished)

Brees, I. (2008), 'Towards sustainable livelihoods: Vocational training and access to work on the Thai-Burmese border'. *ZOA issue paper no. 1*. Maesot, Thailand: ZOA Refugee Care Thailand.

Brooks, H. K. (2004), 'Burmese Refugees in Thailand: the Provision of Humanitarian Relief to Karen Refugees on the Thai-Burmese Border', in Bolesta, A. (ed.), *Conflict and Displacement in the Developing World*. Poland: Libra, pp. 95–112.

Brown, T. (2001), 'Improving Quality and Attainment in Refugee Schools: The Case of the Bhutanese Refugees in Nepal', in Crisp, J. and Cipollone, D.B. (eds), *Learning for a Future: Refugee Education in Developing Countries*. Geneva: UNHCR, pp. 109–61.

Buckland, P. (2005), *Reshaping the Future: Education and Postconflict Reconstruction*. Washington, DC: World Bank.

Bush, K. D. and Saltarelli, D. (2000), *The Two Faces of Education in Ethnic Conflict: Towards a Peacebuilding Education for Children*. Florence, Italy: UNICEF.

Chambers, R. and Conway, G. R. (1991), *Sustainable Rural Livelihoods: Practical Concepts for the 21st Century*. Discussion Paper 296. Brighton: IDS.

Coulby, D. and Jones, C. (2001), *Education and Warfare in Europe*. London: Ashgate.

Davies, L. (2004), *Conflict and Education: Complexity and Chaos*. London: Routledge.

Davies, L. (2005), 'Schools and War: Urgent Agendas for Comparative and International Education'. *Compare*, 35(4), 357–71.

Decha, T. (2007), '"Temporary Shelter Areas" and the Paradox of Perceptibility: Imperceptible Naked-Karens in the Thai-Burmese Border Zones', in Prem Kumar Rajaram and Grundy-Warr, C. (eds), *Borderscapes: Hidden Geographies and Politics at Territory's Edge*. Minneapolis: University of Minnesota Press, pp. 231–62.

Eyber, C. (2002), Psychosocial Issues. *FMO Research Guide*. Available from http://www.forcedmigration.org/guides/fmo004/ (accessed 4 August 2010).

Freedman, S. W., Harvey, M. W., Murphy, K and Longman, T. (2008), 'Teaching History after Identity-Based Conflicts: The Rwanda Experience'. *Comparative Education Review*, 52(4), 663–90.

Fountain, S. (1999), *Peace Education in UNICEF*. Working Paper. New York: UNICEF.

Metro, R. (2006), 'Developing history curricula to support multi-ethnic civil society among Burmese refugees and migrants'. *New Issues in Refugee Research*, Research Paper No. 139. UNHCR.

Karen Human Rights Group (KHRG) (2008), *Growing Up Under Militarisation: Abuse and Agency of Children in Karen State*. Thailand: KHRG.

Kirk, J. (2009), *Certification Counts: Recognizing the Learning Attainments of Displaced and Refugee Students*. Paris: IIEP-UNESCO.

Lang, H. J. (2002), *Fear and Sanctuary: Burmese Refugees in Thailand*. Ithaca, NY: Southeast Asia Program Publications, Southeast Asia Program, Cornell University.

LeBlanc, K. and Waters, T. (2005), 'Schooling in refugee camps'. *Humanitarian Exchange Magazine*. Issue 29. Available from http://www.odihpn.org/report.asp?id=2654 (accessed 22 June 2010).

Loescher, G. (1994), *Beyond Charity: International Cooperation and the Global Refugee Crisis*. New York: Oxford University Press.

McCallin, M. (2001), 'Understanding the Psychosocial Needs of Refugee Children and Adolescents', in Loughry, M. and Ager, A. (eds), *The Refugee Experience. Psychosocial Training Module*, 1, 73–103 (2nd edn). Oxford: Refugee Studies Centre, University of Oxford, 2001. Available from http://earlybird.qeh.ox.ac.uk/rfgexp/rsp_tre/student/children/toc.htm.

Machel, G. (1996), *Impact of Armed Conflict on Children*, in Report of the Expert of the Secretary-General, Submitted Pursuant to UN General Assembly Resolution 48/157. New York: United Nations.

Nicolai, S. and Triplehorn, C. (2003), *The Role of Education in Protecting Children in Conflict*. Save the Children US. ODI, Humanitarian Practice Network 42.

Oh, S.-A. (forthcoming a), *Education in Refugee Camps in Thailand: Policy, Practice and Paucity*. UNESCO

Oh, S.-A. (forthcoming b), 'Identity and Inclusion: Education in Refugee Camps in Thailand'. Book chapter.

Oh, S.-A. and Pakdeekhunthum, T. T. (2007), *The Learning Landscape: Adult Learning in Seven Refugee Camps along the Thai-Burmese Border*. Maesot, Thailand: ZOA Refugee Care Thailand.

Oh, S.-A., Rattanasamakkee, S., Sukhikhachornphrai, P., Ochalumthan, S. and Purnell, P. (2010), *Education Survey 2009*. Maesot, Thailand: ZOA Refugee Care Thailand.

Oh, S.-A. and Roberts, R. (2006), 'Palestinians and Education in Lebanon', in Griffin, R. (ed.), *Education in the Muslim World: Different Perspectives*. Oxford: Symposium Books, pp. 239–56.

Oh, S.-A. and Van der Stouwe, M. (2008), 'Education, Diversity, and Inclusion in Burmese Refugee Camps in Thailand'. *Comparative Education Review*, 52(4), 589–618.

Oh, S.-A., and Van der Stouwe (2009), 'Towards the certification of learning achievements for Burmese refugees in Thailand: a nongovernmental organization perspective', in Kirk, J. (ed.), *Certification Counts: Recognizing the Learning Attainments of Displaced and Refugee Students*. Paris: IIEP-UNESCO, pp. 149–59.

Oh, S.-A., with Ochalumthan, S., Saw Pla Law La and Htoo, J. (2006), *ZOA Education Survey 2005*. Maesot, Thailand: ZOA Refugee Care Thailand.

Pigozzi, M. J. (1999), 'Education in Emergencies and for Reconstruction: Strategic Guidelines with a Developmental Approach', in Retamal, G. and Aedo-Richmond, R. (eds), *Education as a Humanitarian Response*. London: Cassell, pp. 342–59.

Preston, R. (1988), *Educational Needs of West Irian Refugees in the East Awin Relocation Site in Papua New Guinea*. Boroko, Papua New Guinea: National Research Institute, Educational Research Division.

Preston, R. (1991), 'The Provision of Education to Refugees in Places of Temporary Asylum: Some Implications for Development'. *Comparative Education*, 27(1), 61–81.

Rajah, A. (1990), 'Ethnicity, Nationalism, and the Nation-State: The Karen in Burma and Thailand' in Wijeyewardene, G. (ed.), *Ethnic Groups across National Boundaries in Mainland Southeast Asia*. Singapore: ISEAS, pp. 102–133.

Rajah, A. (2002), 'A "nation of intent" in Burma: Karen ethno-nationalism, nationalism and narrations of nation'. *The Pacific Review*, 15(4), 517–37.

Retamal, G. and Aedo-Richmond, R. (1998), 'Introduction', in Retamal, G. and Aedo-Richmond, R. (eds), *Education as a Humanitarian Response*. London: Cassell, pp. 1–20.

Save the Children Alliance (1996), *Promoting Psychosocial Well-being among Children Affected by Armed Conflict and Displacement: Principles and Approaches*. International Save the Children Alliance, 14.

Sawade, O. (2008), Educational certification for refugees from Burma living in Thailand. *ZOA issue paper* no. 2. Mae Sot, Thailand: *ZOA* Refugee Care Thailand.

Seitz, K. (2004), *Education and Conflict. The role of education in the creation, prevention and resolution of societal crises – Consequences for development cooperation.* Eschborn: Deutsche Gesellschaft für Technische Zusammenarbeit (GTZ).

Sinclair, M. (2001), 'Education in Emergencies', in Crisp, J., Talbot, C. and Cipollone, D. B. (eds), *Learning for a Future: Refugee Education in Developing Countries.* Geneva: UNHCR, pp. 1–83.

Smith, A. and Vaux, T. (2003), *Education, Conflict and International Development.* London: Department for International Development (DFID).

Smith, M. (1991), *Burma: Insurgency and the Politics of Ethnicity.* London: Zed Books.

Sommers, M. (2002), 'Children, Education and War: Reaching Education for All (EFA) Objectives in Countries Affected by Conflict', *Conflict Prevention and Reconstruction Unit Working Papers.* Paper No. 1. The World Bank.

Sommers, M. (2000), *The Dynamics of Coordination.* Providence, RI: Thomas J. Watson Jr. Institute for International Studies, Occasional Paper #40.

Sommers, M. (1999), *Emergency Education for Children.* Cambridge, MA: Center for International Studies, MIT Working Paper.

Sommers, M. (2001), 'Peace Education and Refugee Youth', in Crisp, J., Talbot, C. and Cipollone, D. B. (eds), *Learning for a Future: Refugee Education in Developing Countries.* Geneva: UNHCR, pp. 163–216.

South, A. (2007), 'Karen Nationalist Communities: The "Problem" of Diversity'. *Contemporary Southeast Asia,* 29(1), 55–76.

Summerfield, D. (1996), *The Impact of War and Atrocity on Civilian Populations: Basic Principles for NGO Intervention and a Critique of Psychosocial Trauma Projects.* Relief and Rehabilitation Network Paper no. 14. London: Overseas Development Institute.

Tefferi, H. (1999), *Psychosocial Needs of Children in Armed Conflict and Displacement. A Module for Training Teachers and Caregivers.* Stockholm: Radda Barnen.

TBBC (Thailand Burma Border Consortium) (2010), *Burmese border refugee sites with population figures: July 2010.* Available from http://www.tbbc.org/camps/2010-05-may-map-tbbc-unhcr.pdf (accessed 5 July 2010).

Tillman, D. G (2001), Educating for a Culture of Peace in Refugee Camps. International Focus Issue 2001. Available from http://www.livingvalues.net/reference/docs-pdf/lvrefugee.pdf. (accessed 1 August 2010).

Tolfree, D. (1996), *Restoring Playfulness. Different Approaches to Assisting Children who are Psychologically Affected by War or Displacement.* Stockholm: Radda Barnen.

US Committee for Refugees and Immigrants (USCRI) (2009), *World Refugee Survey 2009.* Washington, DC: USCRI.

WCRCW (Women's Commission for Refugee Women and Children) (2006), '*We Want to Work*': *Providing Livelihood Opportunities for Refugees in Thailand.* New York: Women's Commission for Refugee Women and Children.

ZOA (2009), *Annual Report 2009: Promoting Inclusive Education.* Thailand: ZOA Refugee Care.

3

The Provision of Education in the Palestinian Refugee Camps, in Lebanon

Lala Demirdjian

Chapter Outline

Introduction

This case study aims to explore the provision of education in the Palestinian camps in Lebanon, with focus on the relevance of content to refugee education. The harsh living conditions of Palestinian refugees in Lebanon as opposed to those in other host countries raises an interest in exploring the current situation in schools and among the youth. The case study discussed in this chapter is the result of fieldwork conducted in three Palestinian camps – Rashidiyeh, Sabra and Shatila – in Lebanon in 2007. It also relies on data gathered from the UNRWA, the main international body responsible for the provision of education to Palestinian refugees in Lebanon. Data derived from qualitative empirical research and primary documentary research, as well as secondary sources, have been used for this study. The writer has relied strongly on her empirical research, which mainly comprises interviews with various parties interested in the content of the education of Palestinian refugees in Lebanon and the challenges formal and non-formal education faces in this context. It is perhaps in the nature of the problem under examination here that there is a dearth of published information. The author has updated the information, where possible, for the purpose of this chapter.

Definitions and historical background

For children living in vulnerable conditions, education secures a sense of normalcy and stability. The 1948 Universal Declaration of Human Rights, the 1951 Convention Relating to the Status of Refugees, the 1989 Convention of the Rights of the Child and the 1990 World Declaration of Education for All highly value educational quality and equity for children in crises. The International Network for Education in Emergencies (INEE), the UNESCO-affiliated International Institute for Educational Planning (IIEP) and non-governmental organizations such as the Save the Children have worked tremendously hard to establish guidelines and promote well-planned and established responses for educational provision in emergency situations (Brock and Demirdjian, 2010).

> Education serves to restore a sense of structure and organisation to the refugee community, and as a group activity helps meet the psychosocial needs of students who have often seen or suffered traumatic experiences. [It] contributes to the social and economic development of refugee community. (Sinclair, 1998, p. 264)

Unfortunately, in times of crises, education gets disrupted. In addition to the destruction of school buildings and the lack of administration, teaching materials are no longer available, there is a shortage of qualified teachers and a lack of funds, schools are used as shelters, there is the risk of landmines around the schools' premises and many students do not have the motivation to study. In the case of refugee camps, there are no guaranteed means to start an education system without humanitarian assistance from the host country or other local and international organizations. Providing education to children affected by crises is crucial because it can support their psychosocial well-being, defined as the 'intimate relationship between psycho-social and social factors' (UNHCR, 1994). Moreover, education develops conflict resolution and peace-building skills and leads populations towards reconstruction and socio-economic development (Sinclair, 2002). UNESCO defines *emergency education* as a 'crisis situation created by conflicts or disasters which have destabilized or destroyed the education system . . . [that] require an integrated process of crisis and post-crisis response' (UNESCO, 1999 in UNHCR, 2001, p. 4). Nicolai defines *education in emergencies* as a 'set of linked project activities that enable structured learning to continue in times of acute crisis of long-term instability' (2003, p. 11).

The Guidelines on Protection and Care of Refugee Children adopted by UNHCR emphasize that the disruption and insecurity in certain refugee situations can harm children's physical, intellectual, psychosocial and cultural development. Therefore, organizing and supporting educational activities helps to lessen the negative effects of trauma and protect at-risk groups. Various UN bodies such as UNESCO and UNICEF, together with UNHCR and other NGOs, aim to assist children in crisis by providing teacher training, school supplies, psychosocial support and various programmes to enhance the well-being of children. Many communities affected by crisis consider the provision of education as a top priority of assistance. Among all the refugee groups, Palestinian refugees who fled their homes as a result of the Arab-Israeli War in 1948 and have since been using education as a survival tool are a unique case.

UNRWA is the main provider of relief, health and educational services to this refugee population.[1] The financial constraints on the agency, together with the lack of student and teacher motivation, have left Palestinians in Lebanon with the lowest enrolment and highest dropout rates in education compared to their compatriots in the other areas where the UNRWA is active, namely Jordan, Syria, the West Bank and Gaza (Tyldum and Bashour, 2003). Unlike other refugee groups, for whom repatriation is highly significant and the provision of education is in accordance with their country of origin, the Palestinian refugees in Lebanon follow the national curriculum of Lebanon (Tyldum and Bashour, 2003). In fact, the living conditions of Palestinian refugees in Lebanon are not as favourable as those in other host countries; in fact, the educational achievements of the refugee population are severely affected by the restrictions the Lebanese government imposes on them.

Because education systems of UNRWA follow the curriculum of the host country, it is important to determine whether the needs of refugee students and the youth are being met through the implementation of existing educational services. This case study examines the challenges both NGOs and UNRWA schools face in the process of providing educational services. Two primary research questions are being explored: How relevant is the provision of education to the needs of Palestinian refugee children in Lebanon?[2] What are the main educational challenges in the camps? First, this study attempts to evaluate the extent to which the education provided is relevant to the needs of Palestinian refugees. Secondly, it aims to examine educational problems in depth. This entails discussion the reason why this particular refugee group is excluded from the programmes of the UNHCR that deal with ameliorating the situation in refugee camps worldwide.

The 1951 United Nations (UN) Convention Relating to the Status of Refugees defines a refugee as a person 'who owing to well-founded fear of being persecuted for reasons of race, religion, nationality, membership of a particular social group or political opinion, is outside the country of his nationality and is unable or, owing to such fear, is unwilling to avail himself of the protection of that country; Or who, not having a nationality and being outside the country of his former habitual residence as a result of such events, is unable, or, owing to such fear, is unable to return to it' (Parvathaneni, 2004, p. 8).

UNHCR followed the International Refugee Organization as the main UN agency concerned with the issue of refugees. The UNHCR was established by the UN General Assembly in 1950 on the basis of Article 22 of the Charter of the UN, in order to provide 'international protection' as well as to seek 'permanent solutions for the problems of refugees', especially after the Second World War (Goodwin-Gill, 2007, p. 21). Article 1 of the UNHCR Statute states that UNHCR:

> shall assume the function of providing international protection . . . to refugees who fall within the scope of the present Statute and of seeking permanent solutions for the problem of refugees by assisting Governments and . . . private organisations to facilitate the voluntary repatriation of such refugees, or their assimilation within new national communities. (Parvathaneni, 2004, p. 7)

The statute recognizes as refugees within UNHCR's purview those who were previously covered by various treaties and arrangements. It includes various categories of refugees such as those who became refugees as a result of events that took place before 1 January 1951 and refugees who are outside their own country of origin and are not able, or not willing, to benefit from its protection (Parvathaneni, 2004, p. 7). UNHCR's field presence has become very significant as it establishes a way of preventing forced displacement and reinforces national protection (Zieck, 2006). The current number of refugees receiving aid from UNHCR reaches 10.5 million (UNHCR, 'Refugee Figures').[3]

There are an additional 4.7 million Palestinian refugees living in approximately 60 camps in host countries in the Middle East and receiving assistance from UNRWA (UNHCR, 'Refugee Figures'). Palestinian refugees living *inside* the UNRWA operation areas are excluded from the protection regime of the UNHCR Statute and the 1951 Convention.[4] For political and practical reasons, Palestinians were not accepted in the UNHCR's Statute, which was drafted during a period when the Palestinian problem was very sensitive in the international arena (Goodwill-Gill and McAdam, 2007).

The United Nations Conciliation Commission for Palestine (UNCCP), and later the UNRWA, were created to protect and assist Palestinian refugees *prior* to the establishment of UNHCR. Hence, Palestinian refugees do not fall under the category of refugees protected by UNHCR, based on Article 1D of the 1951 Convention, which states:

> This Convention shall not apply to persons who are at present receiving from organs or agencies of the United Nations other than the United Nations High Commissioner for Refugees protection or assistance. When such protection or assistance has ceased for any reason . . . these persons shall ipso facto be entitled to the benefits of this Convention. (UNHCR, 2009, p. 1)

According to the UN General Assembly Resolution 302 (IV), UNRWA was mandated to collaborate with local governments in order to implement relief and works programmes, and to consult with governments in the Near East to take measures when the relief and work projects are no longer available (El Malak, 2006). Created on 8 December 1949, as a result of the 1948 Arab-Israeli conflict, UNRWA defines Palestine refugees as 'persons whose normal place of residence was Palestine between June 1946 and May 1948, who lost both their homes and means of livelihood as a result of the 1948 Arab-Israeli conflict' (UNRWA undated c).

In addition, UNRWA's definition of *refugee* includes the descendants of persons who became refugees in 1948. UNRWA provides services to

Palestinians who meet the above definition and are registered with the agency. The operations of the agency are supervised and supported by the headquarters, currently located in Gaza. UNRWA is considered to be the largest UN agency in the Middle East, with thousands of staff members who themselves are refugees (UNRWA, 2007b). UNRWA was accorded a short mandate with the belief that the refugees would soon be able to return to their homes. The relief operations were to be terminated by the middle of 1951, but UNRWA's mandate continues to be regularly extended due to the lack of sustainable solutions for Palestinian refugees (BADIL, 2007). Presently, around 595,000 refugees reside in Libya, Saudi Arabia, Kuwait, and other Gulf and Arab countries; these do not receive assistance from UNRWA because they live outside the host countries where the agency operates (BADIL, 2005).

The status of Palestinian refugees in Lebanon

In order to understand the education provided to Palestinian refugee in Lebanon, it is crucial to be familiar with the background of Palestinian refugees, in general. Palestinian refugees who fled to Lebanon came mainly from coastal and other northern Israeli towns such as Haifa, Acre, Safad and Galilee. An estimated 104,000 refugees fled into Lebanon in 1948. Initially, the Palestinians found refuge in southern Lebanon, but subsequently, they were relocated to refugee camps across the country due to the Lebanese government's fears of smuggling and infiltration (Sayigh, 1998 in Schulz, 2003). In the absence of UNRWA, the International League of Red Cross Societies initially provided tents, clothes and food to the Palestinian refugees.

Despite the fact that UNRWA supports the refugees in Lebanon, their living conditions have become the worst among all Palestinian refugees in all host countries (Howe, 2005). Due to restrictions on ownership, employment, education, health care and social services, the Palestinian refugees in Lebanon live in extremely unfavourable conditions in the camps (Bowker, 2003). Haddad (2003) explains the long-term difficulty of integrating Palestinian refugees into Lebanese society, referring to 'the precariousness of the Lebanese confessional political and social make-up' (p. 29). Because of the long-standing political weakness of the Lebanese state, Palestinians were destined to experience many obstacles in order to survive (Talhami, 2003). Sayigh (1995) mentions the marginalization of Palestinian refugees as a phenomenon that grew after the signing of the Ta'if Agreement in 1989 that ended the Lebanese civil war. The rejection of *tawteen* by the Lebanese community has excluded Palestinian refugees from many benefits in Lebanon, one of them being the right to employment (Sayigh, 1995).[5] In August 2010, the Lebanese government finally agreed to grant work permits to Palestinian refugees. However, refugees are still unable to practice a number of professions, such as medicine, engineering and law, due to their 'stateless' status which does not allow refugees join the syndicates (Hall, 2010).[6]

The legal status of Palestinian refugees in Lebanon is ambiguous; over the years various committees have been established by the Lebanese government to deal with the status of the refugees. However, UNRWA has remained the only body responsible for providing services to registered refugees. As of 30 June 2010, the number of registered refugees in Lebanon totals 416,608; however, only around half that number (220,809) live in the 14 official camps run by UNRWA (UNRWA, 2008).[7] The rest of the registered refugees live in gatherings throughout Lebanon with no access to UNRWA services such as water, sanitation and electricity (Shafie, 2007).

Sayigh (1995) refers to constraints on space and shelter as one of the most serious problems in the camps. Overpopulation has intensified since the civil war years.[8] There were official vetoes on rebuilding the camps, on establishing new camps, and even on UNRWA reconstruction in the existing camps. Consequently, refugees left the destroyed camps to find shelter in the existing, crowded camps (Sayigh, 1995).

Such struggles are continuous challenges for Palestinian refugees in Lebanon. A recent example of the ongoing difficulties was the July 2006 war between Hezbollah and Israel. The refugees in southern Lebanon were directly affected by the Israeli attacks (UN, 2006). The camps became isolated, and the inhabitants were unable to access basic supplies due to the extreme danger of leaving the camps (Shafie, 2007). Another recent example of the complex conditions of Palestinian refugees was the fighting between the Lebanese army and Fatah al-Islam militants in Nahr el-Bared camp in northern Lebanon in 2007.[9] Out of 30,000 refugees residing in Nahr el-Bared, the majority found refuge in neighbouring camps or fled to Tyre with the assistance of UNRWA and other UN agencies (UNICEF, 2007). Unfortunately, the further displacement of refugee children, together with the threat of conflicts and political instability, has left many of them traumatized. The fighting in the camp began during a critical time in the academic calendar since the official dates of Brevet and Baccalaureate examinations were approaching for students 14–18 years old.[10] Classes in Beddawi camp had to stop because the schools were accommodating refugees from Nahr el-Bared camp. Approximately 1,000 Palestinian students and teachers, living in the nearby Beddawi refugee camp, were transported to UNRWA schools in the Tripoli area, where there were three school shifts each day in order to continue the classes (UNICEF, 2007).

Educational opportunities for Palestinian refugees in Lebanon

Lebanon is the only host country where UNRWA provides both elementary and secondary education to Palestinian refugee students, as a result of the refugees' limited access to secondary schools in Lebanon. The public schools' quota system allows only 10 per cent of the openings to be filled by foreign students, and high tuition fees and the sectarian division of private schools limit the opportunities of enrolling in private education (Talhami, 2003).[11] UNRWA also provides vocational and technical education and training, as well as teacher training. Based on the UN Convention on the Rights of the Child, it also raises awareness of basic human rights (UN, 2004).

The objectives of the UNRWA education programme, as stated in the *Report of the Commissioner-General of the UNRWA*, are:

> to help Palestine refugee children and youth acquire the basic knowledge and skills needed to become productive members of their community in accordance with their needs, identity and cultural heritage . . . and to prepare them to encounter and adjust efficiently to the multifaceted challenges and uncertainties of the rapidly changing world and compete successfully at higher levels of education and in the job market. (UNRWA, in Oh and Roberts, 2006, p. 245)

Considering the significance of educational services to the refugee population, UNRWA allocates the greatest portion of its yearly expenditure to education. The total budget of core activities in 2010 was $60,192 million, out of which $33,621 million was allocated to education services. Of that amount, $40,642 million was used to maintain UNRWA schools in Lebanon (UNRWA, 2010a).

As part of the *Human Rights, Conflict Resolution and Tolerance* programme, in 2005 UNRWA began training teachers, headteachers and school supervisors in addition to providing workbooks and teacher training guides.

The programme enhanced the establishment of 'student parliaments' in some of the schools (UN, 2006).

To further improve the quality of UNRWA education staff, UNRWA provided additional training courses in June 2010 to headteachers and elementary teachers. Moreover, elementary English teachers began a three-week training course on the methodology of teaching English, sponsored by the British Council (UNRWA, 2010b).

In the case of long-term crises, like that of the Palestinian refugees, education can be seen as an important factor of giving meaning to life (Nicolai, 2003). Above all, education is a human right, as stated by Article 26 of the Declaration of Human Rights, hence it should be available to all people without exception.

The *Guidelines on Protection and Care of Refugee Children* emphasize that the disruption and insecurity in certain refugee situations can harm children's physical, intellectual, psychosocial and cultural development. Therefore, organizing and supporting educational activities helps lessen the impact of trauma and protect at-risk groups. UNRWA and NGOs in the Palestinian camps in Lebanon work towards implementing activities that enhance the psychosocial and cultural development of young children. For instance, in the July 2006 war – and later, during the war in Nahr el-Bared refugee camp – NGOs focused on projects that supported traumatized children in need of psychosocial assistance. Extracurricular activities were strongly emphasized, to assist children and the youth in overcoming the trauma of conflict and further displacement (UNICEF, 2007).

Structure of UNRWA's Education Department

The staff membership of the UNRWA Education Department in Lebanon consists of teachers, headteachers, assistant headteachers, area education officers, area education clerks, school counsellors and learning resource centre assistants (UNRWA, undated). It is worth noting that UNRWA provides job opportunities to its own refugee community. As a result, the above mentioned staff members include Palestinian refugees themselves. The department also has an Administrative Unit, Training and Enrichment Material Unit, Placement and Career Guidance Office, an Education Development Centre and the Vocational Education/Siblin Training Centre (ibid.). As of January 2010, the educational staff in Lebanon numbered 2,190 (UNRWA, 2010a).

The School Education Division monitors the daily operation of the schools and the students. It prepares annual class formation such as class designations, teachers and staff. Moreover, it designs strategic plans with a focus on staff development, construction of premises, promotion of human rights, and school health activities, and finally, keeps in contact with the education sector NGOs and the Ministry of Education (UNRWA, undated). The provision of quality education is highly related to teacher preparedness. UNRWA is responsible for a pre-service and in-service teacher training. The trainees follow a UNRWA-designed curriculum that runs on a two-year cycle for basic education elementary teachers. Upon the completion of the course, teachers are employed by the agency (UN, 2004).

Formal education

Formal education constitutes a major part of UNRWA services to Palestinian refugees in Lebanon. Students attending formal education in UNRWA schools are between 6 and 18 years of age. NGOs coordinate with UNRWA in order to strengthen the community's commitment to schooling and to education in general. UNRWA's provision of education began informally in tents, with older generations teaching the younger people. Eventually, the educational structure was developed; school buildings were constructed within or outside the refugee camps; sufficient school equipment and teaching material was provided; and qualified teachers were hired to provide instruction.

Over the years, due to the growing population in the refugee camps and the lack of sufficient school buildings, UNRWA schools operate on a double shift. Two different school administrations use the buildings, one in the morning and the other in the afternoon. Consequently, the average teaching session is only 40 minutes, which is insufficient, especially in the higher grades when students prepare for the official state examinations. Moreover, the limited budget forced UNRWA to begin charging a small fee (approximately US$60 per year) for expenses such as books and stationery.[12]

Currently, the total number of students is 32,892, but there are only 75 UNRWA schools (UNRWA, 2010a). What Alami (1996) highlighted about an acute and increasing need for space to build new schools remains a valid concern to date. Teachers mentioned that, due to overcrowded classrooms, they cannot meet the needs of each individual student. An NGO official commented on the same issue, stating that teachers pay attention only to high-achieving students, whereas the rest are ignored. Headteachers mentioned that in many classrooms, especially in the camps in southern Lebanon such as the one in Ain El-Helwe, the ratio of teachers per student is 1:50.[13]

Due to limited funding and government restrictions, many UNRWA schools use rented premises to accommodate the growing student population. The replacement of rented schools with UNRWA-built schools depends on the availability of funding. In some cases, there are more than 40 students in each classroom, leading to a high student–teacher ratio and an insufficient quality of education.

Students in UNRWA schools take the official state examinations just as any other Lebanese student. The Lebanese Brevet and Baccalaureate exams are taken at the preparatory and secondary levels, respectively. Classes in 1st–4th grade are conducted in Arabic, whereas the English language is introduced in grade five. UNRWA's latest figures from July 2010 indicate a significant improvement in the results of Brevet exams in UNRWA schools throughout Lebanon. Students' pass rates have shown an 11-point increase with 50.75 per cent of students passing. Currently, UNRWA's Education Department is focusing on the causes of the improved results and looking for ways to raise the student pass rate even further (UNRWA, 2010b).

Preparatory teachers participating in the interviews perceived their students as having low standards. These teachers were mostly concerned about the lack of creativity and poor work ethic among students. These are also seen as weaknesses of the teachers who do not reinforce creativity and active learning in the classroom. The weak basis in English is also perceived as a cause for low student achievement. Some teachers criticized a system that does not allow students to fail and enables automatic promotion, even if they lack the basic skills to go on to the next level. Unfortunately, the system in UNRWA schools supports automatic promotion as a means to decrease the dropout rate and encourage student enrolment. 'Teachers blame this policy as a major cause of lowering academic standards and raising drop-out rates' (Sirhan, 1996, p. 17).

UNRWA also has scholarship programmes that enable successful students to continue their higher education in accredited universities in Lebanon (Talhami, 2003). Due to the limitations by the Lebanese government, Palestinian refugees holding university degrees cannot practice employments as doctors, lawyers, engineers or accountants, unless they work in the camps. As a result, many young people drop out of school before graduating high school to join the job market in the camps. The education services of UNRWA have helped Palestinians adapt to life as refugees and keep alive the expectation of returning home (Alzaroo and Hunt, 2003). Interviews conducted by Alzaroo and Hunt in the West Bank, show that young Palestinians perceive education as a tool to build the Palestinian identity and achieve the eventual goal of return. However, many Palestinian refugees in Lebanon have lost interest in education. Fewer refugee students are likely to attend secondary and higher education in Lebanon than in any other host country. In Lebanon, the illiteracy rate of refugees aged 15 years and over is 25.5 per cent, which is the highest among all host countries. In addition, educational attainment is lowest in Lebanon; many from the adult population have not even completed basic education (BADIL, 2010). The enrolment level of Palestinian students between the ages of 7 and 14 is above 96 per cent; however, by the age of 15–17, enrolment levels drop to 58 per cent for males and 68.7 per cent for females (BADIL, 2010).[14]

Since 2006, UNRWA has been working towards decreasing the dropout rate in its schools. One of the objectives of the European Commission's education project is reintegrating early dropouts back into the UNRWA school system. The dropout rates vary between camps depending on the camp's character. For instance, the dropout rate in Shatila camp is almost eight times higher than the rate in Mar Elias camp (interviewee). The main reasons for dropouts are early marriages, poverty, family background, apprenticeship, vocational education, low achievement and laziness. Dropout rates reach their peak among 7th grade students, consisting of students between the ages of 13 and 15. Figures also indicate that more boys than girls leave school before reaching the high school level (interviewee). The statements made agree with the literature that identifies frustration and insecurity as causes of dropout. Lack of motivation and poor incentives were explained as the consequences of the arsh living conditions in the camps, especially for the older generations.

Even though UNRWA's main role in the provision of education consists of formal education in the primary, preparatory and secondary levels, the agency runs four kindergartens (KG) sponsored by the French embassy in Lebanon. The kindergartens are located in primary school buildings. The Arabic and French languages are given equal importance at the KG level. Unlike the primary and secondary schools, the KG system is based on a single shift, accommodating students between the ages of 4 and 6.

According to officials, it is very important to improve links with the elementary schools in order not to lose the benefit of KG education. NGOs based in the camps also provide non-compulsory preschool education to refugee children. For instance, Beit Atfal Assomood, a local NGO, runs a nursery for 3 to 4-year-old children and provides a non-compulsory preschool education for refugee children. The teachers hold either a university degree or are participants of a pre-service teacher training programme provided by the NGO and the American Community School in Lebanon. Additionally, in-service teacher training, introducing new teaching methods, is provided to teachers annually.

Some NGOs develop and follow their own KG curriculum, whereas the rest follow the Lebanese curriculum. In the second case, students are introduced to Palestinian culture through songs, folklore, dances and poems, in addition to special events and celebrations.

As young Palestinian children begin their first year of schooling, they face two major problems in relation to their academic background. First, they are integrated into heterogeneous classrooms of children with mixed abilities and skills. Second, both students who have attended preschool and those who have not are in the same classroom, which makes it hard for teachers to deliver the same material to both groups. As a consequence of the difficulties arising due to the differences in the provision of preschool education, UNRWA and NGOs are collaborating to develop a common KG curriculum to bridge the gap between students' academic levels.

Meetings with the Ministry of Education are held in order to discuss curriculum matters and gain access to further information related to changes of curriculum and instruction methods. The KGs hire qualified teachers, and in-service teacher training takes place regularly. During an official interview with the author, a UNRWA staff member from the Education Department said, 'We provide two kinds of training to the preschool teachers: in-service teacher training on subjects defined together and short summer training which takes place in France'.

Human rights and citizenship

Elements of human rights and citizenship are currently being introduced in school programmes in Lebanon. The lack of trained teachers limits the possibilities of teaching these concepts in a professional and well-planned manner. UNRWA schools also face the same problem, but to a greater degree; because refugees have not internalized the concept of human rights values, implementation becomes difficult. UNRWA receives some minor funding from UNESCO, and recently from the EU, to train teachers and introduce human rights programmes in schools. When asked about the ways of integrating the idea of human rights in the curriculum, one intermediate class teacher mentioned that students take part in activities reinforcing their ideas of civic duties and human rights. For example, one of the preparatory schools has created a 'Parliament of the School'. The committee of the parliament consists of 16 students, elected on an annual basis. The committee organizes field trips and open days, raises awareness on health and other issues, and plans campaigns targeting children's rights. Another primary teacher acknowledged that schools are making efforts to introduce these elements, but he also specified that in order to see positive changes, the mentality of the parents has to change:

> The schools are working towards human rights issues, but there is nothing on peace education. Students believe they have rights, but they do not know the way to use them. Also, the value of human rights is not important for the parents because they (the parents) are not rights oriented and this kind of mentality is not part of their culture. This creates conflicts. (interview with a primary school teacher, 2007)

An officer from UNRWA was more pessimistic about the issue. He did not see any reason why people should work towards human rights education when they do not even have access to universal human rights. One primary teacher had the same approach. Her viewpoint was as follows:

> How can you teach human rights to a refugee who faces a lot of discrimination from the international and Lebanese society? We cannot talk about human rights education. The problem is that a lot of teachers have lost hope; they feel they cannot teach much to children. We have to acknowledge that we have to be humans before being Palestinians. (interviewee, 2007)

However, this kind of answer was not typical of the interviewees. Most teachers and NGO officials said they try to find ways to introduce the concept inside and outside the classroom through activities and various events.

The findings indicated that peace education and citizenship are not taught in UNRWA schools on a regular basis. Teachers are not well trained in the subject, and, as the teaching hours are limited, there is lack of time for students to become engaged in activities that can enhance their conflict resolution skills. Teachers noted that there is a limited use of storybooks, workbooks, and other materials for activities that can result to the enhancement of the peace education program. They agree that NGOs have a key role in the implementation of projects that deal with human rights issues and community awareness. The literature on education in emergencies emphasizes the need to introduce human rights and citizenship concepts as a tool for enhancing the individual and community development of any population affected by crisis. The non-formal activities supported by NGOs in the refugee camps in Lebanon are essential for the promotion of human rights values. They are also important in raising community awareness on health and environmental issues, including the dangers of landmines and other unexploded munitions. NGOs have the potential to develop the skills for peace and civic participation, an element which is still absent in UNRWA schools. It is well understood that the implementation of citizenship education in UNRWA schools remains a challenge.

Parental attitude towards education

The most important factor indicating parental attitudes towards education was their own academic background. The findings show that the more literate the parents are, the stronger their relationship with the school. Educated parents value education highly and encourage their children to pursue their studies. According to the teachers, illiterate parents, who have dropped out of school or do not provide an appropriate home environment, affect their children's academic progress adversely. A teacher from Sabra camp indicated that most parents are not optimistic about their children: 'When students return to school they are worse off. Parents are ignorant about their children's education and there is a huge gap between UNRWA and the parents' (interview with a primary school teacher, 2007).

The same teacher raised the issue of too few school hours to raise awareness among children. A preparatory teacher described her relationship with parents as 'official, not intimate'. On the other hand, a primary teacher had an opposing standpoint concerning parental involvement. During the interview, she said:

> Very few parents are uneducated. Many of them care about the achievement of their children and they come to school to ask about them. The parents of my students belong to the generation of the (Lebanese) civil war; they did not pursue their education because they had to stay at home. In order to improve the situation we have to work with parents. (interviewee, 2007)

An NGO officer mentioned the financial status of the family as a second factor affecting the parents' attitude towards education: 'If there is money then the students are able to study, if not, then they have to drop out of school to start working.'

In the case of parents whose children are in KG, the findings show that they are more cooperative with the teachers and are more involved in organizing events. Teachers in Shatila camp agreed that nowadays it is easier for parents to send their children to KGs due to the increasing number of KGs in each camp. They also added that more and more parents are assisting teachers in preparing events and taking children on field trips. They described teachers' relations with parents as being very good. NGOs and UNRWA schools communicate with parents through letters and home visits, and engage them in extra-curricular activities and events. The vocational training coordinator of the NGO stressed the parents' interest in sending their children to vocational training centres with the hope that vocational skills will guarantee job opportunities for their children. In this sense, parents cooperate with NGOs and are aware of NGO importance in the provision of vocational education.

Parents do not cooperate with UNRWA teachers as well as with NGO staff. Teachers mentioned that most parents are 'indifferent' towards their children's academic achievement, and they hardly attend school meetings. Cases were mentioned of parents not even knowing the grade level of their own children.

The headteacher of one UNRWA school mentioned that the school administration follows up in cases of low-achieving students, regularly sending letters home, but there is hardly any response from the parents. However, these are extreme cases. One teacher mentioned that there is a great need for parents to work closely with teachers and school administration alike, to achieve the school's objectives and decrease UNRWA schools' dropout rates. 'Education is also within the family. If families do not prioritize education, then students may just grow up learning to do things the easy way rather than trying something on their own', responded one elementary teacher.

European Union Education Project

In 2006, the European Commission initiated a four-year project to improve living conditions for Palestinian refugees in Lebanon. One of the project's main objectives is improvement of educational services in UNRWA schools. The project aims to enhance the learning environment in schools, providing teacher training, constructing new schools and outfitting new classrooms in existing schools. Recreational and remedial teaching rooms, science equipment and laboratories are planned to be available to students in 40 UNRWA schools by 2010. Great emphasis is put on providing psychosocial support, better learning environments to students with educational needs, enhanced health education and so on. The EU project encourages NGOs and UNRWA to cooperatively improve vocational training, reduce the dropout rates, provide remedial classes and meet the needs of students with special needs, and provide quality kindergarten education to refugee children (UNRWA, 2007c).

Relevance to refugee needs

The education in UNRWA schools follows the curriculum of the host country with almost no relevance to refugee needs. Consequently, the principles of peace education and citizenship are not well addressed during class hours.

The Lebanese system does not include the geography and history of Palestine. However, teachers and the refugee community make sure the new generations are aware of their roots and history, and so Palestinian history is taught during extra-curricular activities or at home by older generations, who narrate the stories of how and why they fled to Lebanon. A UNRWA officer from the Education Department, when interviewed, opined that the curriculum does not promote the individual needs and personal development of the children in the camps, as refugee education should. Concerning the enhancement of cultural identity, one of the preparatory school teachers said, 'Neither issues of Palestinian refugees, nor the Palestinian case are considered in the curriculum. The lessons deal with tourism . . . or with anything that concerns the Lebanese government. There is no lesson or importance of Palestinian history; we have to raise the memories during special events like the Remembrance Day.'

The changes to the Lebanese national curriculum did not make it any more relevant to the needs of refugees. UNRWA schools still struggle to deal with refugee-specific issues during limited teaching hours. In the words of an officer of the Education Department, 'The changes of the curriculum had to do with the Lebanese government and not the Palestinian refugees. . . .

UNRWA teachers had to be trained to teach with new methods, whereas students had to get used to those methods.'

Teachers in UNRWA schools see education as a 'double-edged weapon', believing that it can be a tool for liberation when provided in the right way. Education widens the students' ability to think creatively and independently, hence making positive changes in their lives. On the other hand, some believe education can be misused if teachers impose their own ideas on the students without enabling them to develop their thinking in a society that needs to experience changes in a constructive way. An elementary teacher responded by stating, 'I want to give the students the things I missed as a student, so it can be a tool of opening new doors and broadening their minds which might be narrow due to the limited exposure to the outside world'.

Counselling services are uncommon in the schools. In some schools, counselling services were introduced for the first time during the academic year 2006–07. Other schools have established a counselling committee that holds sessions with students, helping them make decisions about enhancing their career prospects, giving up smoking and preventing their friends from dropping out of school. Meetings with parents are also arranged on an ad hoc basis if deemed necessary.

Refugee students with special needs

Article 23 of the Convention on the Rights of the Child (OHCHR, 1989), states that a mentally or physically disabled child should enjoy a full and decent life, in conditions which ensure dignity, promote self-reliance and facilitate the child's active participation in the community' (p. 7). Unfortunately, Palestinian refugee children with disabilities are not granted the educational and health services available to Lebanese children with disabilities. In addition, they suffer from a lack of the extra-curricular activities needed to raise their self-esteem and dignity (Grondahl, 2006).

Children in the camps with disabilities are included in the UNRWA school system. The lack of additional support acts as a major cause of dropout by such pupils. There is a great need to change the attitude of teachers and social workers and provide greater support to children with disabilities in the refugee camps (Grondahl, 2006). Despite limited funding for special education, the agency has tried to offer opportunities to children with learning difficulties by providing them with remedial and special education services in order to maintain achievement levels (UN, 2004).

Under the EU project, UNRWA schools have been working to strengthen and enhance the mainstreaming of children with disabilities. Hence, the project aims to adapt the schools to the needs of disabled students and provide necessary learning equipment at school and at home. In the last academic year, two visually impaired students were able to pass the Brevet official exam thanks to the special support of an EU-funded project that improves educational access for blind and visually impaired students. Schools are gradually being equipped with materials for the visually impaired students. Moreover, the special support is also being extended to visually impaired students attending universities (UNRWA, 2010d). However, there is still a great need for awareness of students with disabilities byUNRWA teachers, social workers and parents (interviewee).

Vocational education

In addition to formal schooling, UNRWA also runs a pre-service teacher training, vocational and technical education centre in the region of Siblin. The Siblin Training Centre (STC) provides courses to both male and female trainees. The main trade and post-preparatory courses offered include carpentry, auto mechanics, industrial mechanics, hairdressing and beauty culture, computer typing, data processing, plumbing and central heating. Some of the semi-professional courses and post-secondary courses are business administration, electromechanical engineering, medical laboratory science and architectural engineering. Such courses lead to employment opportunities mostly within the refugee camps (UNRWA, undated). Lately, additional classrooms and a learning resource centre were constructed in Siblin. The courses not only focus on training the students, but they also target the employability of female refugees (UNRWA, 2010c).

Non-governmental organizations

The majority of NGOs and grassroots organizations that function in the camps were established in the late 1980s (Aidun, undated). NGOs, such as Association Najdeh, Beit Atfal Assomood Association and Developmental Action without Borders/Naba'a fill the gap left by UNRWA as far as basic services are concerned (Aidun). UNRWA schools cannot afford the implementation of extra-curricular activities at the end of a school day. First, the limited teaching hours do not permit the system to introduce other activities, especially when students have to leave the school premises to allow the start of the next shift. Second, the outdoor spaces in the schools are too small to adequately accommodate sports, dance classes and other activities. One of the interviewees, an NGO official said, 'You cannot implement any extra-curricular activities in the school because there is another shift afterwards. Ramallah School has a very small playground and there are columns in the playground so children cannot play.' According to the same official, the new EU budget includes an amount for recreational activities. Recently, some pilot programmes have begun offering extra-curricular activities in UNRWA schools during the summer vacation.

Naba'a, an NGO, works with Palestinians in the refugee camps and gatherings in Lebanon. Its main offerings for children from birth to 18 years of age include dance, music, theatre, handicraft, home economics, remedial and computer classes, field trips, psychosocial support to children and families, teacher training and, finally, community awareness (including landmine awareness, child protection and human rights). The 'Child-to-Child Activities', 'Child Right Awareness', and 'Sports Games' are a few of the extra-curricular activities the NGO offers to refugee children (Al Turkey and Awayed, 2007).

The Community Development Project aims to develop the personal and social abilities and enhance the creativity of children and youth, whereas the Learning and Playing programme gives psychological support to children through play and enables them, both educationally and socially, to enter school (Naba'a, 2007).

The Children and Youth Centre (CYC) teaches and practices 'International Child and Human Rights' policies. The main aim of the programme is to teach children the rights they have and the ways they have to fight for them in addition to respecting and valuing the rights of others. CYC emphasizes gender equality, religious tolerance and non-discrimination through various activities run in the Shatila camp (CYC, undated). The Centre is open daily to children aged 9–18. Some other activities include dancing, music, remedial classes, gender courses, workshops, summer camps and early childhood education (Howe, 2005).

The Ghassan Kanafani Centre for Children with Disabilities (GKFC) provides therapy for children affected by cerebral palsy, heart problems and other disabilities. The foundation also runs kindergartens, two rehabilitation centres and two children's libraries in camps around the country. GKCF follows a policy of integrating children with special needs into its KGs (KRSF, 2007).

The importance of play and informal activities in helping children deal with and understand their traumatic experiences is strongly emphasized in the findings of this study. During the July 2006 war, NGOs planned activities such as music, drama, sports and social events in order to provide children with adequate psychosocial support and help them overcome the events of the war by raising their self-esteem and reducing the level of stress. These activities of the NGOs are in accordance with what Aguilar and Retamal (1998) have discussed concerning the importance of recreational activities in emergency situations which are crucial for: 'bolstering cultural identity and self-esteem and providing informal support to those living in the most extreme adversity' (p. 12).

The input of NGOs in the camps contributes a great deal to the progress and development of the younger generations, since vocational education and training is one of the primary responsibilities of the NGOs. UNRWA schools do not provide any remedial classes due to the limited teaching hours per school day; therefore, NGOs collaborate with the schools for planning remedial classes in English, Arabic and math. English is highly emphasized due to the need of improving English-language proficiency in UNRWA schools. Volunteers in each camp work with NGOs to meet the needs of low-achieving students and marginalized groups.

Students and young volunteers contribute to NGO publications. Education provided by these NGOs reaches the vulnerable populations in the camps, such as girls, children with disabilities and out-of-school children. In addition, human rights, citizenship and community awareness on health and environmental issues are highly emphasized in the NGO activities.

The NGOs have professional counsellors and psychologists who work with families and children with special needs. After the July 2006 war, many NGOs introduced additional psychosocial activities to support children in the camps: 'We brought the children to the Centre so they could play and forget about the war. The fear of the parents affected the children. . . . all these cause health and social problems in the community' (interviewee).

Generally, NGOs are working towards filling the gaps of UNRWA schools. However, better cooperation is required in order to avoid the duplication of services by both.

Conclusion

The literature available on the provision of education to Palestinian refugees is limited, and what is available varies greatly between the different organizations involved. This case study was based on observations, interviews, and – occasionally – on UNRWA resources and NGO activities in the refugee camps. NGOs are seen as the link between UNRWA schools and the refugee community. This case study recommends further action to be taken for the improvement of the education system in the camps:

- Further encouragement of parental involvement in UNRWA schools. Organized activities and events may be used to bring parents closer to the school environment and develop means of communication between both parties.
- Improved and expanded English-language support by well-trained teachers.
- Construction of new school buildings in order to abolish the double-shift system, hence extending the teaching hours and permitting extra-curricular work.
- Improved outdoor space in the schools to encourage the physical development of children and young people.
- Additional workshops and seminars for teachers to develop better understanding of the needs of refugee students.
- An improved and consistent curriculum in kindergartens that is more helpful to heterogeneous groups in the first grade of primary school.
- Well-planned teacher training in the subjects of human rights, citizenship and conflict resolution.
- Professional assistance in building self-esteem and developing the well being of children.
- Enhanced school programmes and educational trips to make education fun for refugee students and encourage their enrolment in formal education.

To enhance formal and non-formal education, ensure better education standards and avoid duplication of educational services, it is recommended that UNRWA and NGOs develop an efficient cooperation among themselves and with the Ministry of Education of Lebanon.

The status of most Palestinian refugees has trapped them in a protracted refugee setting where repatriation, return or integration remain unpredictable. Given that the sectarian society of Lebanon is politically volatile, it seems almost impossible to acknowledge a permanent solution for those refugees residing in Lebanon.

Key Questions

1. If one considers assimilation to be the solution to the Palestinian refugee problem in Lebanon, then how can the provision of formal and non-formal education support the needs of refugees throughout the process of assimilation?
2. How can schools, organizations and individuals encourage refugee students' enrolment in formal education as the path to a 'better future' when the ongoing experience of their immediate environment has not been a promising one throughout the decades?

Notes

1 UNRWA's relief and social services programme supports those refugees who are unable to meet their need for food or shelter. The agency runs health care facilities and clinics in the camps. For more information, visit www.unrwa.org.

2 In this study, the term *Palestinian refugee* is used to refer to UNRWA's operational definition of Palestine refugees, that is, all the people who fled or left Palestine as a result of the Arab-Israeli war in 1948, and the descendants of persons who became refugees in 1948.

3 Figures as of the beginning of 2009; 8 per cent less than the year before.

4 UNRWA's areas of operation include the West Bank, Gaza, Syria, Lebanon and Jordan.

5 The literal meaning of *Tawteen* is 'naturalization'.

6 Employees must join syndicates to be able to practice certain professions such as medicine, engineering and others.

7 Two of the camps were completely destroyed in the 1970s; however, refugees originally registered in the camps still maintain their status.

8 The Lebanese Civil War lasted 16 years (1975–91).

9 For more information on the relief and early recovery appeal (RERA) for Nahr el-Bared, visit http://www.unrwa.org/userfiles/201007133727.pdf.

10 The Lebanese system of education follows the French system of official exams.

11 The Lebanese Constitution considers Palestinian refugees to be non-Lebanese or 'foreigners', with few exceptions (Sayigh, 1988).

12 Information accessed through a formal interview between the author and an UNRWA officer.

13 Formal interview conducted by the author.

14 For detailed statistical figures, visit http://www.badil.org/index.php?page=shop.product_details&flypage=garden_flypage.tpl&product_id=119&category_id=2&vmcchk=1&option=com_virtuemart&Itemid=4,

Further reading

Chatty, D. and Hundt, G. L. (eds) (2005), *Children of Palestine: Experiencing Forced Migration in the Middle East*. Studies in Forced Migration. New York; Oxford: Berghahn.

Demirdjian, L. (2007), *The Case of Palestinian Refugee Education in Lebanon*. MSc Dissertation. Oxford University.

INEE (2004), *Minimum Standards for Education in Emergencies, Chronic Crises and Early Reconstruction*. London: DS Print/Redesign.

Schulz, L. H. (2003). *The Palestinian Diaspora: Formation of Identities and Politics of Homeland*. London: Routledge.

References

Aidun, M.E.-A. (2005), 'Palestinian Refugees in Camps in Lebanon: A Controversial Autonomy', *Security when the State Fails: Community Responses to Armed Violence*. Netherlands: Pax Christi.

Al Turkey, A. and Awayed, S. (2007), *Children Need Social Care That 'Naba'a' Initiate to Involve Them in Its Activities*. Beirut: Naba'a.

Alami, L. (1996), 'Educating Palestinian Refugees: The Role of UNRWA'. *Palestine-Israel Journal of Politics, Economics and Culture*, 3(2), 68–74.

Alzaroo, S. and Hunt, L. G. (2003), 'Education in the Context of Conflict and Instability: The Palestinian Case'. *Social Policy and Administration*, 37(2), 165–80.

BADIL (2005), *Closing Protection Gaps; Handbook on Protection of Palestinian Refugees in States Signatories to the 1951 Refugee Convention*(1st edn). Bethlehem, Palestine: Al-Ayyam Press.

BADIL (2010), 'Population Size, Distribution and Characteristics', in Ingrid Jaradat Gassnen (ed.), *Survey of Palestine Refugees and Internally Displaced Persons 2008–2009*. Ramallah: al-ayyam, pp. 56–87.

BADIL (2007), *The UN Relief and Works Agency for Palestine Refugees (UNRWA)*. Available from http://www.badil.org/Assistance/UNRWA.htm (accessed 7 August 2007).

Bowker, R. (2003), *Palestinian Refugees: Mythology, Identity, and the Search for Peace*. London: Lynne Rienner Publishers.

Brock, C. and Demirdjian, L. (2010), 'Education as a humanitarian response as applied to the Arab world, with special reference to the Palestinian case', in Abi-Mershed, O. (ed.), *Trajectories of Education in the Arab World: Legacies and Challenges*. London; New York: Routledge, pp. 185–98.

CYC (undated), Children and Youth Centre. Beirut: UNICEF, Radda Barnen, Welfare Association, Palestina Solidaritet.

El-Malak, L. (2006), 'Palestinian Refugees in International Law: Status, Challenges, and Solutions'. *Immigration, Asylum and Nationality Law*, 20(3), 179–96 Goodwin-Gill, S. G. and McAdam, J. (2007), *The Refugee in International Law* (3rd edn). Oxford: Oxford University Press.

Grondahl, M. (2006), *Refugees in Lebanon: Palestinian Children's Voices*. Beirut: Save the Children.

Haddad, S. (2003), *The Palestinian Impasse in Lebanon: The Politics of Refugee Integration*. Brighton/Portland: Sussex Academic Press.

Hall (2010), 'Mired in poverty: Palestinian refugees in Lebanon see little hope in new law'. *Guardian Weekly*, 24 August 2010. Available from http://www.guardian.co.uk/world/2010/aug/24/palestinian-refugees-lebanon-rights (accessed 28 September 2010).

Howe, M. (2005), 'Palestinians in Lebanon'. *Middle East Policy*, 12(4), 145–55.

KRSF (2007), Developmental Action Without Borders. Available from http://www.krsf.org/project.php?proj_id=50&HiddenRegion_map_lebanon=true (accessed 15 August 2007).

Naba'a (2007). http://www.nabaa-lb.org/articles/templates/bzabout.asp?articleid=2&zoneid=6 (accessed 8 August 2007).

Nicolai, S. (2003), *Education in Emergencies: a Tool Kit for Starting and Managing Education in Emergencies*. London, UK: Save the Children.

Oh, S.-A. and Roberts, R. (2006), 'Palestinians and Education in Lebanon', in Griffin, R. (ed.), *Education in the Muslim World: Different Perspectives*. Didcot, UK: Symposium Books, pp. 191–210.

OHCHR (1989), 'Convention on the Rights of the Child'. Available from http://www2.ohchr.org/english/law/pdf/crc.pdf (accessed 24 August 2010).

Parvathaneni, H. (2004), 'UNRWA's Role in Protecting Palestine Refugees'. Badil Resource Center for Palestinian Residency & Refugee Rights.

Retamal, G., Devadoss, M. and Richmond, M. (1998), 'UNESCO-PEER: Lessons Learned in Eastern Africa', in Retamal, G. and Aedo-Richmond, R. (eds), *Education as a Humanitatian Response*. London: Cassell, pp. 210–22.

Sayigh, R. (1995), 'Palestinians in Lebanon: Harsh present, uncertain future'. *Journal of Palestine Studies*, 25(1), 37–53.

Shafie, S. (2007), FMO Research Guide: 'Palestinian Refugees in Lebanon'. Available from http://www.forcedmigration.org/guides/fmo018/ (accessed 30 August 2007).

Sinclair, M. (2002), Planning Education in and after Emergencies. Paris: UNESCO/IIEP.

Sirhan, B. (September 1996), 'Education and the Palestinians in Lebanon', in *Palestinians in Lebanon*. University of Oxford: Refugee Studies Programme, Queen Elizabeth House.

Talhami, H.G. (2003), *Palestinian Refugees: Pawns to Political Actors*. New York: Nova Science Publishers, Inc.

Tyldum, G. and Bashour, N. (2003), 'Education', in Ugland Fr., O. (ed.) *Difficult Past Uncertain Future: Living Conditions Among Palestinian Refugees in Camps and Gatherings in Lebanon*. FAFO report 409. Norway: Centraltrykkeriet AS.

UNHCR (2001), *Learning for a Future: Refugee Education in Developing Countries*. Geneva: UNHCR.

UNHCR (1994), 'Refugee children: Guidelines on Protection and Care'. Geneva: UNHCR. Available from http://www.unhcr.org/refworld/docid/3ae6b3470.html (accessed 4 August 2010).

UNHCR, 'Refugee Figures'. Available from http://www.unhcr.org/pages/49c3646c1d.html (accessed 15 August 2010).

UNHCR (2009), 'Revised Note on the Applicability of Article 1D of the 1951 Convention Relating to the Status of Refugees to Palestinian Refugees'. Available from http://www.unhcr.org/refworld/pdfid/4add77d42.pdf (accessed 29 September 2010).

UNICEF (2007), 'Palestinian Youth in Northern Lebanon Head Back to School Two Weeks Into Refugee Camp Crisis'. Available from http://www.unicef.org/media/media_39905.html (accessed 10 June 2007).

United Nations (2004), Report of the Commissioner-General of the United Nations Relief and Works Agency for Palestine Refugees in the Near East. New York: United Nations.

United Nations (2006), Report of the Commissioner-General of the United Nations Relief and Works Agency for Palestine Refugees in the Near East: 1 January–31 December 2005. New York: United Nations.

UNRWA (2008). www.unrwa-lebanon.org/refugees.aspx (accessed 17 July 2010).

UNRWA (undated a), Department of Education. Beirut: UNRWA.

UNRWA (2007a), The European Commission and UNRWA: Improving the lives of Palestine refugees.

UNRWA (2007b). Organization. http://www.un.org/unrwa/organization/index.html (accessed 1 August, 2007).

UNRWA (2010a), 'Figures'. Available from www.unrwa.org/userfiles/20100628261.pdf (accessed 19 July 2010).

UNRWA (undated b), 'Lebanon Camp Profiles'. Available from http://www.unrwa.org/etemplate.php?id=73 (accessed 8August 2010).

UNRWA (undated c) 'Who is a Palestine Refugee?' Available from http://www.un.org/unrwa/refugees/whois.html (accessed 12 August, 2007).

UNRWA (2010b), 'NBC Latest Updates'. Available from http://www.unrwa.org/userfiles/file/publications/nahrelbared/NBC%20Updates%20July%209%20Eng.pdf (accessed 21July 2010).

UNRWA (2010c), 'Projects in Lebanon'. Available from http://www.unrwa.org/etemplate.php?id=72 (accessed 29 July 2010).

UNRWA (2010d), 'Visually impaired students from Nahr el Bared achieve high school success'. Available from http://www.unrwa.org/etemplate.php?id=824 (17 accessed October 2010).

Zieck, M. (2006). *UNHCR's worldwide presence in the field: A legal analysis of UNHCR's cooperation agreements*. Nijmegen: Wolf Legal Publishers.

4

Non-Formal Education as a Means of Supporting the Well-Being of Resettled Refugees: Case Studies of Community Approaches in Denver, Colorado

Janet Shriberg, Susan Downs-Karkos and Stacey Weisberg

Chapter Outline

Introduction

This chapter explores the potential contributions of non-formal educational programmes in the context of refugee resettlement in the United States.

Framed within an ecological perspective, the chapter highlights school-based and community approaches to serving refugee children, youth and adults in order to promote psychosocial well-being and increased access to economic resources. These approaches are explored through case studies of the WorkStyles programme at the Spring Institute for Intercultural Learning and the International KidSuccess programme at Jewish Family Services, both located in Denver, Colorado. The conclusion stresses the importance of a flexible programme that recognizes the direct interests and concerns of diverse refugee populations.

Background and ecological perspective on well-being

Children and youth affected by armed conflict and/or natural disasters are among the world's most vulnerable populations. A 2009 UNHCR report estimates that there are approximately 10.5 million refugees worldwide, at least half of whom are children.[1] A significant number of these refugees arrive in the United States annually. Over the past decade, increasing numbers of refugees from Africa, the Americas, Asia, Europe and the Middle East have immigrated to the United States. As survivors of disaster, refugee children and youth arrive on American ground after enduring varying levels of conflict, trauma and disruption to their education and lives. Their experiences may include the loss of loved ones, economic decline, flight, hunger, rape, conscription into fighting forces and/or torture. As these children adjust to their new social, political, linguistic and cultural contexts, their lives may be fraught with the psychological and social consequences of war. Once resettled in the United States, refugee children and youth often face significant challenges associated with adjusting to their new surroundings. Studies have demonstrated that trauma, grief and loss are common concerns for refugee children (Kinzie et al., 1986; Reichenberg and Friedman, 1996; McBrien, 2005; Miller et al., 2008). Often, these children must confront the challenge of learning English. Some have not had the opportunity to attend school regularly prior to coming to the United States.

Adolescent and older youth refugees may face the hardship of entering a school environment after a long period of being out of school. Due to war and other disasters, their experience with formal schooling may be limited to nonexistent; thus, they may be placed at a school grade level lower than is typical for their age. At the same time, they may be adapting to a new language and culture, in addition to contending with the usual adolescent concerns of peer acceptance, sexual development, and future educational and career interests. Meanwhile, the parents and other caregivers of refugee children, themselves survivors of war, may be struggling to learn English while coping with financial concerns and adapting to a new culture. Isolated from their communities of origin, adult refugees are often on their own in navigating new social systems such as those associated with employment, health and education. Their struggles can be particularly acute during economic downturn, such as is the current situation in the United States, where unemployment rates have surged in recent years and there is significant competition for jobs.

To date, research on refugee populations has focused largely on the prevalence of poor outcomes and psychopathology rather than on resiliency in refugees (Crowley, 2009). In addition to assessing the direct effects of violence, there is growing interest among researchers and practitioners in examining protective factors that can mediate or moderate the effects of violence and/or displacement for individuals (Miller et al., 2008). Such a focus on social factors may be found in an ecological perspective, which enables one to examine social factors – such as family, community and state institutions – outside of individuals' inner processes, and to consider how they can influence individual health and behaviour. Broadly stated, this perspective enables one to explore the confluence of family, community and institutional factors in human behaviour. As such, it posits that traumatic events may be mitigated by restoring the support offered within 'social ecologies' created by the interaction of the familial, community, cultural, spiritual and geopolitical factors that surround and influence individuals. In short, the community-based psychosocial response focuses on strengthening opportunities in social ecologies that restore and build individual and community capacities. Increasing access to quality education, both formal and non-formal, as a way to enhance individual and community well-being is a particularly important goal for those employing the ecological perspective.

Non-formal educational programmes and refugee resettlement in Denver, Colorado

There is a burgeoning body of literature that describes the role education can play in supporting the well-being of resettled refugees (McBrien, 2005; Rutter, 2006; Kia-Keating and Ellis, 2007). In addition to advancing literacy and numeracy skills, schooling offers young people developmental and psychosocial opportunities for structure, stimulation and socialization with peers and adults. For young refugees who were forced to migrate due to war and other disasters, opportunities for cognitive, psychosocial and physical development are particularly important in building new systems of social support. However, young refugee students often make up only a small portion of a school's population; thus, specialized language and/or psychosocial support for refugee students may be limited. Moreover, formal education, by definition, requires approved curricula that lead to credentials. In meeting these demands, schools are regularly challenged by the need for trained staff, funding, time schedules, and meeting state and federal mandates regarding curriculum, student achievement and outcomes.

For refugee adults, opportunities to learn basic English and to successfully navigate local systems for employment, transportation and financial services can contribute to greater self-sufficiency. Such opportunities can contribute to increasing refugees' overall economic, psychological and social well-being. Such adult programmes, however, exist outside of formal schooling. Therefore, activities that may complement the work of schools and further benefit refugee children, youth and adults often benefit from non-formal education programmes developed by community agencies. Such activities, which extend beyond the boundaries of the school, make non-formal education programmes critical supports to the overall well-being of resettled refugees.

Non-formal education is defined as follows:

> Any organized and sustained educational activities that do not correspond exactly to the definition of formal education. Non-formal education may therefore take place both within and outside education institutions, and cater to persons of all ages. Depending on country contexts, it may cover educational programmes to impart adult literacy, basic education for out-of-school children, life-skills, work-skills, and general culture. Non-formal education programmes do not necessarily follow the 'ladder' system, and may have differing durations, and may not confer certification of the learning achieved.[2]

Non-formal education has been discussed in the literature chiefly in relation to adult education, art and music education, rural development and humanitarian contexts (where it is used to support displaced populations). However, despite the important contribution of non-formal educational programming, there is a paucity of available literature that describes in detail the development and intent of programmes for resettled refugees. Each year a significant number of refugees are relocated to the United States. According to the national Office of Refugee Resettlement, 60,193 refugees entered the United States in 2008, and 1,264 of those resettled directly in Colorado. Since 1980, over 39,000 have been directly resettled in Colorado. While the majority of foreign-born students in Colorado are classified as immigrants and originate from Mexico, there are many special considerations for educators to take into account when working with refugee children and parents, given the challenging circumstances under which refugees leave their country of origin.

In the next section, two extended case studies provide examples of how non-formal education programmes offered in Denver effectively promote well-being among resettled refugees. A discussion of the context and the response to the community interests are presented, as are innovative approaches to supporting well-being. Particular attention is given the specific strategies, considerations and techniques developed by two community agencies – Spring Institute for Intercultural Learning and Jewish Family Services – in order to give detailed information on these non-formal educational approaches to supporting the well-being of resettled refugees in Denver.

Case studies of non-formal education programmes for refugees in Denver

International KidSuccess at Jewish Family Services

Founded in 1872, Jewish Family Service of Colorado (JFS) offers a broad range of over 40 programmes for people in need, including the economically disadvantaged, the elderly, refugees, the disabled, people living with chronic illness, families, youth and those facing life-altering losses. All of JFS's services are offered to anyone seeking help – regardless of faith, race, creed, sexual orientation, gender expression or economic status. The services JFS provides help promote self-sufficiency, improve coping skills, positively change behaviours, increase awareness of available resources, improve well-being, decrease isolation and stress, increase client safety and avert and manage crises.

JFS has a long and rich history of serving newcomers to the United States. JFS has provided resettlement services to émigrés and refugees for 35 years, offering a variety of services to assist people from diverse cultures settling in a new country, helping them locate housing, find employment and learn English. As émigrés developed their skills and found their way in this new country, other needs surfaced. JFS developed further programming to meet these emerging needs, including citizenship classes and services for elderly émigrés who needed medical care and case management. As families' basic needs were met, other issues came to light, such as the need for mental health services. JFS offers bilingual and bicultural mental health services, case management and psychiatry.

As time progressed, JFS received calls from local schools inquiring about immigrant and refugee students that were struggling or parents the school could not access. JFS provided outreach to that student or family. Often the school staff assumed the family was disinterested in their child's education; this was usually not the case. JFS realized there was an enormous gap in cultural understanding, in addition to general misunderstandings due to language and familial/role issues. JFS observed schools assuming students had learning disabilities when they were unclear as to the nature of the academic, behavioural and attendance problems. After years of providing services primarily for immigrant and refugee adults, JFS began to develop a programme for refugee and immigrant youth. The programme would be housed in the schools to foster close cooperation with school staff and administrators, and to limit any barriers to service such as transportation, financial resources or stigma. More importantly, many of the acculturative struggles of refugee youth unfold in the school setting.

JFS started its work providing cultural adjustment groups for refugee and immigrant students at Denver's South High School in 2000 to a culturally diverse group of students. Roughly one-third of the school's 1,500 students were refugees. This population represented over 60 different languages and cultures. There was growing tension both among refugee youth and between refugees and mainstream youth. The school's vice principal called JFS petitioning for assistance in resolving these issues. South High School was chosen, as it served as a magnet school for refugee youth. JFS began by meeting with the school's staff to determine the scope of the issues, particularly the concerns of the English Language Acquisition (ELA) teachers. This meeting became the start of a formal needs assessment. JFS staff discovered that many issues were rooted in refugee students' poor understanding of basic school rules or unfamiliarity with school culture. The same was true for their parents. Some students were very frightened and therefore did not participate in school activities. Other students were very angry and were often in the disciplinarian's office. Regular school attendance was also a significant problem. The school staff was frustrated with the parents who did not return calls, and therefore seemed apathetic; in reality, they could not speak English. Parents were frequently working multiple jobs and often used their high-school-age students to provide childcare to younger siblings.

JFS determined that a massive amount of education was required on multiple levels. School staff needed to be taught about refugee/immigrant struggles and ethnic styles as related to education and parent participation, and refugee parents needed education regarding the roles of parents in the United States with respect to their child's education and communication with teachers. Students needed to understand school rules and culture and, most importantly, their adjustment to life in the US school system needed to be facilitated.

From the experience garnered by JFS at South High School evolved International KidSuccess (IKS), a programme to help refugee and immigrant children and adolescents adjust to a new school, culture and home in the United States. The overarching goal of this programme is to provide support to immigrant and refugee children through the major life transition of immigration so that they are better able to focus on and succeed in school.

Presently, IKS students attend local K–12 schools and include elementary, middle and high school age groups. The students served come from all over the world with significant subgroups coming from over 60 countries. Currently, the largest groups of refugee students are from Burma, Nepal, Eritrea, Iraq, Congo, Somalia and Mexico.

In each school, the programme begins with a needs assessment conducted by JFS with ELA teachers, school staff and school administration. JFS conducts an initial survey of the immigrant and refugee students. The information gathered from this survey includes basic demographic information (e.g. country of origin, native language, length of time in the United States) as well as areas of concern (e.g. adjustment to the United States, conflicts with other students at school, academic progress). These surveys enable IKS to plan tailored curricula, as well as to track the progress at each school.

The main objectives of the International KidSuccess programme are to:

1. Address developmental issues within the context of the adjustment process for refugee and immigrant students.
2. Empower refugee and immigrant students for leadership opportunities and increase their interaction with the general population.
3. Address social, emotional and mental health needs of refugee and immigrant students that occur concurrently to the adjustment process.

4. Educate refugee parents about the Colorado school system and facilitate better understanding between refugee and immigrant parents and youth.
5. Educate school administrators, ELA teachers and other school staff about issues and resources for refugee and immigrant families.
6. Collaborate with schools and other community agencies in order to address the unique needs of refugees and immigrants.

The school support services provided include:

1. Adjustment and other group interventions: Adjustment groups consist of psycho-educational as well as psychotherapeutic activities and interventions geared towards facilitating adjustment to school and to life in the United States.
2. Individual intervention: Referrals for students needing individual treatment originate from teachers, school counselors and administrative staff, as well as from the mental health counselors leading adjustment groups. Services offered to individual students include individual therapy, case management, triage and referral. Students are followed as long as needed throughout an academic year.
3. Teacher and school staff interventions: Services provided to teachers and school staff include consultation and in-service and/or workshop training on immigrant/refugee issues. The focus of this training is typically on enhancing the staff's understanding of the psychological, cultural and practical issues affecting immigrant and refugee students and their families, as well as increasing awareness of how these issues often impede a child's ability to succeed in school.
4. Parent support and education: Parental support includes providing parents with information about child and adolescent immigrant and refugee development (e.g. the effects of trauma, warning signs of emotional distress). In addition, school-based programming is available to provide information to families about community resources available to assist them with their adjustment to the United States.

Over time, the IKS programme grew and – based on the needs identified by refugees, immigrant students and school staff – additional school-based counselling services were developed. Currently, the IKS programme serves seven K–12 schools with culturally diverse student populations in three school districts: Denver public schools, Cherry Creek schools and Aurora public schools.

Over the past ten years the IKS programme has found that approximately 10 to 15 per cent of refugee students are referred to or seek out individual school based counselling. Referrals for students needing individual counselling originate from teachers, school counselors and administrative staff, as well as from the mental health counselors leading adjustment groups.

Students requiring more extensive services are referred to the refugee mental health programme of JFS or other community resources and agencies.

Young refugees/immigrants face a variety of challenges. Birman and Chan (2008) identify migration stress, acculturative stress, traumatic stress and learning disabilities or developmental disorders exacerbated by migration and acculturation. These challenges cannot be overestimated. IKS provides ongoing education for school staff and mainstream American students to help create a supportive and successful school environment for refugee and immigrant students.

The cultural adjustment groups provided by JFS utilize, in part, components of art expression and social support within group settings. The most critical responsibility of the group facilitator is to create an atmosphere of trust, support and safety. The importance of providing this foundation for students who have been uprooted – many of whom have seen war violence, lived in refugee camps, are in a strange environment and do not speak the language – cannot be emphasized enough. The facilitator provides this foundation by establishing clear group rules and norms and emphasizing respect for each other's experiences and traditions. Within the group setting may be the first time a student has had the opportunity to tell their story from their point of view. The facilitator and other group participants may be the first to validate a student's life events. The act of 'storytelling' of traumatic events can be a healing experience. Creating and expressing a linear and coherent 'story' of an experience that otherwise has left an individual fragmented, is an integrating experience. Bringing thoughts and feelings together in a place of support can be liberating. These thoughts and feelings may have been unacceptable to family members who are struggling to forget their own traumatic experiences and rebuild their lives in a new country. Students are allowed to adjust to their new school without the burden of intrusive, upsetting thoughts and feelings which can distract them from their studies, from making friends or from other developmentally appropriate tasks. Most students are able to complete the adjustment groups and report very positive outcomes. Students have reported that they better understand themselves and school expectations as a result of having completed the group. Participants also say they have improved their ability to communicate with teachers and are better able to make American friends. Students are able to communicate their needs and to ask for help when they are struggling with school work. Students report greater involvement in school activities and feel more positively about their school environment.

Due to the cultural differences in terms of communication between group members (some cultural groups are more verbally expressive than others), as well as the fact that English is a second language for all participants, the IKS programme uses activities as a base for students discussions. That way, each student is given the chance to participate in the discussion. The primary means of organizing groups is to cover the following overarching topics throughout each set of adjustment group sessions: pre-migration, resettlement and current life experiences. Several groups are conducted in very low-level English proficiency classes. Groups conducted in the Newcomer's Centre and in Level I ELA classes are more heavily weighted towards non-verbal activities and enhancing basic social-emotional English vocabulary. For example, photographs might be used to label feelings in English and to discuss what kinds of experiences cause these feelings, *always focusing on the immigration experience.* Even in very broken English, students in these levels are able to identify feelings, choose pictures, and create art projects – connecting these to their immigration experiences.

Adjustment groups are offered to ELA classes identified by school staff as needing additional support. The group sessions are approximately 45 minutes long and run for 8 to 12 weeks. The purpose of the group is to provide a place at school where students can get to know other students, thus reducing isolation and promoting mutual support. Group facilitator(s) help create a safe, supportive environment where students can express their concerns, feelings and thoughts about their migration experiences and process of acculturation. Groups are organized around the themes of pre-migration, migration and post-migration life experiences. Issues raised in groups include memories and feelings associated with student's country of origin, such as losses, trauma and uncertainties. Other themes addressed in the adolescent groups are cultural adjustments; language difficulties; understanding diversity; the nature of prejudice and racism; bicultural or multicultural identity; and relationships with families, friends, teachers and so on. It is critical not to overwhelm or re-traumatize students in the adjustment groups. Facilitators never force students to do anything they are uncomfortable with. Facilitators encourage participation by all students, but the level of participation is ultimately the choice of each student. Group facilitators may point out students' strengths, teach coping skills and model problem solving.

A central activity of the group student sharing of memories, thoughts and feelings about their journey to the United States. There is tremendous variation in how ready and willing students are to share their stories. Some students describe a long journey, travelling through many countries before arriving in the United States. Some students have great difficulty talking about their journey and require significant help from the facilitator and group in order to reconnect with their thoughts, memories and feelings. It is extremely important for the facilitator and group participants to respect these difficulties. It is critical for the facilitator to model respect and patience for the struggles of each person.

A common theme among students is the longing for pets, friends, grandparents and other family members left in their country of origin. They also miss the comforts of home, like language, food, climate and holidays. These common themes help group members see the similarities among them. They feel a common bond with the other students. This helps them make sense of their feelings and makes their feelings of loss more bearable. Sometimes students express feelings that are ambiguous and complex. A Somali boy shared his sense of ambivalence about living in the United States because his brothers were unable to come with him. He was plagued by the guilt of being safe in the United States while his brothers were still in harm's way.

The Tree of Life[3] activity encourages refugee students to reflect on their past, present and future; integrate previous experiences from their countries of origin with current life in America; and articulate their hopes and plans for the future. The activity aims to build on their strengths and resilience by thinking about what they have overcome in life and achieved so far. It enhances their confidence regarding future opportunities and motivates them to keep working on their goals and accomplishments.

WorkStyles programme at Spring Institute: A pre-employment programme for refugee adults

Spring Institute for Intercultural Learning is a Denver-based NGO providing services to help adult refugees rebuild livelihoods, recognizing the opportunity non-formal education provides not only to strengthen refugees' economic outlooks, but to improve their psychosocial well-being as well.

Spring Institute for Intercultural Learning was created in 1979 and began working within the United States' emerging refugee resettlement network, with a focus on meeting the English language and pre-employment needs of refugee arrivals. While providing these direct services to refugees resettled to the Denver area, Spring Institute also began consulting nationally on ESL curriculum design and teacher training. That consultation continues, as teachers request assistance in addressing cultural, language and mental health challenges that emerge in the adult classroom.

Spring Institute's overarching goal is to help individuals, organizations and communities recognize cultural differences as assets and to provide services promoting integration and inclusion. In order to do so, Spring Institute delivers direct services, training and technical assistance to help newcomers integrate into communities and to help longer-term residents benefit from the country's changing demographic landscape. Many of Spring Institute's clients are refugees resettling in Colorado from across the globe. These refugees are very diverse, with some of the most common countries of origin including Somalia, Ethiopia, Bhutan, Burma, Iran and Congo, among many others.

Many refugees come to Spring Institute after languishing in refugee camps for years, where they may or may not have experienced a safe environment and where few were able to proactively build their livelihoods. Others have been displaced and living in urban areas while trying to find a permanent home. Over time, many have become dispirited and less confident, lacking a sense of control over their lives. They come to the United States with a sense of euphoria and hope, but typically enter a period of disillusionment as they struggle financially, face tensions within their family dynamics and become overwhelmed by the new language and culture. While many felt perfectly capable until their world fell apart and they became refugees, that period of self-sufficiency may feel very long ago. Refugees need to develop a sense of control over their lives again. Language and cross-cultural training give them the tools to do this, so that they have the opportunity to gain employment and language skills and eventually feel at home in their American community.

Spring Institute's non-formal education programmes for adult learners are designed to promote well-being. They embrace a strength-based approach, recognizing that most students were very successful in their own country and know a tremendous amount. Not only do students learn core content, but an atmosphere of trust, inclusion and well-being is established that builds their confidence and creates a positive foundation for strengthening their livelihoods. One of Spring Institute's programmes that embodies this spirit is WorkStyles.

The WorkStyles programme

Spring Institute first began offering WorkStyles in the mid-1980s to Southeast Asian refugees, who needed to develop confidence in order to secure jobs. Whether they were highly educated professionals or had worked more menial jobs, refugees were petrified by the prospect of facing job interviews, writing resumes and interacting in the American workforce. It was clear that helping them develop cross-cultural skills and giving them an understanding of the American work culture were fundamental to their employment success and longer-term livelihoods.

WorkStyles is one of Spring Institute's longest-running programmes and is a pre-employment, competency-based training targeted to refugees. WorkStyles is designed to help limited English speakers learn, in a challenging but supportive classroom environment, how to gain and retain employment in the United States. Classes ideally have about 20 participants, typically contain people from a variety of ethnic backgrounds and are conducted in English. They are two-week, 60-hour intensives led by a team of professional trainers. Most refugees have been in the country two to three months when their resettlement agency employment specialist/job developer refers them to the programme.

In order to successfully engage diverse adult learners, an interactive class format is employed that includes the use of lectures, small group discussions, brainstorming, case studies, role play and videotaped exercises. Core class content is focused on the following aspects of employment: effective communication, the job search, resume writing, job applications, online applications, interviews, problem-solving at work, American workplace values, stress management and employee rights and responsibilities. However, while the core content addresses the skills and knowledge to find and retain a job, much of the class process focuses on helping refugees rebuild their confidence and gain a sense of control over their lives.

WorkStyles incorporates a teaching philosophy that emphasizes eliciting content from participants by demonstrating skills, rather than giving information through lectures. Teachers actively involve people in the class, drawing on what the refugees already know and showing how they can contribute to the class community, thereby reinforcing their potential to be contributing members of a broader community.

WorkStyles stresses the following training approaches:

1. Content is generated by participants as much as possible, written on flipcharts, and placed on walls around the room to emphasize how much participants do know and how they are contributing to class.

2. Strong connections between students of all cultures are fostered due to the intensive nature, both in terms of time and content, of the training.
3. High participant involvement is promoted throughout. By challenging themselves through hands-on learning activities, students discover they can handle new and unfamiliar situations.
4. Active listening – a communication feedback technique in which the listener repeats what has been heard and understood and re-states or asks questions to check for understanding – is promoted and practiced regularly among all students. This is an empowering skill that helps refugees verify that they fully understand the relayed information, and it reassures the speaker that the listener is engaged in the conversation.

At its core, WorkStyles is about psychosocial adjustment, helping refugees explore how to present themselves in the US workforce in a way that is true to who they are and preserves their sense of self, but also helps them consider adaptations that will allow them to be more effective in their jobs and the broader community. A few of the cultural challenges many ethnic groups face include understanding the emphasis placed on individualism, being comfortable expressing one's own positive attributes, being assertive, understanding time management and a sense of urgency on the job, and being willing to ask a question of an authority figure. Where possible, teachers demonstrate and discuss these explicitly, such as demonstrating and practicing a firm handshake and talking about what it implies, or demonstrating and discussing the use of eye contact. There is always an element of choice: students are not told they must follow these behaviours, but they at least develop an understanding of American expectations. Those who are able to adopt these cultural behaviours in a way that feels real and authentic will be most successful. Perhaps most importantly, given the traumatic backgrounds of many refugees, teachers try to set a tone from the first day of class that WorkStyles is a safe place. As much as possible, people work in small groups. When students are asked to perform a task in front of a larger group, the teacher uses a scaffolding technique, always physically demonstrating what is requested, then verbally repeating the request and finally asking students to repeat the task instructions verbally. The idea is to convey that it is a safe environment where no one will fail. One of the first activities is an introduction activity. The teacher typically begins by providing a list of nine questions for students to ask each other. After pairing off with a partner from a different ethnic or linguistic background, students ask questions of and then introduce their partner to the full class. Typically, speaking in front of a group like this is rather daunting for limited English speakers, but this exercise introduces the idea of risk-taking and is the first step towards rebuilding self-confidence. By that afternoon, each will be taking on an additional challenge: introducing themselves on video. Activities are designed to challenge the participants and to build on each other, always introducing a new element of risk. Each time students meet those challenges, they gain confidence to take on additional ones.

Over two weeks of interactive class activities, participants become very close. Typically the classroom spirit becomes a very supportive one, where people know they are cared for and also recognize that they will be held accountable for high standards. Time and again participants report that they deeply appreciate this class. People feel successful and can identify what they are learning. After each activity, teachers ask, 'Why did we do this?', so that students explore how each task can help them with their job and their life. When possible, at the beginning of each class, participants brainstorm about what they learned from the day before. At the end of each class, they practice something that they learned, such as a firm handshake or identifying three positive qualities about themselves. All of this contributes to them 'owning' their learning. For some participants, WorkStyles will be the first time in a long time that they have had a chance to shine. On occasion, people are resistant to programme participation, and often those who are the most defensive are the most scared. Finding ways to connect with them, through their talents and skills, is a first step in helping them break down those defenses. One class session, significantly, is devoted to culture shock, which falls on day nine of the ten-day programme. In a supportive environment, a discussion begins by eliciting from participants what culture means for them. They talk about how they felt upon their initial arrival in the United States, what is stressful for them now, what they miss about their home country and how to cope. Students often talk about missing the smells, the feel of the air, or even the way the moon looked back at home. Teachers actively listen during this portion, careful not to overstep their bounds by asking probing questions. They do emphasize coping strategies. For example, if refugees miss certain foods, teachers suggest where they might be able to purchase them. This helps participants again try and establish a measure of control. Through this conversation, students also learn about the typical stages of euphoria and discouragement that refugees face after resettlement, approaches to managing such feelings, and when and how to seek outside help. The last day of class is the graduation, where students share their culture and what they have learned with the broader community. Graduations are celebrations, honoring the accomplishments of participants and giving them an opportunity to contribute something that no one else can – their culture – through dance, music, poetry or whatever method they prefer. The class selects two participants, typically those who have naturally emerged as class leaders, to serve as the masters of ceremony for the graduation. After the cultural sharing, teachers recognize each graduate by saying something positive about them and giving them a certificate. Food prepared by students is shared by all. Many leave WorkStyles with a renewed sense of hope for their future.

The changing landscape of workforce initiatives

Since WorkStyles' inception 25 years ago, the mechanics of securing a job have changed tremendously, the needs of students have grown more varied and the emphasis on workforce development has also expanded. First, the internet has changed the job search process, and employers are increasingly using online procedures in their hiring practices. Many employers only accept resumes electronically or they have their own online job application system. This emphasis on technology can be challenging for refugees. While some refugees have existing email and even Facebook accounts, many of those who have lived in refugee camps for years have a much steeper learning curve. WorkStyles has struggled at times to find the best way to address the increased emphasis on technology in the job market in a way that is responsive to participants' needs.

In addition to the challenges of increased technology use, there is also the issue of the wide ranges in the abilities of students who enter the class. Some hold numerous college degrees, while others may have never held a pair of scissors. In response, WorkStyles is attempting to create a new curriculum which covers the basics, including the development of fine motor skills, so that students can learn to perform the most simple of tasks. These demonstrable tasks include measuring objects, counting money and performing tasks under time pressures. Helping students master the wide range of skills required in today's workforce – from fine motor to internet usage – is a significant challenge.

For many refugees, coming to WorkStyles class for two weeks is a welcome respite from the challenge of uprooting their lives and beginning the process of securing employment in the United States. Indeed, the country's economic downturn and heightened unemployment rate have an enormous impact on their ability to find jobs and secure livelihoods. Organizations working to resettle refugees also experience increased pressure to help refugees prepare for, secure and retain employment. Certainly, WorkStyles has not been immune to this shifting employment landscape.

The trend in workforce efforts in general is towards sector-specific training, especially for fields where there are labour shortages. With projected job growth in industries such as health care, green energy and technology, there is less emphasis at times on the broader approaches to job preparation that WorkStyles offers. The programme has worked diligently to position itself as a precursor to such programmes, believing that students can benefit from sector-specific approaches once they have the foundation of WorkStyles. However, with the increased sense of urgency for refugees to secure jobs, it is possible that referring clients to pre-employment education followed by sector trainings will be unattractive because it may slow down the hiring process. Enrolments in WorkStyles remain at record levels, though there is an awareness that the programme needs to stay relevant so that it is not replaced by sector-specific approaches.

Perhaps the greatest challenge for WorkStyles is the tension between helping people build livelihoods and addressing their psychosocial needs. In the current environment, there is such an emphasis on the former, and a chance that psychosocial adjustment is being ignored, to the detriment of securing livelihoods in the longer term. With the huge emphasis on job placement by NGOs, programmes with a psychosocial component may seem commendable but perhaps not essential. However, Spring Institute would argue that for their longer-term employment and community integration, nurturing psychosocial adjustment early in the resettlement process is fundamental.

Conclusion

The resettlement process provides refugees with opportunities to build a new future despite their many losses in their countries of origin. However, even when they can overcome the anguish of their histories, they must face new challenges brought on by the acculturation process. Non-formal educational programmes play an important role in facilitating their adaptation. Many refugee adolescents need an avenue for sharing their worries about their family's future in America, talking about the burden of interpreting for limited-English-speaking parents, exploring new family dynamics as they are thrust into the role of cultural broker, and understanding and overcoming the sense of isolation that prevents them from utilizing their parents as a source of knowledge and comfort. Refugee students tend to be eager to reflect on questions such as the following: How do I see myself? How am I perceived by others? Where do I belong? Where is my home now? Beyond the traditional classroom, refugee youth need opportunities to learn from each other about the variety of ways to answer these seemingly simple questions. Non-formal education can provide these special opportunities. For adults, much of the emphasis of the resettlement process is on employment. Refugees are encouraged to secure jobs as soon as possible so that they can support their families and avoid receiving public benefits. This emphasis on early self-sufficiency is a significant aspect of the culture of the United States. At the same time, many who work with refugee populations struggle to meet the psychosocial needs of adult refugees who have experienced great loss, but may need help to grieve fully. Too often, a blind eye is turned towards the painful histories of young refugees as adults focus on meeting their most immediate needs for work, housing and shelter. The unintended consequence is that underlying psychosocial issues can fester and become exacerbated in the future. To the extent possible, a variety of formal and non-formal educational efforts can work together to promote a comprehensive, collaborative approach to meeting refugee families' needs.

People within a network of refugee service organizations, such as the network that exists in Colorado and many other places, can recognize emerging needs among the members of refugee populations and consider how to be most flexible in meeting them. Given the focus in the United States on self-reliance, however, there may never be enough funding available to cover all of the supports from which refugees would benefit. At the same time, given the American cultural gestalt involving individual opportunity and the American Dream, one could say that refugees in the United States have come to a place where starting over has been honored for generations.

Key Questions

1. How do we encourage the independence/identity formation of refugee adolescents when their parents are asking them to perform many roles that are directed towards family concerns?

2. How might we help parents allow their children to talk about their feelings when many parents are hoping that if their children don't talk about their experiences, the pain might go away?
3. If one recognizes that both learning the language of the host community and gaining employment are critical for supporting refugees' livelihoods and supporting positive psychosocial adjustment, how can the two be balanced optimally, given the time and energy constraints facing refugee families?
4. How might we prioritize funding for resettled refugee populations, given that in comparison to the total population of Colorado, they represent a small number?

Notes

1 Statistic taken from http://www.unhcr.org/pages/49c3646c1d.html.

2 Source: UNESCO (1997, 41). Available at http://www.iiep.unesco.org/fileadmin/user_upload/Research_Highlights_Emergencies/Chapter12.pdf.

3 Activity is adapted from the Life Book Trainer's Guide by the IOM Nepal, Cultural Orientation Resource Center – Center for Applied Linguistics.

Further reading

Kia-Keating, M. and Ellis, H. (2007), 'Belonging and Connection to School in Resettlement: Young Refugees, School Belonging and Psychosocial Adjustment'. *Clinical Child Psychology and Psychiatry*, 12, 29–43.

McBrien, J. (2005), 'Educational Needs and Barriers for Refugee Students in the United States: a Review of the Literature'. *Review of Educational Research*, 75(3), 329–64.

Miller, K., Kushner, H., McCall, J., Martell, Z. and Kulkarni, M. (2008), 'Growing Up in Exile: Psychosocial Challenges Facing Refugee Youth in the United States', in Hart, J. (ed.), *Years of Conflict: Adolescence, Political Violence, and Displacement*. New York: Berghahn Books, pp. 59–86.

Miller, K. and Rasco, K. (eds) (2004), *The Mental Health of Refugees: Ecological Approaches to Healing and Adaption*. Mahwa, NJ: Lawrence Erlbaum Associates, Inc Publishers.

References

Birman, D. and Chan, W. Y. (2008), Screening and Assessing Immigrant and Refugee Youth in School-Based Mental Health Programs. Center for Health and Health Care in School, Issue Brief #1, May. Available at www.healthinschools.org.

Crowley, C. (2009), 'The Mental Health Needs of Refugee Children: a Review of Literature and Implications for Nurse Practitioners'. *Journal of the American Academy of Nurse Practitioners*, 21, 322–31.

Kia-Keating, M. and Ellis, H. (2007), 'Belonging and Connection to School in Resettlement: Young Refugees, School Belonging and Psychosocial Adjustment'. *Clinical Child Psychology and Psychiatry*, 12, 29–43.

Kinzie, J., Sack, W., Angell, R., Manson, S. and Rath, B. (1986), 'The Psychiatric Effects of Massive Trauma on Cambodian Children: ii. The Family, the Home, and the School'. *Journal of the American Academy of Child Psychiatry*, 25(3), 377–83.

McBrien, J. (2005), 'Educational Needs and Barriers for Refugee Students in the United States: a Review of the Literature'. *Review of Educational Research*, 75(3), 329–64.

Miller, K., Kushner, H., McCall, J., Martell, Z. and Kulkarni, M. (2008), 'Growing Up in Exile: Psychosocial Challenges Facing Refugee Youth in the United States', in Hart, J. (ed.), *Years of Conflict: Adolescence, Political Violence, and Displacement*. New York: Berghahn Books, pp. 59–86.

Miller, K. and Rasco, K. (eds) (2004), *The Mental Health of Refugees: Ecological Approaches to Healing and Adaption*. NJ: Lawrence Erlbaum Associates, Inc Publishers.

Reichenberg, D., and Friedman, S. (1996), 'Healing the Invisible Wounds of Children in War: a Rights Approach', in Danieli, Y., Rodley, N. S. and Weisaeth, L. (eds), *International Responses to Traumatic Stress: Humanitarian, Human Rights, Justice, Peace and Development Contributions, Collaborative Actions and Future Initiatives*. Amityville, NY: Baywood Publishing, pp. 307–26.

Rutter, J. (2006), *Refugee Children in the UK*. Maidenhead, Berkshire: Open University Press.

5

Refugees and Education in Kent in England

Dr. James Dada

Chapter Outline

Introduction

This chapter seeks to discuss refugees and education in Kent in England, which is a county to the southeast of London popularly known as the 'Garden of England' because of its natural beauty. Refugees and asylum seekers there have experienced forced migration due to wars, famine, economic oppression, religious persecution and other factors that have placed them under severe pressure. First, they seek security but then they begin to seek a better life. Refugees and their education have been of international concern such that the United Nations, central and local governments, NGOs and voluntary organizations have been working together to address their urgent needs. A growing literature is apparent, provoking discussion from many practitioners and academics, giving their experiences from different perspectives in different countries, but all striving to find solutions to the problems of refugees. Experiences of refugees from Europe, Africa, Asia and the Americas are discussed below. Special projects such as the Finding Your Feet project in Kent are examples of initiatives for acquiring and teaching skills. Through this programme, refugees from different nationalities learn skills that will help them gain employment. This chapter also discusses the Sunlight Centre, which provides facilities for the community of refugees and asylum seekers. Such initiatives have provided for the health, nourishment and even entertainment of refugees in Kent. Interaction between refugees and their host communities has become possible in a meaningful way. Such services are constrained by finance, however, and are rarely sufficient for existing need. Throughout this chapter, issues relating to refugees who have been assisted in Kent are discussed, interspersed in the broader context of refugee experiences in general.

Refugees

Refugees are defined by the Geneva Convention of 1951 to be persons who have a well-founded fear of being persecuted for a variety of reasons and who are outside the country of their nationality and are unwilling or unable to avail themselves of the protection of that country. Since they are removed from normal home circumstances, many writers, observers, agencies and governments are concerned about refugees' educational needs and standards. Global refugee figures are difficult to determine, but likely run into hundreds of millions. It is generally accepted that most refugees flee their countries of origin because of religious, tribal or political oppression, sometimes to the point of ethnic cleansing and even genocide. Examples of countries where these incidences have taken place include Kosovo, where the Serbs were in conflict with the Albanians, and Central Africa, where the conflict was between the Hutu and Tutsi. There are many other examples around the world in recent decades – such as Zimbabwe, Somalia and Uganda – where ethnic cleansing experiences have led people to flee their homelands as refugees. Such ethnic cleansing and persecution has been evident throughout human history; religious-based examples include tensions between Islamic and Christian factions, Sikhs and Hindus in India, and persecution of Jews that led to a massive diaspora due to late nineteenth-century pogroms in Eastern Europe and the Holocaust in the mid-twentieth century.

Religion is one of the two prime components of culture; the other is language. The combination, together with the issue of territory, sometimes makes for violent conflict such as the Nigerian-Biafran War in Nigeria in the late 1960s. Internal displacements in Nigeria took place significantly during the Nigerian-Biafran War, which was precipitated by several factors such as ethnic rivalries, imbalance of political power at the federal legislative level, religious bickering and competition over oil revenue. At Nigerian independence on 1 October 1960, the north had the Fulani and Hausa; the west, Yoruba; and the east was dominated by the Igbo. The Muslims and the Christians have often had clashes in the north with reprisals in the east and the west (Dada, 1986). A military coup in 1966 by Iqbo leaders led to the creation of an unofficial new state, Biafra, in 1967 which survived for nearly three years before being crushed militarily. This in turn led to a significant exodus of refugees to many countries, especially the United States, the former USSR and the United Kingdom, where the entry point was often Kent, through the port of Dover. Coming from the most-affected part of Nigeria, the writer has personally experienced the disruption of education in his homeland at that time, as well as the efforts to assist refugees being made in the area of England in which he now resides.

Vijayshree (2005) studied how asylum seekers and refugees tend to access education in four local education authorities in England: Doncaster, Haringey, Greenwich and Kent. The majority of the children interviewed for the project were positive about their school experiences and they were enthusiastic to learn. They had strong aspirations and were positive about their futures. Schools generally provide not only education but also a gateway for leading a new and peaceful life and being a part of a wider community. The government, local authorities and schools in the United Kingdom attempt to work closely together and provide a safe and fair environment for these children to flourish. While it is important for schools to have the freedom to choose how best to use their resources, it is equally important that the local authorities have refugee education teams with special skills. The key recommendations from Vijayshree were that:

> the government must ensure that all school-aged asylum seekers and refugees can access their right to education by being allocated school places quickly; local authorities should collect detailed statistics on the education attainment of school-aged asylum seekers and refugees so that Local Education Authorities (LEA) and schools can review current practice and share good practice; schools

> need to explore mechanisms for allowing parents to understand schools' delivery of the curriculum. (Vijayshree, 2005, pp. 1–2)

It was also recommended that the government should ensure that all school-aged asylum seekers and refugees are allocated school places quickly, and collect detailed data on their educational attainment, so that LEAs and schools can review their current procedures and share best practices. The resettlement experiences of refugees in the United Kingdom was also researched by the Home Office Research Planning Unit, according to Duke (1996a). The sample size was 263 and interviews were the chosen method of investigation. The sample population was restricted to those people who had applied for asylum when they were aged 18 or over. The research was exploratory and it investigated the general problems that refugees encountered in adjusting to their new social and economic environment.

Refugees in Kent in England

Kent has a special place in modern refugee flows to the United Kingdom due to its proximity to the mainland of Europe. More refugees have entered the country through the port of Dover than through any other entry point. Given the nature of the transportation routes from Dover, the first major conurbation reached on the journey inland towards London is that of the Medway towns. This is a cluster of five towns on the river Medway that flows into the Thames estuary. They are Rochester, Chatham, Gillingham, Rainham and Strood. A few cases known to the writer will be selected here to illustrate the variety of refugees and experiences.

The writer has lived in Medway for nearly 20 years, and during this period he has known many of the refugees in his area. He has not been a member not only of the Medway Refugee Support Group and the Kent Refugee Support Group but also the Kent Refugee Asylum Network and Monitoring Group. The knowledge gained from his activities in these organizations has been valuable in writing this study, which emanates from his interest and experiences in mentoring, supporting and learning from refugees such as those mentioned below.

One such refugee was an ex-military Russian who had worked in the aviation department and was a specialist in parachute systems. Due to continued wars in his part of the country he transported members of his family from Grozny (Chechnya) to Linda (Byelorussia) and then escaped to England alone. He left behind a wife and five children (three daughters and two sons). He arrived at Dover on 2 April 2000 and stayed there for five days until he was moved to Rochester prison for 15 months. He had a General Certificate of Education (ordinary level) and wanted to improve his skills for employment. After he was released from prison, he obtained poor accommodation and spoke little English. Yet, because of the lack of security and the oppressive regime in Russia, he did not want to return to his home country.

Another Russian, aged 35, fled with his father, brother and sister who were forced out of Russia after refusing an order to shoot at a peaceful demonstration. He understood that his mother and brother were in London but he had not been able to trace them during a period of five years. His problems were depression, poor accommodation, food shortage and poor physical health.

A further example was an 82-year-old Polish man from a longstanding refugee family. His parents had migrated from Poland in 1850. His father was from Poland, but his mother was from Portugal. He spoke English, Hebrew and Russian. He did not like to recall his past, handed down to him by his parents, because of the unpleasant memories. He spoke briefly of the difficulties the Jews had encountered in Europe as a result of World War II. He commended the people of Medway for treating Jewish children very well as they passed through the towns, some of them settling permanently. According to him, as early as the twentieth century, there had been families of Jews living in Medway. He spoke of the contributions made by the Jews to Medway. Some notable personalities included Daniel Barnard, who founded the Chatham 'Fire Brigade', and Captain Lazarus Magnus, who was instrumental in bringing the railway to Sheerness and Queen's borough. He was later a mayor of Queen's borough on the Isle of Sheppey. Another Jew interviewed was a mechanical engineer. He came to work at the Chatham Dockyard and, after his retirement, he found himself a suitable home in Chatham. He held public offices such as a magistrate, school governor local councillor, chairman of the local Racial Equality Council, and Advisory Councils for Religious Education. He truly appreciated the National Health Service (NHS), although he had no health problems himself.

Such examples show how the longstanding experience of the Medway conurbation has created a relatively favourable environment for successive waves of refugees. There have also been many refugees from Africa, especially from Uganda, Zimbabwe, Nigeria, Sierra Leone and Somalia. All of them had similar stories to tell about war, oppression, repression, nepotism, conflicts, human rights abuses, and arbitrary and deliberate killings. Women and girls were often raped. There were cruel amputations and genocide targeting opponent clans in continual civil wars. These refugees have come to the Medway towns for sanctuary. One woman from Somalia fled to the United Kingdom with other destitute women and children after the 1977–78 war between Ethiopia and Somalia. She suffered from depressiion, psychotic disorders and suicidal tendencies, but while she was recovering she worked to get into a Midwifery Studies Course at the University of Kent in Canterbury.

Two people interviewed for this study from Uganda were originally from India; the husband was aged 85, while the wife was 82. The couple fled Uganda when Idi Amin came to power and expelled all Ugandan Asians in 1971. All their businesses and properties were confiscated without compensation. Becoming refugees was unavoidable as Idi Amin consolidated his brutal dictatorship by imprisoning and executing all political opponents. This couple arrived in the United Kingdom in 1975. The husband was a well-qualified accountant holding a university degree. Consequently, he gained employment at the Barclays Bank head office in London. He was in charge of the foreign accounts before he retired with a pension. The couple lived in a quiet, primarily Asian and Indian suburb of Chatham. The Medway towns are within London's commuter range, and it is important to recognize cases like this in which some refugees have been very successful and indeed contributed significantly to the UK economy.

Fewer refugees in Medway were from Asia. One 71-year-old respondent was originally from India but became a Pakistani when the subcontinent was partitioned in 1947. After graduating from Lahore University with a BSc in social studies, he came to Britain in 1992 and lived in London. He had suffered religious persecution in Pakistan and had to flee for his life after his wife was kidnapped, a memory that he still finds distressing as he has not seen her since. At times, he nearly broke down, trembling in trepidation as he recounted his memories. Another refugee respondent from Asia speaks Urdu, Punjabi, Arabic, Persian and English. He is able to mingle with people freely but found little sympathy and support from the indigenous population in London. He recapitulated how he slept with others under bridges and in the railway tunnels in London. There, he met different kinds of people and quickly established friendships. Food was a problem, and he had to rely on the charity of others. He later secured a job as a night watchman at the detention centre itself, earning a pound a day. That did not offer him the standard of life he had wanted. Soon he developed asthma and, on his doctor's recommendation, he moved from London to Chatham. He became a British citizen in 2002. He enjoys this status now that he is retired and lives alone in Chatham. His son lives in Germany, but he would not like to talk about the rest of his family members. The son suffers from loneliness, but has no accommodation issues. He is aware of voluntary organizations offering help and the social services organized by ethnic minorities, but according to him, these organizations are opportunists looking for grants to line their pockets. He is now a man of all faiths, for he believes that all faiths lead to the same place and the same God.

Refugees appear to find it relatively easy to settle in Medway, possibly because the region is very close to Dover, which is the main seaport of passenger entry to the United Kingdom from Europe and because they find Medway an easy route to the hinterland of England and other UK destinations. Medway is one of the urban areas outside of London where refugees form a significant proportion of the population. An accurate refugee population there is difficult to obtain, as admitted by the Home Office, but it is estimated to be about 4.2 per cent of the overall population. One challenge to estimating the refugee population is that they often move from place to place in search of opportunities.

Initiatives for refugees in Medway

The Inclusive Education Centre

Children of refugees and asylum seekers have the opportunity of receiving education at Medway's own Inclusive Education Centre, which is established at the New Road School in Chatham. The school works with the Medway Council and admits children irrespective of race, background, ethnicity or disability. The school is inclusive, embracing all cultures and social expectations. Le Touze (2003) reminds us that refugees and asylum seekers in United Kingdom are entitled to free state education from preschool age to 16. Those 16 to 18-year-olds who are seeking asylum or are the dependants of adults claiming asylum are entitled to reduced rates for further education. Schools are legally required to offer places to asylum seekers. Qualifications for entry, especially to higher institutions, have to comply with international requirements. There are facilities at which students can upgrade their qualifications. Teachers or interpreters from the refugees' states of origin are often given preference for teaching employment skills, since they are familiar with the culture of refugees and can easily interact with them. Well-trained nationals are also employed.

There are cases of unaccompanied children sold to prostitution in their own countries. The culture of the children is often a melange of influences derived from religion, cultural bereavement, ancestral worship, ghosts and other beliefs and superstitions. The Inclusive Education Centre in Medway seeks to take into account all such problems of cultural dislocation, discrimination and exploitation by providing both psychosocial and technical support as well as more regular schooling.

Project Sunlight

This is a project established in the Gillingham area in order to fill a gap between the refugees and the public. It was established to enhance the education of the refugees and is not confined only to the classroom, as it was intended to improve the public interaction with the refugees. All members of the local society have access to facilities and free services such as an information centre, services which are beneficial to their general education, a comprehensive health care centre, a community pharmacy, extensive IT facilities, a family centre office, a flexible space for voluntary organizations and community groups, as well as a community café for the social well-being of both the youth and adult members of the community.

The FindingYour Feet project

The Finding Your Feet project took place in Strood and Rochester. The general objective was to understand the problems faced by refugees in Kent, so that these problems can be properly addressed over time. The method of investigation used was qualitative research comprising observations and unstructured interviews. It explored in-depth the situations of two of the refugees as indications of what they tend to encounter.

The refugees and asylum seekers, who came from several countries, were not interviewed as fully as would have been ideal because of language problems – there were no interpreters. Basic questions focused on the statistics of the refugees and their countries of origin, programmes of study, problems of the organization, and suggestions to ameliorate their problems. The names of the two officials interviewed were Brenda Joyce and David Woodward. Other information provided was from the records kept in refugee files. The number of refugees registered in the project was 204. They were from seven different countries: Russia, Egypt, Poland, India, Sierra-Leone, Somalia and Zimbabwe. All the resident refugees were offered instruction in the English language, as well as plumbing, building, hairdressing or computer literacy, and business studies in their programmes of study. All were being prepared to work in the community.

Problems experienced by the refugees and possible responses

Writing about public attitude and the media, Ingleby and Watters (2002) suggested that the public opinion in Western countries seems to have hardened against refugees. Such opinions tend to dissuade the general public from helping the refugees as they ought to do. The same sentiment was expressed by a Mori Research Institute survey (June 2002); the majority of respondents overestimated the number of refugees in the United Kingdom. Respondents felt that England was housing nearly a quarter of the world's refugees and that this trend was wrong. In actual fact, the total number of refugees being assisted by the United Kingdom is about 1.98 per cent of the global total. The media often describe refugees as illegal and scroungers. This angered the public, who thought that political agendas directed the attitudes in the newspapers. For example, some typical complaints from residents in Kent and their explanations in the mass media follow.

Complaint: Why should Kent County have to support so many refugees?

Explanation: The central government is now responsible for the benefits paid to the refugees and any benefits paid previously by counties are being refunded.

Complaint: Refugees tend to get everything, like council homes, ahead of the local people.

Explanation: They have never been put in council houses, but in privately rented accommodation and refurbished poor-quality houses that local people decline to occupy.

Complaint: They are aggressive and demanding and are often being pushed or pushing themselves to the front of queues.

Explanation: This is often a problem of cultural conflict, and it takes time for them to get used to and adjust to the English way of life.

Complaint: Refugees are illegal immigrants.

Explanation: The 1951 Convention on Refugees signed by the United Kingdom stipulates that anyone has the right to apply for asylum and remain in the United Kingdom until a final decision is made. Illegal entry is understandable in view of motivating circumstances such as escaping from persecution or from oppressive/discriminatory regimes like those in Zimbabwe, Afghanistan, Iraq and Somalia. In these difficult circumstances, it is possible that refugees will enter a country without valid documents. In realizing this fact, Article 31 of the 1951 Convention on Refugees prohibits governments from penalizing refugees who, seeking asylum, use false documents to enter their countries.

The complaints mentioned above have contributed to a lack of interest by the general public – who would have otherwise generally assisted the refugees – in helping the refugees in their education and other aspects of life.

One of the problems refugees face is integrating into the British way of life. Many of them suffered from trauma, change of environment, cultural conflicts, language problems and unreasonably high expectations of life in Britain. In many instances, asylum seekers interviewed in France often said, 'We just want to go to London. There is job there. There is money there.' Another problem encountered is the difficulty of controlling three or four young people living in a house without an older person. There was a case at Gravesend in Kent in which two youngsters stabbed each other while eating! According to a detective, one youngster complained that the other was making rude remarks about his mother. He also noted that if an older person had been present, the stabbing could have been averted. Lack of adequate financial resources to provide necessary services for the refugees has also caused some problems. In addition, the public and the media need to work cooperatively with the refugees as there are still misgivings about their presence in Kent.

There is an ongoing need to promote good relationships between communities and asylum seekers. The host communities should understand that refugees can bring benefits to the country and that the problem of refugees is an international one, not easily solved. Attempts should therefore be made to integrate them into the community as much as and as soon as possible. In our research in Medway, local arrangements have been made for over 200 refugees to be integrated into youth clubs and organizations where they can mingle and socialize with their peers. Football and other sports can often bring refugees closer to communities and enable them to improve their English language skills as they interact with their peer groups. A youth worker will normally help to organize series of sporting activities and social events to help integrate refugees with the communities. Thus, appointment of a mentor is highly advantageous to the refugees as a mentor will help to plan and provide support for them. Mentors also assist in other areas, such as adjustment to the new environment, counselling, health, food, accommodation and opportunities for education and employment.

Mutual understanding between refugees and host communities is encouraged by various NGOs. Some refugees have complained that they do not want to be called 'refugees' because of how refugees in the community are perceived and the derogatory remarks sometimes made. It is important to remember that refugees are just people who, because of harsh experiences in their home countries, fled for security and better lives in the host countries. If things were normal in their home countries, most refugees would prefer to live there. The majority of refugees would like to study and improve their positions and skillsRegarding the all-important matter of finance, the Home Office presently provides the funding for towards the education of refugees, but with the change of government in May 2010 this may be in question. There may be moves to privatize parts of the public services with as yet unforeseen results. A possible negative outcome is that criminal activities may increase and cause unwanted problems and further hostility from the host community.

Meeting the educational needs of refugees in Kent

Throughout this discussion we can see that the problems refugees pose are global, be it in developed or developing countries. The United Nations – through some of its agencies such as UNESCO, UNICEF, UNIFEM and UNHCR – is concerned with multifaceted problems, including education. Education is often considered a solution in itself for societal problems. It is sometimes asked whether it is possible, through education, to stop wars, poverty, disease, intertribal hostilities, religious persecutions, slavery, oppression of minorities and other vices that force people out of their places of origin. This is, of course, impossible and unrealistic. The educational needs of refugees in Kent are similar to the needs of refugees all over the world. The approach to solving the problems may differ, but the solutions can sometimes be transferred to similar situations elsewhere. This is one reason why a comparative study of different educational needs of refugees is advantageous. The main educational needs of refugees in Kent will be discussed briefly under a number of headings below, though in practice they are interconnected.

Language for communication and studies

The language problem is crucial because refugees need to communicate with the host communities for assistance, food, health facilities, accommodation and employment possibilities. Therefore, teaching the language should be a priority and ought to be tailored to the individual refugee. Although language is part of the culture of a community, education providers must remember that the new arrivals have their own imported cultures that their hosts need to respect. Of course, the new arrivals also need to adjust to the new cultures of their hosts. Failure to adjust, on the part of the refugees, often causes friction and protests by the indigenous population, as illustrated above. However, in some cases, the host communities expect too many changes from the refugees, or too much too soon. Clearly a key issue here is to maintain, and – if possible – increase, the provision of classes and facilities for learning English as a second language by adult immigrants.

Education for employment

New refugees tend to be desperate for employment but are often frustrated by the need to assess their credentials, and – worse still – the new communities they are in are concerned that their jobs will be taken away from them, depriving them of their livelihood. In many cases, refugees need to retrain for accreditation. Adequate education is the solution for work in the interest of both the refugees and their hosts. This study suggests that harmonization of credentials be achieved at an international level to ensure consistency. People with secondary education should have access to open competition to occupations where knowledge of the host language may not be made a prerequisite for employment, unless a good mastery of it is really necessary to perform the job properly.

Loss of documents

Refugees often report having lost their original academic credentials obtained from their home countries; an alternative to this situation is for educational certificates be given to them in the host country after an assessment of their competencies. Educational agencies should be in charge of this process, in view of the nature of the problems involved. Often, it is easier to make policy recommendations than implement them.

Financial support by other authorities and Kent County Council

Adequate financial support is crucial for educational provision for refugees. There are those who need short-term education to supplement their existing qualifications and some others who need longer-term education and/or training to overcome the limitations of their original qualifications. They need financial support for payment of fees and travel costs to study where there may not be residential facilities. Although the European Education Fund has been made available for refugee support, this has proved insufficient for all expenses to be met. The more specific European Refugees Fund was established in September 2000, but this also has not sufficiently met the needs of the refugees in the member states. The implementation of the policy of the wider European Council is subject to differing standards by participating countries. So, there has been considerable inconsistency in respect of and support by European governments, especially relating to financial support for refugee education. McCorriston (2006), in her study of refugees and their education in London, mentions that there were three levels of regulations to be referred to relating to provision of education for newly arrived refugees: (a) European, (b) United Kingdom, and (c) local authority. In practice, most headteachers would overlook these bureaucracies and admit refugee children immediately as far as they possibly could and try to sort out the maze of rules and regulations subsequently.

Nonetheless, the host government should be encouraged to give more financial support than is being provided at present. Education for post-secondary or professional courses should also be provided in order to enable refugees to be employed where there are shortages of manpower. Unfortunately, on 21 October 2010, the UK Chancellor of the Exchequer announced drastic cuts in public sector funding by the government. This included a 27 per cent reduction in the funding of local authorities such as Kent County Council. This will bring additional problems for the support of refugees and place more pressure on cooperation between the private sector and the authorities who provide education and work for refugees. In the case of refugees from universities in conflict situations, the World University Service (WUS) (UK), has a long history of providing assistance (Brock, 1995), including in Kent, but as a result of the public expenditure cuts mentioned above, grants to NGOs and charities from central government will also be reduced or even abolished.

Conclusion

This discussion has shown how one relatively small community, the Medway towns in Kent in England, has responded to the needs of refugees who naturally flow into this area from the major entry port of Dover. The location of the Medway towns has given them many decades of experience in receiving refugees from many parts of the world. This is a challenge they have taken up both within these communities and through both local and countrywide authorities. The nearby University of Kent at Canterbury has played a significant role in this positive humanitarian response by creating the 'European MA in Migration, Mental Health and Social Care', which the author completed (Dada, 2004). This programme is provided in cooperation with Orebro University of Sweden, the University of Utrecht in the Netherlands and the Alberta University of Portugal. It includes interactive provision that assists cooperation and understanding in the provision of education for refugees in Europe.

Key Questions

1. What has been the broad pattern of refugee flow to the United Kingdom (or to your selected country) over the last 25 years?
2. Select one category of refugee's to United Kingdom (e.g. Somali, Congolese, Iraqi Afghan) and investigate their educational experience.
3. Find out what you can about the work of WUS (UK) in support of higher education refugees in the United Kingdom.
4. In this chapter some special local initiatives to help refugees were mentioned. Find other examples in your locality.
5. What problems do refugee children bring to host country classrooms, and what advantages too?

Further reading

Balloch, S. (1993), *Refugees in the Inner City: A Study of Refugees and Service Provision in the London Borough of Lewisham*. London: Centre for Inner City Studies, Goldsmiths College, University of London.

Harvey, C. (2000), *Seeking Asylum in the UK. Problems and Prospects*. London: Butterworths.

References

Brock, C. (1995), 'Educational Support for Refugees in the UK: The Case of the WUS (UK) Ethiopean Refugee Student Scheme', in Aedo-Richmond, R., Brock, C. and Lewis, A. (eds), *Refugee Education in International Perspective*. University of Hull Occasional Paper of the British Comparative and International Education Society, pp. 80–5.

Dada, J. A. (2004), *Aspects of Educational and Social Service Provisions in Medway, Kent, England*. MA Dissertation, University of Kent.

Dada, J. A. (1986), *Educational Development and Religion in Northern Nigeria, with special reference to Kwara State*. PhD Thesis, University of Hull.

Duke, K. (1996a, 1996b), 'The resettlement experiences of refugees in the UK: main findings from an interview study'. 0047–9586/96/030461-18© Journal of Oxford Ltd. Published on behalf of ERCOMER.

Ingleby, D. and Watters, C. (2005), 'The Mental Health and Social Care for Asylum Seekers and Refugees: A Comparative Study', in Ingleby, D., *Forced Migration and Mental Health*. International and Cultural Psychology Series, SpringerLink, pp. 193–212.

Ingleby, D. and Waters, C. (2002), 'Public Attitude and the Media about Refugees'. Tizard Centre: University of Kent.

Le Touze, D. (2003:35), in A Report of the European Commission Project led by Dr Charles Watters of the University of Kent and Professor David Ingleby of Utrecht University Nigerian Civil War. Available at http://en.wikipedia.org/wiki/ (accessed 31 August 2010).

McCorriston, M. (2006), *Refugees and Education in England: Examining the Educational Needs of Refugees and Asylum Seekers in Two West London Boroughs*. Doctoral thesis. Oxford University.

'Refugees' contribution to Europe: Netherlands'. Available from http:// www.uaf.nl (accessed 8 September 2009).

Vijayshree, A. (2005), 'A Study on How Asylum Seekers and Refugees Access Education in Four Local Authorities in England'. Available from www.researchasylum.or.uk (accessed 24 July 2009).

6

Twenty-first-century Learning: The Role of Community Cohesion in Refugee Education

Megan McCorriston

Chapter Outline

Introduction

Inclusive education for England's refugee and asylum-seeker population has been widely researched in England in the past decade (Doyle and McCorriston, 2008; McCorriston, 2006; McKenna, 2005). Much of this research has emphasized the barriers that refugees and asylum seekers face upon entry to the United Kingdom, including challenges for social integration in their new communities. In 2006, the UK Education and Inspections Act introduced a new duty on all maintained schools in England to promote community cohesion in support of student achievement for the most vulnerable in society, including the focus of the present study: refugees and asylum seekers. This chapter explores how secondary schools in England provide inclusive education for refugees and asylum seekers, with a focus on curriculum, instruction and extended school services within the policy framework of the new duty of schools to promote community cohesion. The lessons drawn from the following case studies highlight examples of best practice in respect to this type of education, demonstrating that community cohesion is a useful policy framework in which schools can promote both inclusive education and social cohesion for at-risk pupils such as refugees.

The rationale for the study

The duty on schools in England to promote community cohesion, which was enacted in 2007, encourages schools to partner with the community to support student achievement and gives detailed guidance on how to improve student services to foster greater social cohesion. The rationale for this study draws upon previous research which demonstrates that, with respect to refugees and asylum seekers, there are many secondary schools which already demonstrate curricular, instructional and extended initiatives that promote community cohesion and build upon best practice:

> Many schools already work in ways that promote community cohesion and the Department for Children, Schools and Families (DCSF) wants all schools to build on the best of that practice, so that all pupils understand and appreciate others from different backgrounds with a sense of shared values, fulfilling their potential and feeling part of a community, at a local, national and international level. (DCSF, 2007, pp. 9–10)

The two case studies presented in this chapter examine how selected secondary schools in London are meeting the educational needs of refugees and asylum seekers, thereby increasing social cohesion in their communities, as evidenced in innovative school activities and visionary school leadership.

School activities that promote community cohesion can be grouped into three broad categories, which form the basis of the empirical investigation:

1. teaching, learning and curriculum
2. equity and excellence
3. engagement and extended services (DCSF, 2007, pp. 9–10)

The empirical research, carried out from 2005 to 2008, investigates the relationship between the school's duty to promote community cohesion and the work of school leadership and instructional staff to promote an inclusive, high-achieving learning environment for refugees, asylum seekers and their families. It also examines the extent to which educational provision in England overcomes barriers to refugee student achievement. Moreover, the following case studies aim to supplement ongoing case study research conducted by the Department for Education (DfE) and the Office for Standards in Education (Ofsted), highlighting examples of best practice in respect of the duty to promote community cohesion.

The policy context: why does community cohesion matter?

While England has long been home to multicultural and multilingual school communities, the United Kingdom's immigration policy reaction to the events of 11 September 2001 adversely impacted access to education and other social services for England's refugee population. Some researchers have even criticized the United Kingdom's current immigration policies and procedures as 'restrictive', with a higher proportion of asylum-seeking persons receiving delayed decisions, outright refusals or detention (perhaps worst of all for children and adults) with regard to their legal status (Stanley, 2001). Furthermore, some researchers argue that refugee social and educational exclusion is a result of punitive immigration policies which also cause divided, non-cohesive communities (Jones and Rutter, 1998). In contrast to these subjectively punitive policies, the DfE introduced the new duty on schools to promote 'community cohesion' (DCSF, 2007) to bridge the chasm between England's increasingly diverse communities and a lack of appropriate educational responses in the school system to their unique educational needs in a distinctly twenty-first-century learning environment.

The duty, which was enacted in 2008, promotes the notion of community cohesion as a means of combatting racism and bullying and promoting tolerance:

> As a starting point, schools build community cohesion by promoting equality of opportunity and inclusion for different groups of pupils within a school. But alongside this focus on inequalities and a strong respect for diversity, they also have a role in promoting shared values and encouraging their pupils to actively engage with others to understand what they all hold in common . . . All schools, whatever the mix of pupils they serve, are responsible for equipping those pupils to live and thrive alongside people from many different backgrounds. For some schools with diverse pupil populations, existing activities and work aimed at supporting pupils from different ethnic or socioeconomic backgrounds to learn with, from and about each other, will already be contributing towards community cohesion. (DCSF, 2007, p. 7)

The main research questions

The present study attempts to answer the following overarching research question:

> How do secondary schools in England comply with the duty to promote community cohesion by providing inclusive education for refugees and asylum seekers?

Subsidiary research questions were also addressed in order to explore various aspects of refugee education and community cohesion, specifically in three main categories: teaching and learning, equity and excellence, engagement and extended services.

1. How do secondary schools provide effective teaching and learning at the secondary school level to refugee and asylum-seeker pupils and thus foster greater social inclusion?
2. How can increased community participation lead to equity and excellence in refugee education?
3. How do schools use extended day services to increase learning opportunities for refugees and asylum seekers and their families?
4. How does the new duty on schools to promote community cohesion work effectively to enhance 'education for all children', with an emphasis on refugees?

Documentation from secondary schools, local authorities, government department agencies and NGOs were 'quarried' for responses to the above questions.

A review of the literature found that, overwhelmingly, refugee and asylum-seeker pupils aged 14–16 have a more difficult time accessing mainstream education for a variety of reasons, including discriminatory school practices, lack of available school places or a combination of these reasons (McKenna, 2005). The fact of pupil mobility and out-of-borough transfers also results in the disruption of their education, and possible exclusion from school in their new place of residence.

Research from the Refugee Council supports these assertions:

> Practitioners from a variety of settings generally agree that a continuing problem for 14 to 16 year old refugee pupils is accessing their entitlement to full-time mainstream education in a school . . . Families and carers can find admission systems complex and inscrutable; administrators may lack understanding and flexibility; systems and processes may be structurally discriminatory; schools may be reluctant to accept what are perceived to be additional problems without additional resources within a competitive system. Yet this was felt to be exacerbated by uncontrollable mobility that impacts directly on schools. Another major issue was inclusion. For example, equal access to the curriculum for refugee children in the same way as for all children, and the support needed to meet their needs. (McKenna, 2005, p. 12)

As the above quotation indicates, resources are important in helping refugees to access their entitlement to a free public education; however, it is the responsibility of the school and its leadership team, including teachers and community volunteers, to support these individuals using innovative measures to help them succeed. The present study explores these innovative mechanisms to help refugee students achieve success in education and inclusion in their school communities.

The methodology

The empirical research took place in four secondary schools in two west London boroughs. This dimension involved 29 detailed interviews with three categories of informants: first, governmental and non-governmental agencies including the DfE, The Children's Society, Refugee Council and Save the Children UK; second, local authority representatives, including heads of local education services where possible and Ethnic Minority and Traveller

Achievement Service (EMTAS) team representatives; thirdly – and not least – headteachers, teachers (both ESL and non-specialist teachers), induction mentors and heads of Refugee Unit classrooms.

The research presented in this exploratory study utilized multiple methods, namely, documentary analysis, the case-study method and the open-ended interview method (Robson, 2002). Multiple case studies were used to analyse educational provision on the local level for refugees and asylum seekers in four secondary schools in West London and the extent to which promoting community cohesion generated increased and effective learning opportunities for refugees. Two secondary schools were selected within each local authority on the basis of documentary research which mainly included an evaluation of the most recent Ofsted reports of the schools. The Jameson Technology College and the Corpus Community School were selected in Bradwell, and the Cranwell School and Heathcliffe Manor School (HMS) in Heathcliffe. Four case studies in four secondary schools were used as units of analysis to arrive at a more robust understanding of the way in which local and school-level initiatives drive educational provision and social inclusion with respect to refugee and asylum-seeker pupils.

Barriers to refugee education and community cohesion

The literature of NGOs operating in the United Kingdom and elsewhere has noted that refugees and asylum seekers experience significant barriers to accessible, quality education at the secondary level, not least because they recognize the shortage of available school places for refugees at this level of education.

> [M]any asylum-seeking and refugee children do not receive the level of care and protection that they need. This is despite the fact that by law, unaccompanied asylum-seeking and refugee children in England have the same legal entitlements as citizen children. This includes the right to education and healthcare and the rights enshrined in the Children Act (1989) and Human Rights Act (1998). (Stanley, 2001, p. 11)

The data on refugee education is particularly significant at the secondary school level, as it demonstrates increased chances of school exclusions, higher dropout rates and lack of access to school places and/or the curriculum (Doyle and McCorriston, 2008).

In addition to these challenges to access and inclusion at the secondary level, young refugees and asylum seekers face a number of insecurities once they are granted leave to remain in the country. They include issues involving age disputes, pupil mobility ('out-of-borough' transfers), victimization by racism and bullying in school, racial stereotyping and profiling in the media, risk of deportation on a young person's 18th birthday and – perhaps above all else – a lack of proficiency in the English language (McCorriston et al., 2008).

The lack of proficiency in English is especially problematic for young people of secondary school age. Young teenagers who arrive with parents are often forced to learn English quickly, whereas refugee parents are often reluctant to learn and rely on their children for language support (McCorriston et al., 2008). The refugee or asylum-seeking child is often responsible for translating on behalf of their parents: to the Home Office, doctors, lawyers, and school administrators and teachers. The young people who are considered most 'at risk' or challenged in secondary education are Unaccompanied Asylum Seeking Children (UASCs), particularly those who arrive without any caregiver in England. Some of these young people arrive with children of their own, which can lead to increased doubts from Home Office officials about a young person's age and legal status.

These troubling factors in refugee education underscore the empirical investigation. They present challenges to existing policy and the new duty on schools to promote community cohesion, and indeed challenge the very notion of social cohesion in England's twenty-first-century learning communities. The UK Commission on Integration and Cohesion cites recent research on public perception of community cohesion in England:

1. Eighteen per cent of people surveyed identified immigration/migrants as the main issue facing Britain today – with this answer overtaking crime in MORI's regular surveys in May 2006.
2. More than half of respondents (56 per cent) felt that some groups in Britain get unfair priority when it comes to public services like housing, health services and schools. (Although this seems to be a stronger perception nationally rather than locally – locally only 25 per cent feel that some groups get unfair priority.)
3. This gives a sense of the barriers to building cohesion: mistrust of different groups, particularly those new to the local community; a perception that local authorities are giving others special treatment; and a lack of spaces for meaningful interaction (Department for Children, Schools, and Families (DCSF), 2007)

This research raises the issue of why community cohesion is integral to inclusive education policies which allow children from diverse backgrounds to thrive in the British educational system.

The research findings in this chapter are grounded in three main areas, as outlined in figure 6.1. The present study argues that the above categories are possibly strong indicators of student success and the overall well-being of a child, and that the duty of schools to promote community cohesion demonstrably helps schools to meet this goal.

Main research findings

The case of the Bradwell Local Authority

The London Borough of Bradwell is characterized by a high proportion of refugees and asylum seekers and high levels of pupil mobility, which has led to problems at both the primary and secondary level, including pupils being absent from school. Refugee social exclusion is indeed a potential problem in terms of accessing education, as well as social integration. Many schools in this local authority, however, demonstrate best practices in relation to refugee social and educational inclusion.

Two comprehensive schools were selected for this investigation, the Jameson Technology College (JTC) and the Corpus Community School. Both secondary schools focus on EAL provision and other educational needs to support refugee student achievement and social integration. A JTC study of education in the borough found that among the challenges to refugee education in the borough, 'secondary schools were oversubscribed at KS4' and had a 'reluctance to admit students at KS4' owing to the pressures of coursework, inflexible syllabi and General Certificate of Secondary Education (GCSE) preparations (JTC, 2004, p. 1).

Despite challenges, the Bradwell Local Authority promotes community cohesion by employing initiatives that can be grouped into three main clusters, as described below.

Effective teaching and learning

The educational success of refugees relies in large part on the quality of instruction at the school. Refugees and other pupils with learning disabilities, and those who arrive a few grade levels behind their peers, benefit substantially from effective and individualized education plans and additional

Teaching, learning and curriculum

There will be high expectations of success, with all pupils expected and encouraged by teachers and parents to achieve their potential.

1. Opportunities across the curriculum to promote shared values and help pupils to value differences and to challenge prejudice, discrimination and stereotyping. As well as the opportunities in citizenship described above, there are opportunities across the curriculum and in the new programmes of study for Religious Education (RE) and Personal, Social and Health Education (PSHE).
2. Support for pupils for whom English is an additional language (EAL), and specific support for their teaching staff, to remove barriers to effective learning, enabling the pupils to be integrated and achieve the highest possible level in English.
3. Assemblies which involve members of the local and wider community and promote the engagement of learners and shared understanding, as well as a school's ethos and values.

Equity and excellence

In line with existing duties, all schools should have effective approaches in place to deal with incidents of prejudice, discrimination, bullying and harassment.

Monitoring of whether pupils from particular groups are more likely to be excluded or disciplined than others should be accompanied by appropriate behaviour and discipline policies in place to deal with this, and pupils should be involved in evaluating the success of a school in implementing these policies.

Engagement and extended services

1. Working together with community representatives, for example through mentoring schemes or bringing community representatives into school to work with the pupils or to support learning by leading assemblies.
2. Local engagement through links with community groups and organisations, enabling them to play a role in the school and encouraging pupils to make a positive contribution in the local area.
3. Maintaining strong links and multi-agency working between the school and other local agencies, such as the youth support service, the police, different religious groups and social care and health professionals.
4. Placements for pupils in voluntary community based activities.
5. Engagement with parents through curriculum evenings, teaching and learning activities such as parent and child courses, and family liaison work, tailored to suit the needs and requirements of the school and parents. For example, reaching parents who may need additional support through other local bodies and community points of contact.

Figure 6.1 Guidance on the Duty to Promote Community Cohesion (DCSF, 2007, p. 8)

support, such as extra teaching time and regular student assessments throughout the year.

School specialist teachers of refugees cited specific needs such as partnership teaching and general staff support (e.g. an increase in staff support and teaching assistants), as well as community volunteers who can teach in a student's mother tongue, in order to help refugee students access the curriculum. EAL provision was of primary concern as proficiency in English enables refugees to excel in core curricular subjects. The schools in this study revealed that students are initially placed in school on the basis of their age but, more significantly, according to their language ability. Supplementary class time and extra school activities are often needed to meet the heavy academic demands and exam pressure facing these pupils, which is particularly relevant to secondary-level pupils preparing for GCSEs. A lack of proficiency in English can otherwise hinder their academic achievement and even their ability to socially assimilate into their new school environment.

The headmaster at Corpus Community School comments on the success of the school's Saturday school initiative which 500 pupils attend, many of them refugees and asylum seekers. 'They come in every Saturday . . . They actually pay for themselves . . . They pay to come along. These are children from very deprived backgrounds. A lot of them come from the Stockbridge area – which is one of the main educational priority areas in the country for social deprivation' (Corpus Community School headmaster interview, October 2005).

The level of pupil engagement is what is most striking about the school's initiative: it exhibits both the desire and the commitment of the pupils to utilize resources that will benefit them both academically and socially. It is even more interesting that the pupils themselves (or their families, in some cases) are willing to pay for such a service from their own scarce financial resources and ostensibly deal with the hassles of extra travel time.

Equity and excellence

Both secondary schools in this case study exhibited various means of providing equity and excellence in education. In terms of commenting on the 'quality of education' provided by the JTC, especially in relation to refugees and asylum seekers, Ofsted had this to say:

> Equality of access is excellent for all students and ensures full student participation. This is because the college creates a supportive and tolerant atmosphere for students. The climate for learning which the college has developed ensures that the large number of students from minority ethnic groups, students from a travellers background and asylum seekers are integrated effectively into the college. There is a climate of innovation and the curriculum is kept under regular review. (Ofsted, 2005b, p. 22)

The school's equitable policies for refugees and asylum seekers are embedded in the school's ethos, which is one that fosters inclusion. An analysis of the JTC school interviews revealed that an important school policy is the school administration and teaching staff's 'holistic approach' to refugees and asylum seekers in education. More specifically, the college actively engages both parents of refugees and refugee pupils in a clear dialogue about their educational needs and provision for them. For example, the schools in this study engaged parents and carers of refugees in after-school activities, assemblies, parent open evenings and coffee mornings in an effort to educate them about the school system in England, the expectations for the new school year and important calendar events. The meetings were sometimes held in the parents' mother tongue with the help of community volunteers. These inclusive school initiatives have helped both schools promote community cohesion and foster greater awareness about school issues among this population of parents, and the results have been tangible in the way of higher attendance rates and test scores.

The Corpus Community School exhibited a holistic approach to education, working with the parents and carers of refugee and asylum-seeker pupils. The school prioritizes the emotional as well as academic well-being of all its pupils, including its refugees and asylum seekers who may require extra care and facilities.

> The school works extremely effectively with parents, carers and external agencies to safeguard pupils and promote their well-being and achievement. Teachers systematically monitor pupils' academic progress and personal development and pupils know whom to approach when they encounter problems. Pupils have good access to high quality careers advice and guidance which they value highly. Pupils with learning difficulties and disabilities have very effective individual education plans and the support given disaffected pupils and refugees is exemplary. New pupils settle into the life of the school well because of very carefully planned induction arrangements. When pupils from another country join the school, they are helped to settle in quickly by pupils who speak the same language as theirs. All staff are active in the promoting the health and safety of pupils. Good systems for child protection are in place, backed by regular staff training. (Ofsted, 2006b, p. 5)

The Corpus Community School therefore demonstrates that examples of best practice in relation to refugee student achievement and community cohesion for refugees and their families are a result of the school's ethos of inclusion. Notably, school inclusion measures were in place before the legal duty that schools promote community cohesion came into effect in 2008; however, the school continues to build upon its vision under the current policy.

Engagement and extended services

The JTC tries to build and strengthen relationships with the community by increasing support and extended services to its growing refugee and asylum-seeker population, particularly the parents of refugees at the school:

> Parents welcome the inclusive nature of the college and that it looks beyond its boundaries to provide for all and to support students from many different backgrounds or those, like refugees, who are in vulnerable positions. The students reflect these views. They . . . delight in the opportunities given to respect and celebrate the many cultures in the college. They feel that they are valued and their views are listened to and acted on. (Ofsted, 2005b, p. 7)

This is also expounded upon by EMTAS in their publication: *Involving Bilingual Parents in Their Child's Learning: a teachers' handbook* (EMTAS, 2005). The document emphasizes the responsibility of the school to create an environment where there is two-way dialogue between parents and teachers. Measures for ensuring their engagement include: sending bilingual notices home, conducting parent and teacher interviews (involving interpreters, where possible, as it should not be assumed that the child bears the responsibility of interpreting) and inviting parents to informal discussions with teachers where possible.

'Home–school visits' were also considered to be an extremely effective measure of involving parents in their children's education. 'Although these can be very time-consuming the benefits are enormous. Visits to families with limited English work better when the teacher is accompanied by an interpreter; however such visits can be valuable even without an interpreter. Home visits can often transform home–school relations and definitely make future contact easier' (EMTAS, 2005, p. 5).

Moreover, the handbook suggests making links with other refugee organizations, local services and community groups who can support refugee families. It also recommends procedures for supporting staff and a flexible approach to the curriculum. This, again, highlights the important need for coordinated effort and pooling of resources to improve the situation of refugee and asylum-seeker education.

Secondary school induction sessions and school policy documents such as parent and student guidebooks in several languages were cited as critical in helping these pupils integrate more rapidly and successfully to their new academic environment. This was viewed as especially important since refugee and asylum-seeker parents and/or carers, as well as the pupils themselves, often value education as a 'path to success' (JTC EAL teacher interview, July 2005).

The Bradwell Local Authority commented on the importance of linking with local community-based organizations (CBOs) and refugee community organizations (RCOs) that provide additional educational support, and value, to refugees and asylum seekers.

> We work a lot with Salusbury World, which is the charity that was set up at the Salusbury school which is a refugee site which works with families but also provides
>
> support for refugee children in school and for out of school classes like extra homework
>
> support. (Bradwell School Improvement Adviser interview, July 2005)

There is also a school-based support centre and counsellors on hand for pupils in need of such services. Salusbury World (2003) also helps to promote inclusion in the school, providing material resources such as the EMTAS and Salusbury World handbook (2005), which highlights key issues in supporting refugee and asylum-seeker children and their families. It also provides helpful ideas for teachers and others working with them (i.e. refugee mentors and counsellors) and provides a framework for understanding the situation of refugee children and how best to meet their needs in an inclusive learning environment. 'It focuses on a multi-tiered approach to an inclusive education for asylum seeking and refugee children: the role of senior management; teacher awareness; 'risk factors'; and factors which support achievement' (EMTAS and Salusbury World, 2005, p. 3).

This holistic approach to education of refugees and asylum seekers is one the college makes an effort to impress upon their teachers and staff members and can be extended to include community and refugee family participation.

Lessons from Bradwell

Both secondary schools in the Bradwell Local Authority work to promote the inclusion of refugee and asylum-seeker pupils in mainstream secondary classrooms. Furthermore, they each focus on the overall well-being and achievement of pupils, which underpins the duty on schools to promote community cohesion.

> The immediate needs of new arrivals and refugees in school may include: a welcoming, safe and stress-free environment; to know they are valued and belong even if their stay in a school may be short; to have their bilingualism recognised as a positive part of their intellectual development; opportunities to use home language; to feel part of the normal classroom and learning environment – important that they are not further marginalized and excluded; accessible learning opportunities; learning tasks must have relevance and purpose; access to the whole curriculum; opportunities to work with peers; positive social interactions that create opportunities for meaningful communication, sharing of skills and mutual support; opportunities for them to piece together their difficult experiences and restore their self-esteem. (JTC, 2004, p. 12)

Specific ways in which the schools in this case study are seen to be most effective in meeting the needs of refugees and asylum seekers include: whole-school commitment to inclusion and race equality; effective admission and induction arrangements; good background information for parents and pupils; effective initial language assessment; good communication and information sharing with parents; a range of teaching strategies and resources; effective use of support staff; the use of assemblies, festivals and Refugee Week; peer support; and special provision for extra-curricular activities and family learning.

The case of the Heathcliffe Local Authority

The London Borough of Heathcliffe is considered one of the most impoverished boroughs in London; however, it is also characterized as a 'place of refuge' for people of many backgrounds, including refugees and asylum seekers: 'Refugees often return to Heathcliffe, and London, from other dispersal areas because they feel safer here. There are less incidents of racism and harassment' (Heathcliffe School Improvement Adviser interview, November 2005).

Heathcliffe is a multiethnic community in West London very near to Heathrow Airport. It is an important local authority to investigate, not least because of its significant geographic proximity to London's 'drop off centres' or 'detention centres' for unsuccessful asylum seekers or those awaiting a decision on their asylum claim.

This particular local authority has made a significant impact in London because of its grassroots educational policies for refugee and asylum-seeker pupils, especially in terms of quality English as an Additional Language (EAL) provision and its centrally trained EAL teaching staff. The unique Heathcliffe Language Service (HLS), a division of the local authority that houses a central teacher training service offering specially trained part-time teachers to local secondary schools. The HLS also contains an extensive resource centre which is regularly used by teachers and staff members from the borough as well as other local authorities throughout the greater London area.

The local authority prioritizes a school culture of inclusion by offering extended school activities that aim to:

1. increase inclusivity, for example, for children with special needs and disabled children.
2. increase attainment through school enrichment by, for example, extending out-of-school learning opportunities and tackling underachievement in targeted schools (Heathcliffe Council, 2004, pp. 8–9).

The schools visited in Heathcliffe, like those in Bradwell, were selected on the basis of their relatively high percentages of refugee and asylum-seeker pupils compared to other local authorities in the greater London area. The case study research included, significantly, five interviews with the Heathcliffe Authority, two of which involved detailed interviews with representatives at the HLS. The HLS has made major headway in providing refugee and asylum-seeker pupils in the district with multilingual teachers who are trained centrally but work part-time as teaching staff in the authority's secondary schools. They are predominantly EAL support teachers; however, they are also trained in various emotional and care issues involving these pupils.

The first school visited in Heathcliffe was the Cranwell School, where there are 7,000 to 8,000 refugees and asylum seekers (Hounslow Homes, 2009) Furthermore, the school utilizes a teacher from the HLS who works alongside mainstream school teachers to provide additional EAL support especially to refugee and asylum-seeker pupils. The Heathcliffe Manor School (HMS) was the second school visited. It was also selected based on its high proportion of refugees and asylum seekers and its ongoing institutional initiatives to meet the needs of these pupils.

The Heathcliffe Local Authority's School Improvement Adviser explains that refugee and asylum-seeker students in the borough face additional challenges at the secondary level:

> The curriculum presents more challenges at that age, and it's also challenging for teachers. The media has also shown how children at this age pick up stereotypes on ethnicity and gender. We need to deal with it in terms of resources, having teachers from multicultural backgrounds in schools so pupils can know more about their cultures, and where they come from. There are issues of threat: there are external pressures and those present in the curriculum don't help either. There is limited flexibility in the curriculum also in terms of class discussions. Connecting with parents and students in their own language is important. (Heathcliffe School Improvement Adviser interview, November 2005)

Heathcliffe's School Improvement Adviser gave a more detailed account of the LEAs efforts raising achievement levels of refugee and asylum-seeker pupils in secondary schools. 'We work to identify the underachieving groups . . . In terms of educational provision, [refugee] pupils receive special educational help, we try to involve parents of these pupils, look at resources, teacher training needs and so on. We also provide EAL support to teachers in schools' (Heathcliffe School Improvement Adviser interview, November 2005).

Both schools in this study pay particular attention to the needs of underachieving groups and raise performance among these pupils through extra assistance in terms of language provision, teacher resources and outreach to students' families.

Effective teaching and learning

A recent study in the Heathcliffe (2009) addresses the borough's effort to close the achievement gap between refugee and mainstream secondary school pupils by partnering the school and the community and sharing best practices. The report cites additional instructional time and targeted assistance in English language provision as possible mechanisms of support.

The HLS also provides this type of language and curricular support to refugees in education, and leverages additional support from the community:

> Heathcliffe Language Service offers additional teaching support, advice, training and a range of services to Borough schools, which are receiving refugee and asylum seeker pupils. In accordance with Heathcliffe's Social Inclusion Policy, support is focussed on helping target pupils integrate successfully into schools, and access the National Strategies. HLS staff can offer in-school teaching support where there

> are sufficient numbers of refugee/asylum seekers on roll. The Team also offer multilingual liaison and contacts with the community and other agencies for home-school links and pastoral support. (HLS, 2005c, p. 4)

The HLS attributes its achievements to the joint effort of local secondary schools and the LEAs language division to disseminate information about education for refugee and asylum seekers. This allows them to partner effectively with external refugee agencies and CBOs to ensure refugees' overall well-being.

The HLS director states that the service's teachers, who are linked up with local schools on certain days of the week, work well with mainstream school teachers and staff. They offer good quality language support because all HLS teachers are centrally trained, providing continuity and equity in terms of language provision in the borough. HLS also contains a centralized training unit for its specialized teaching staff. The HLS staff is comprised of multilingual teachers, some of whom are former refugees or asylum seekers themselves and therefore provide a mentoring role in addition to their teaching role: 'In-service refugee days and other courses are on offer, certificated courses, including refugees and EALs within them. At the school level, training for new arrivals is offered, specifically for refugee inserts' (Head of HLS interview, November 2005).

Targeted support to new arrivals in education also helps to narrow the achievement gap so that curriculum and instruction is tailored to meet the needs of these pupils as soon as they arrive at the school.

Equity and excellence

Examples of successful measures that both Heathcliffe schools employed to ensure equity and excellence among its refugee pupils are mentorship and/or buddying schemes. Teachers in both schools teamed refugee students with a good role model or 'buddy' in the classroom to ease their transition. In many schools, new arrivals were paired with refugees that had been in the school for a number of years and had been mentored themselves. The borough has noted particular challenges to refugees in secondary school in years 7 and 8. 'The transition to secondary school is particularly difficult as their needs are greater, there is a bigger demand for support and mentorship (in year 7 or 8 especially). They start to deteriorate in terms of achievement at the secondary level' (HLS, Mid Term Admissions Report, 2005d, p. 4).

Support networks may already exist within the school, such as bilingual staff members who speak the child's native language and can therefore assist them with lessons or homework. Schools may also develop resource material that employs creative ways to teach refugee pupils English, for example, labelling equipment bilingually or using common household items to do math and literacy homework.

There is a major focus on the achievement levels of the Cranwell College's Somali refugee population. There are a range of services that provide educational support, such as tutoring and mentorship schemes for those students. The college is a visible part of a community-wide effort at raising awareness about refugees in the community. It promotes good practices to ensure that knowledge of refugees' educational entitlements is communicated to the refugee community:

> [Cranwell is] trying to get the parents involved in education, even though they know they have no experience themselves. Coming to parents' evenings, coming to school is quite threatening if the members of the Somali community don't convince them of the importance. [A mentor] will come and buddy them with the parents, explain induction programmes, give the parents the opportunity to get involved and have access to education – to what the children are doing in school. (EAL headteacher interview, January 2006)

Somali refugee pupils are the fastest-growing group in the area (EAL specialist teacher interview, January 2006). According to the school's headmaster and EAL headteacher, many of them have no previous education. For many of them, their educational needs are very basic: 'We even have to teach some of them how to hold a pencil or a ruler; they have no idea. So, that's the extreme, most or usually students from Somalia would have had no education unless they come from another European country. So the picture is changing slightly' (EAL headteacher interview, January 2006). Teachers commented on these pupils' initial difficulty in the early stages of EAL. But, with quality provision, these pupils are able to succeed as a result of their exposure to other foreign languages.

Both schools in this case study cited their school's ethos of inclusion as being of real importance as this lays the groundwork for refugees to become high academic achievers. The HMS policy of inclusion, for example, is enforced by the school's headmaster and equally upheld by senior management and teachers, thus providing refugee and asylum-seeker pupils with a sense of stability: 'In this school with high pupil mobility, [the headteacher and senior leadership] share with all staff a clear vision for inclusion. This very effectively engages pupils with the school in a supportive and harmonious environment and instils in them a will to succeed' (Ofsted, 2005a, p. 6).

The Cranwell College's ethos is also that of a 'holistic' approach to educating refugees and asylum seekers. The school recognizes the various educational and emotional challenges their pupils face, as well as those of their parents. Partner projects with the local authority and RCOs help the school in its effort to meet the specific needs of refugee and asylum-seeker pupils.

Engagement and extended services

Extended services afford both schools in Heathcliffe an opportunity to engage families of refugees in their education, thereby promoting more cohesion within the community. The HLS regularly holds parents' open evenings and individual discussions and meetings with new parents. It assists the Heathcliffe LA, for example, in developing school policies and implementing parents' notice boards in school (Ofsted, 2005a, p. 6). These strategies proved mutually beneficial for refugee pupils and their parents. The HLS induction programme, for example, is often a refugee's or asylum seeker's first gateway to their new environment and social network. 'One of the things we have is a very structured induction programme . . . they are given an initial needs assessment which includes a language assessment' (HMS induction mentor interview, January 2006).

Parents who are not involved in school activities are often disconnected from the school as a result of their own language difficulties or feelings of exclusion. Secondary school refugee pupils often take on the responsibilities of their parents, especially in instances where the child's command of English is stronger than that of their parents. These are several reasons why the HLS shifts its focus and material resources to parents or carers of refugee pupils as well as the pupils themselves.

The Cranwell teacher added that extended school activities, including extra tutoring time for refugee pupils, has enhanced their ability to learn in other subject areas as well. The school also communicates with the parent of refugees:

> The department for English as an additional language maintains a good liaison with families and carers. Staff make arrangements for other support to become available, especially refugee support with other agencies, that provides effective help for students and their families. (HMS induction mentor interview)

Furthermore, the college's staff maintains strong links with the community and partner agencies that advocate and enforce good practices in educating refugees and asylum seekers.

Lessons from Heathcliffe

The two secondary schools in this case study were aligned in terms of their effort to provide an inclusive education for refugees and asylum seekers, as well as extended services to the refugee community. The schools often referenced EAL provision as an important means of inclusion, whether as part of the curriculum or extended school services such as Saturday school and extra tutoring time.

Community participation and refugee family engagement were also shown to be important means of inclusion. EAL lessons for families of refugees are a focal point of the local authority's outreach to the community. Extended school services, such as English language provision in Saturday school, help parents learn the language of their host country and enable them to engage in their children's education. English language acquisition empowers refugee families to familiarize themselves with the British education system, engage their children's school and better understand expectations for their children's education.

Conclusion: why community cohesion works

A community approach to education for refugees and other marginalized groups, as this study shows, is a successful way to meet the educational needs of these vulnerable pupils. Community cohesion could also potentially serve as a key indicator of success when measuring student achievement and student progress, warranting further investigation of the link between community cohesion and the educational achievement of vulnerable pupils in mainstream schools.

The research findings raise contemporary questions that lend themselves to a more thorough investigation of the correlation between community cohesion in education and increased levels of refugee student achievement. The present study has shown how the duty on schools to promote community cohesion increases engagement of refugees and their families in education and helps refugee students access the curriculum and extended school activities. Thus, some new research questions (see Key Questions at end of this chapter) emerge from these case studies:

The refugee experience potentially poses challenges to educational and social inclusion; however, the examples from the present case studies illustrate how efforts to promote community cohesion can enable and empower even the most vulnerable. Some of these successful strategies to integrate refugees and their families in education are summarized here.

School headmasters in this study highlighted the importance in training teaching staff, not least those who teach mainstream curricular subjects, about the special educational needs of refugees and asylum seekers. This includes basic requirements such as an introduction to the education system in the United Kingdom and the national curriculum. These are novel features for refugees with no previous education, as well as those who may have had prior education in their country of origin.

Teachers and administrators play a critical role in assisting the parents in their transition to their child's new education system. Furthermore, they serve as important intermediaries between the school and the refugee community. Policy documents are a means of outreach to parents and carers of refugees, and ideally educate parents about what they can expect from their child's school experience. Refugee parents' misunderstandings about the school and the British education system generally can lead to the social exclusion of parents sometimes more than the children themselves, especially parents without a significant command of English.

The schools and local authorities that participated in the research consistently produced useful parent handbooks in addition to guidebooks for teaching staff how to deal with the special educational and social needs, and concerns of refugee and asylum-seeker families. Handbooks for parents were also appropriately published in several of the most common languages of refugees and asylum seekers in both communities. Furthermore, all participants agreed that the entire school staff should utilize such resources in order to uphold the school's ethos of inclusion and to encourage good practices in terms of both quality teaching and pastoral care.

The myths and negative stereotypes commonly associated with these vulnerable individuals in education have marginalized their active role and participation in society, and have potentially detrimental effects on their education.

> [The reality of a typical refugee profile] completely undermines this whole myth that many people have about the destitute refugee who is claiming on the system when in fact there are hugely educated people who are here, like there are lawyers, doctors, orthodontists. I guess my point is that we have students who are highly motivated – I mean it's just unbelievable, their motivation and their desire to succeed. Not only because perhaps they've come from an educated family, but even those who haven't come from an educated family have this desire. For example Somali young people come and there's a huge pressure that they will be the first people to have ever had a chance at an education, so they have had to translate everything for their parents: the doctor, the dentist, the lawyers, the home office, they have got to go everywhere with their parents, their daughters, their uncles because they are the only ones who speak the language. (Bradwell Refugee Unit Project coordinator interview, July 2005)

The schools in this study effectively use community cohesion to give refugee pupils, many of whom are indeed highly motivated, the tools they need to succeed in their new school environment.

The curriculum is an important measure of inclusion just as is effective EAL provision. Refugees and asylum seekers are often multilingual, and it has been argued that these individuals can acquire an additional language more readily than those without a second language (HLS, 2005). Thus, with additional teacher and staff support and a moderately flexible approach to the curriculum, schools can improve their job of facilitating inclusion in terms of the curriculum. Also, age-appropriate learning materials were considered indispensable, especially at the secondary school level where most available English language textbooks are geared to primary age pupils.

The three common strands of community cohesion initiatives in education enable schools in this study to realize positive achievement outcomes for refugee and asylum-seeker pupils. In addition, these strands help refugee families to access their children's education and thus better integrate into their local community. Those three main areas are: effective teaching and learning, equity and excellence, and engagement and extended services. A commitment to raising the bar on education for refugees and asylum seekers must involve change on the school level and within local communities. The duty to promote community cohesion identifies specific ways in which schools and local authorities can carry out these duties and, moreover, empower refugees to excel in education.

Key Questions

1. How does the duty to promote community cohesion lead to increased refugee student achievement in respect to the mainstream curriculum?
2. To what extent does the duty to promote community cohesion lead to increased participation of refugee parents and carers in their children's education?
3. How does a more cohesive school community lead to increased community cohesion, generally?

Further reading

Aspinall, P. and Watters, C. (2010), 'Refugees and asylum seekers: A review from an equality and human rights perspective'. Equality and Human Rights Commission Research Report 52. University of Kent.

Brownlees, L. and Finch, N. (2010), 'Levelling the playing field: A UNICEF UK report into provision of services to unaccompanied or separated migrant children in three local authority areas in England'. London: UNICEF UK.

Crawley, H. (2010), *Chance Or Choice? Understanding Why Asylum Seekers Come to the uk*. London: Refugee Council.

JRF (2008), *Community Engagement and Community Cohesion Findings: Informing Change*. London: JRF.

References

Bradwell Refugee Unit Project coordinator interview (2005). London.

Bradwell School Improvement Adviser interview (2005). London.

Corpus Community School (2005), *Towards a Language: Across the Curriculum Policy for Corpus Community School.*Original document.

Department for Children, Schools, and Families (2007), *Guidance on the Duty to Promote Community* Cohesion. DCSF, London.

Doyle, L. and McCorriston, M. (2008), *Beyond the School Gates: Supporting Refugees and Asylum Seekers in Secondary School.* London: Refugee Council.

EMTAS (2005), *Involving Bilingual Parents in Their Child's Learning: Teacher's Handbook.* Bradwell Council, Bradwell School Improvement Services. London.

EMTAS and Salusbury World (2005), *The Inclusion and Attainment of Refugee and Asylum Seeker Pupils.* London: Borough of Bradwell, EMTAS.

Heathcliffe Council (2004), *Education and Development Plan 2002–2007*. London: Borough of Heathcliffe.

Heathcliffe Language Service (2005a), *The Advantages of Being Bilingual: Multilingual Parents' Leaflet*. London: Heathcliffe Language Service.

Heathcliffe Language Service (2005b), *EAL/ESOL Provision for 16± in West London (summary version in Albanian, Arabic, Farsi, Portuguese, Somali, Panjabi, Urdu)*. London: Heathcliffe Language Service.

Heathcliffe Language Service (2005c), *HLS Strategic Plan for Supporting Access and Inclusion for Refugee Pupils in School*. London: Heathcliffe Language Service.

Heathcliffe Language Service (2005d), *Mid Term Admissions Report*. London: Heathcliffe Language Service.

Hounslow Homes (2009), *Refugees and Asylum Seekers in the UK: A Look Inside*. London Borough of Heathcliffe. Jameson Technology College (2004), *Planning for the Inclusion Achievement of Refugee Students*. Bradwell Council and Jameson Technology College.

Jones, C. and Rutter, J. (eds) (1998), *Refugee Education: Mapping the Field*. London: Trentham Books.

McCorriston, M. (2006), *Refugees and Education in England: Examining the Educational Needs of Refugees and Asylum Seekers in Two West London Boroughs*. Doctoral thesis. Oxford University.

McCorriston, M. and Lawton, A. (2008), *Hand in Hand: A Resource Pack to Help Meet the Needs of Refugees and Asylum Seekers in Secondary School*. London: Refugee Council.

McKenna, N. (2005), *Daring to Dream: Raising the Achievement of 14 to 16 Year Old Asylum-Seeking and Refugee Children and Young People*. London: Refugee Council.

Ofsted (2006a), *Bradwell Joint Area Review: Bradwell children's services authority area. Review of Services for Children and Young People*. London: Ofsted.

Ofsted (2006b), *Corpus Community College: Inspection Report*. London: Ofsted.

Ofsted (2005a), *Heathcliffe Manor School: Inspection Report*. London: Ofsted.

Ofsted (2005b), *Jameson Technology College: Inspection Report*. London: Ofsted.

Robson, C. (2002), *Real World Research New Edition*. Oxford: Blackwell.

Salusbury World (2003), *Home from Home: a Guidance and Resource Pack for the Welcome and Inclusion of Refugee Children and Families*, Bolloten, B. (ed.). London: Salusbury World.

Stanley, K. (2001), *Cold Comfort: Young Separated Refugees in England*. London: Save the Children.

Conclusion

Education, the fourth pillar of humanitarian response during emergencies, is vital in establishing a sense of normalcy in the lives of children affected by violence and armed conflicts. In addition to being a basic human right, education acts as a catalyst for development and conflict resolution in the countries where conflict is most often unavoidable. The number of refugees and asylum seekers throughout the world is increasing every year, and sadly, hundreds of thousands of people are leaving their countries of origin to establish themselves in neighbouring countries or move on to 'third countries' where opportunities of living and working are more likely. Many more are uprooted or stay in UNHCR refugee camps for long periods until the conflict is resolved or an agreement of 'permanent solution' is reached.

The UNHCR, the main UN body protecting refugees worldwide, has taken the responsibility of providing food, health, shelter and education to refugees, asylum seekers and IDPs. According to UNHCR's latest figures, by the end of 2009, more than 26 million people were receiving some kind of assistance from UNHCR. The number indicates an increase of one million from the previous year (UNHCR, 2010).

In the last two decades, there has been a great development in the literature discussing the significance of educational provision during and after emergencies. Moreover, a vast amount of research tries to answer questions such as:

1. What is the impact of violence on the psychosocial development of children?
2. How do armed conflicts and displacement affect the cognitive development of children?
3. What is being done to engage affected children in educational programmes?
4. How do children adjust to new learning environments and communities in host countries?

Numerous declarations and conventions protect children's right to education and claim that host countries should provide equal educational opportunities to nationals and refugees. The 1948 Universal Declaration of Human Rights, the Fourth Geneva Convention of 1949, the 1951 Convention Relating to the Status of Refugees, the Convention on the Rights of the Child of 1989 and the Rome Statute of 1998 are just a few examples. However, states do not always respect those conventions for various reasons, two of them being the political and financial/economic conditions of the host country (especially in developing countries where many refugees have settled).

Sadly, during war and armed conflicts, school buildings might not always be safe. For instance, Chechen schools were bombed and grenades were thrown into classrooms during school hours. In other cases, schools may be used as shelters for civilians or for military groups that use schools to gather young men for military service (such as the case in southern Sudan). In the Democratic Republic of Congo, schools were used by Rwandan-backed rebel groups to recruit children. Moreover, in volatile states and regions, education can be 'misused' to manipulate history for political reasons such as the cases of Serbia and Sri Lanka in the 1970s and 1980s (Nicolai and Triplehorn, 2003).

O'Malley (2010), in his UNESCO study *Education Under Attack*, shows how the number of countries where destruction of educational facilities and killing of teachers is occurring is increasing year by year. He gives case studies of 32 countries where such violations have taken place in recent years, many leading to displacement and increased refugee numbers.

Educational systems face numerous obstacles during conflicts and occupations. For instance, Israel imposes heavy taxes on Palestinians and on university books, an action that is against the universal edict exempting educational material from taxation. The occupation has also resulted in denying university degrees to students who have received their higher degree at a period when universities were not 'functioning'. Moreover, the construction of the wall between the West Bank and Israel has adversely affected all sectors of the local economy, in addition to education. As a result of humiliating searches by many soldiers, many teachers and students choose not to cross the checkpoints, a phenomenon which results in teacher and – more frequently – student absenteeism (Brock and Demirdjian, 2010).

While referring to losses of physical buildings, homes and loved ones as a result of war and conflict, one should not ignore the damage to cognitive and psychosocial development children and adults experience as a consequence. The children's experiences during displacement and while residing in refugee camps may result to post-traumatic stress disorder; loss of memory; and regressive, antisocial and destructive behaviour. The school communities in host countries should be responsible for ensuring the well-being of the newly arrived refugees who need to feel protected and welcomed. School administrators, teachers and mainstream students have to be aware of the cultural differences of the newcomers and accept them into the community and society. One should consider the fact that refugees arrive in host countries with great losses and low self-esteem; hence, any expression of prejudice, racial discrimination, stereotypes or bullying may adversely effect them. Councellors and community workers should work closely to help refugees' adaptation to the new school and setting. Special language classes can also be provided to parents of refugee students to encourage their participation in future school activities and support the school–home relationship.

International agencies – UNICEF, IIEP, INEE, UNESCO and NGOs such as Save the Children, Oxfam, IRC and others – play a significant role in promoting the right to education and implementing educational programmes that enhance the well-being of disadvantaged groups, including refugees and asylum seekers.

The case studies presented in this volume are only a small sample of the experiences refugees face in the United States, United Kingdom, the Middle East, Korea and Thailand. The authors' thorough studies can certainly serve as a foundation for further research in the field of education with reference to refugees and asylum seekers.

References

Brock, C. and Demirdjian, L. (2010), 'Education as a Humanitarian Response as Applied to the Arab World, with Special Reference to the Palestinian Case', in Abi-Mershed, O. (ed.), *Trajectories of Education in the Arab World: Legacies and Challenges*. London; New York: Routledge, pp. 185–98.

Nicolai, S. and Triplehorn, C. (2003), *The Role of Education in Protecting Children in Conflict*. Network Paper 42. London: Humanitarian Practice Network.

O'Malley, B. (2010), *Education Under Attack*. Paris: UNESCO.

UNHCR Division of Programme Support and Management (2010), *2009 Global Trends: Refugees, Asylum-Seekers, Returnees, Internally Displaced and Stateless Persons*. UNHCR. Available from www.unhcr.org/statistics (last accessed 2 October 2010).

Index